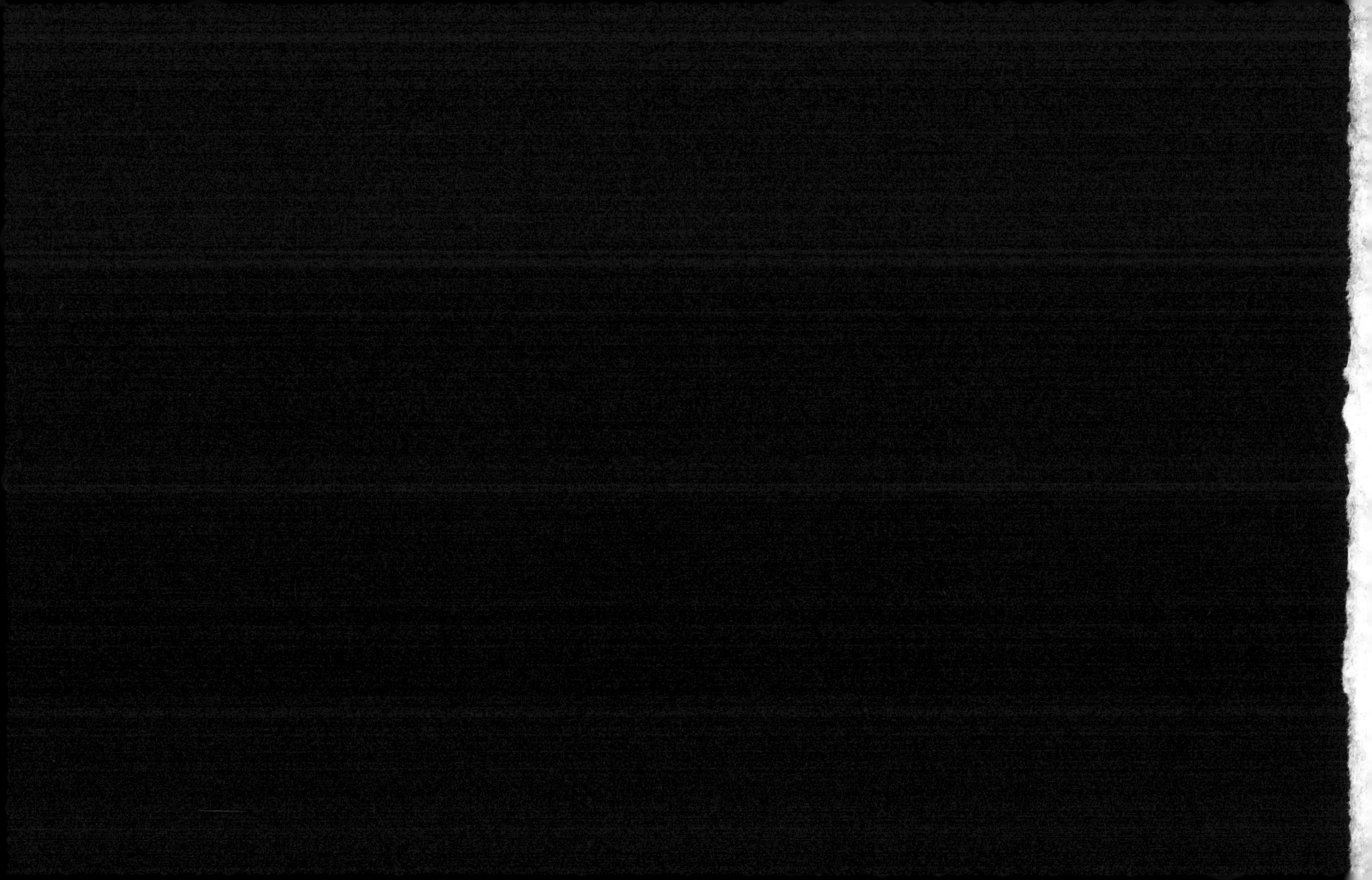

THE ROMAN SKETCHBOOK

MAARTEN VAN HEEMSKERCK

THE ROMAN SKETCHBOOK

Edited by Tatjana Bartsch and Christien Melzer

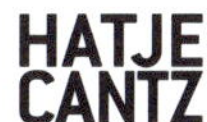

HATJE CANTZ

[INDETERMINATE NUMBER OF MISSING PAGES]

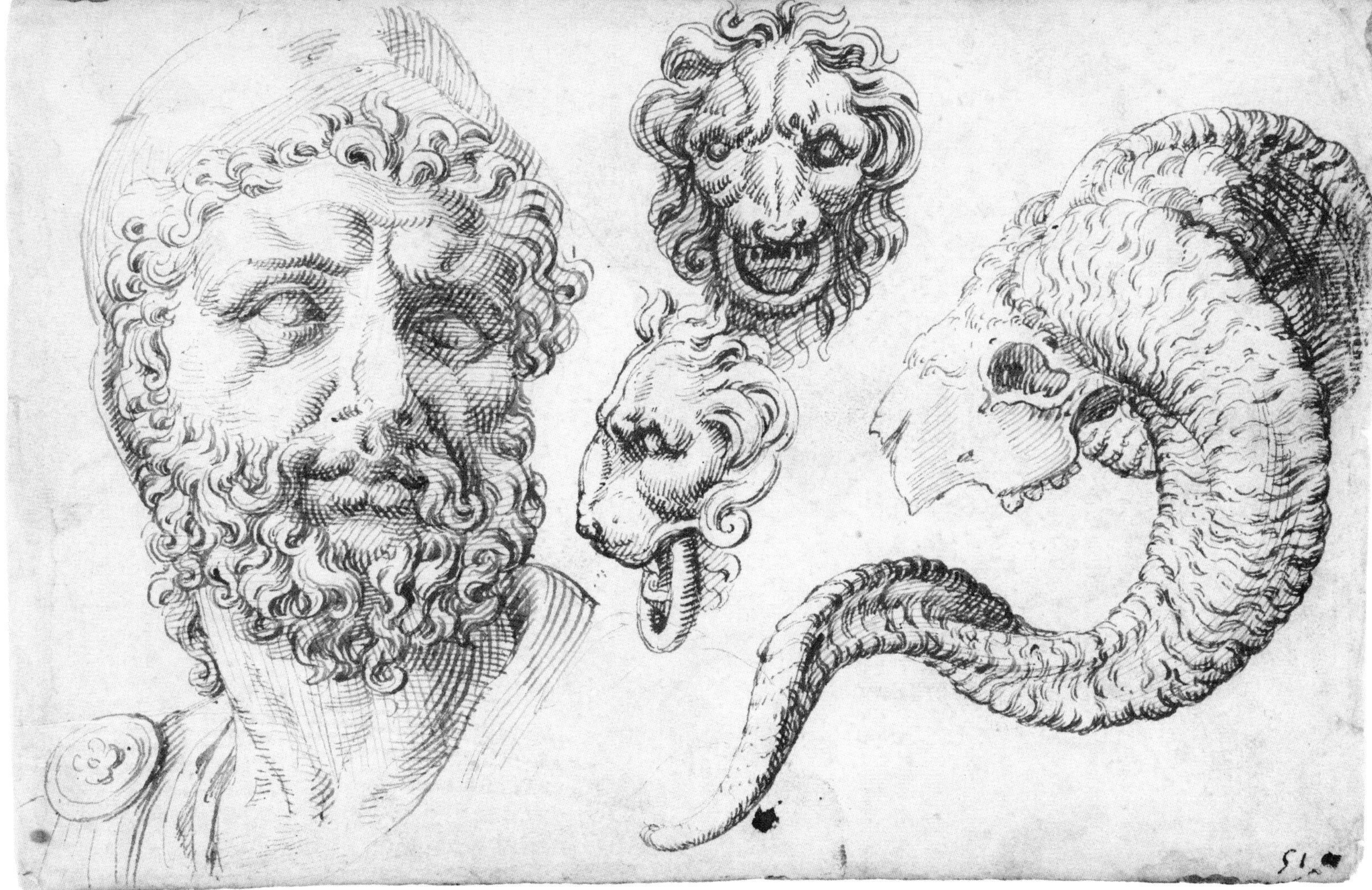
51.

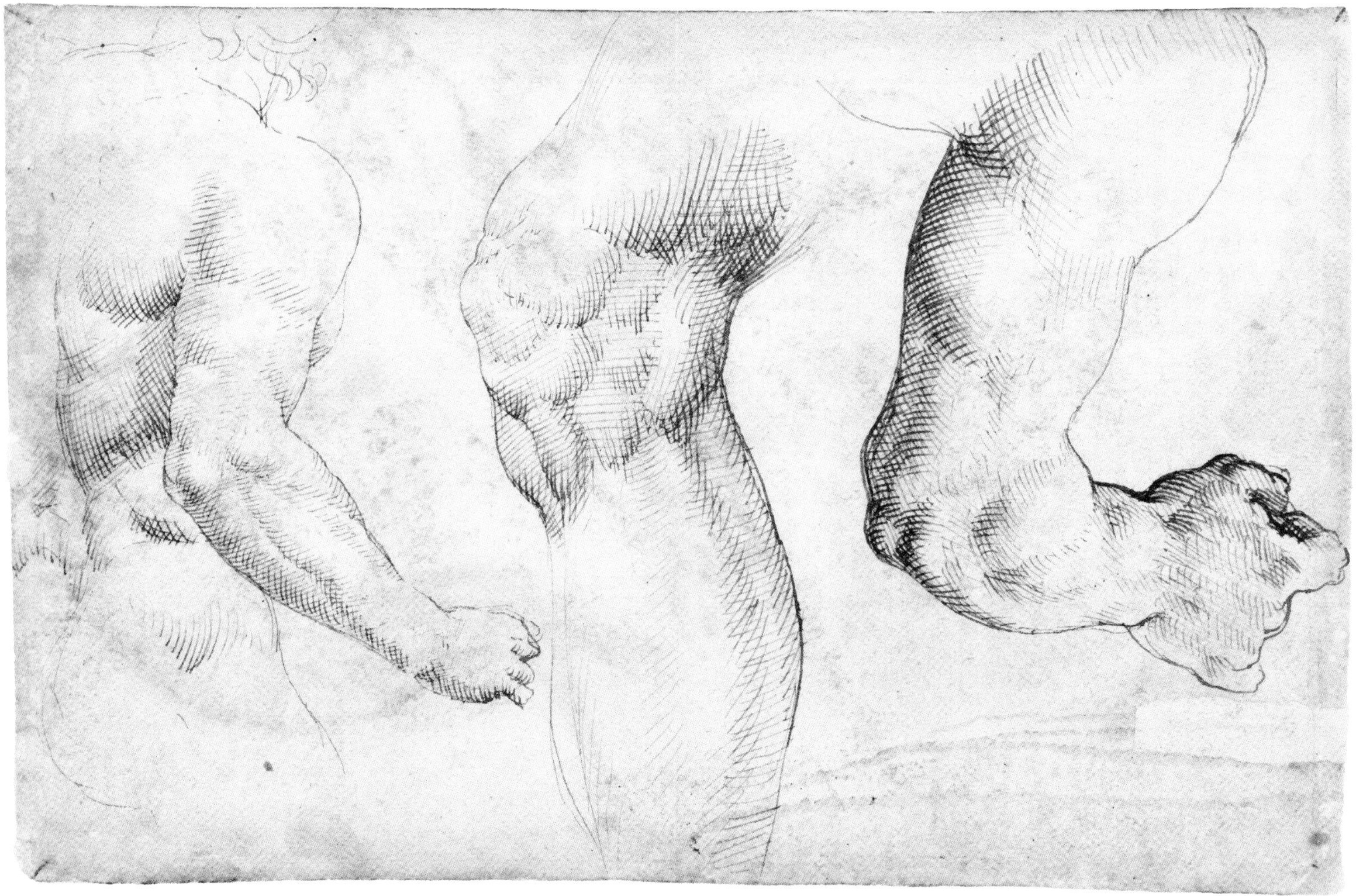

[TWO MISSING PAGES]

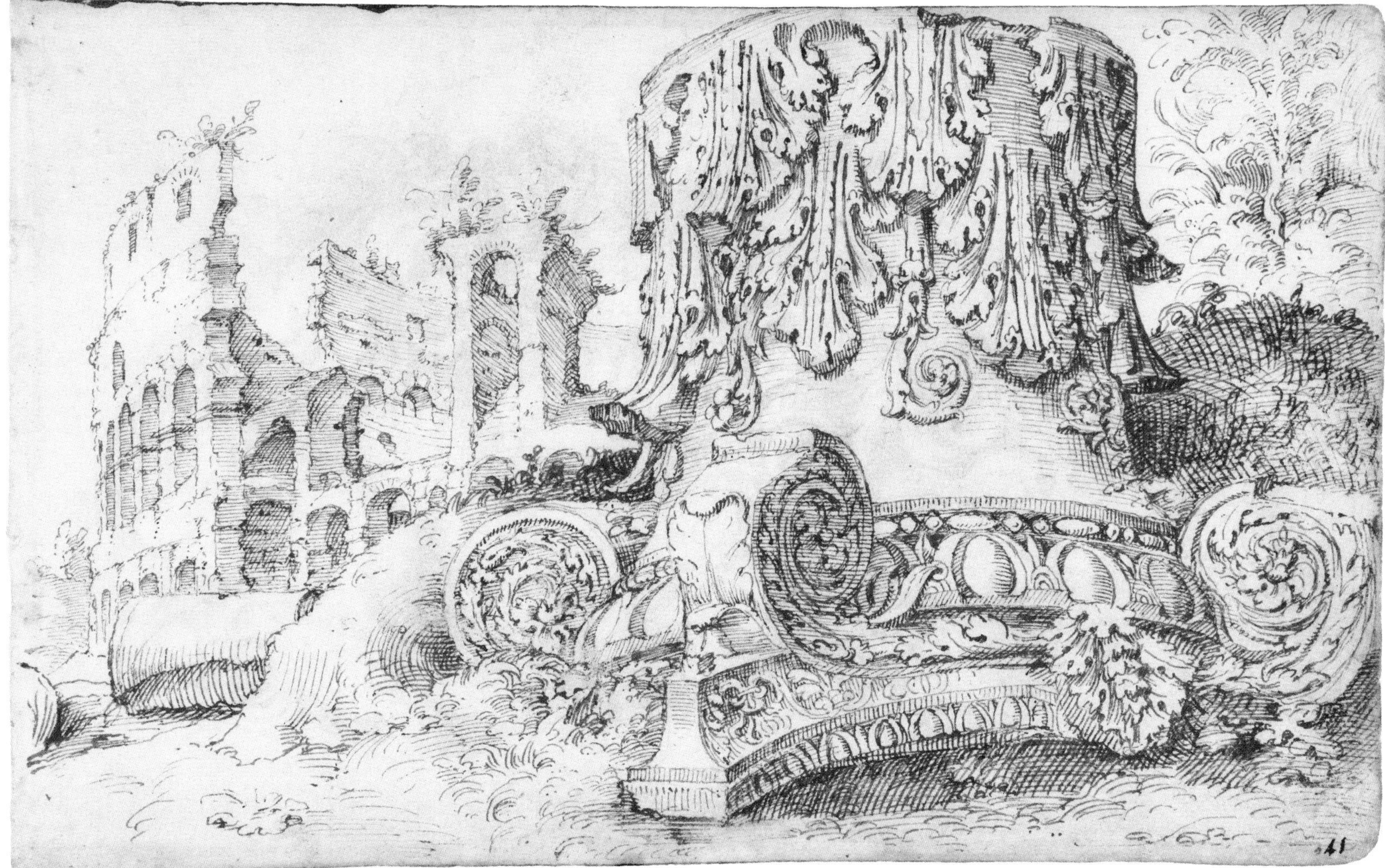

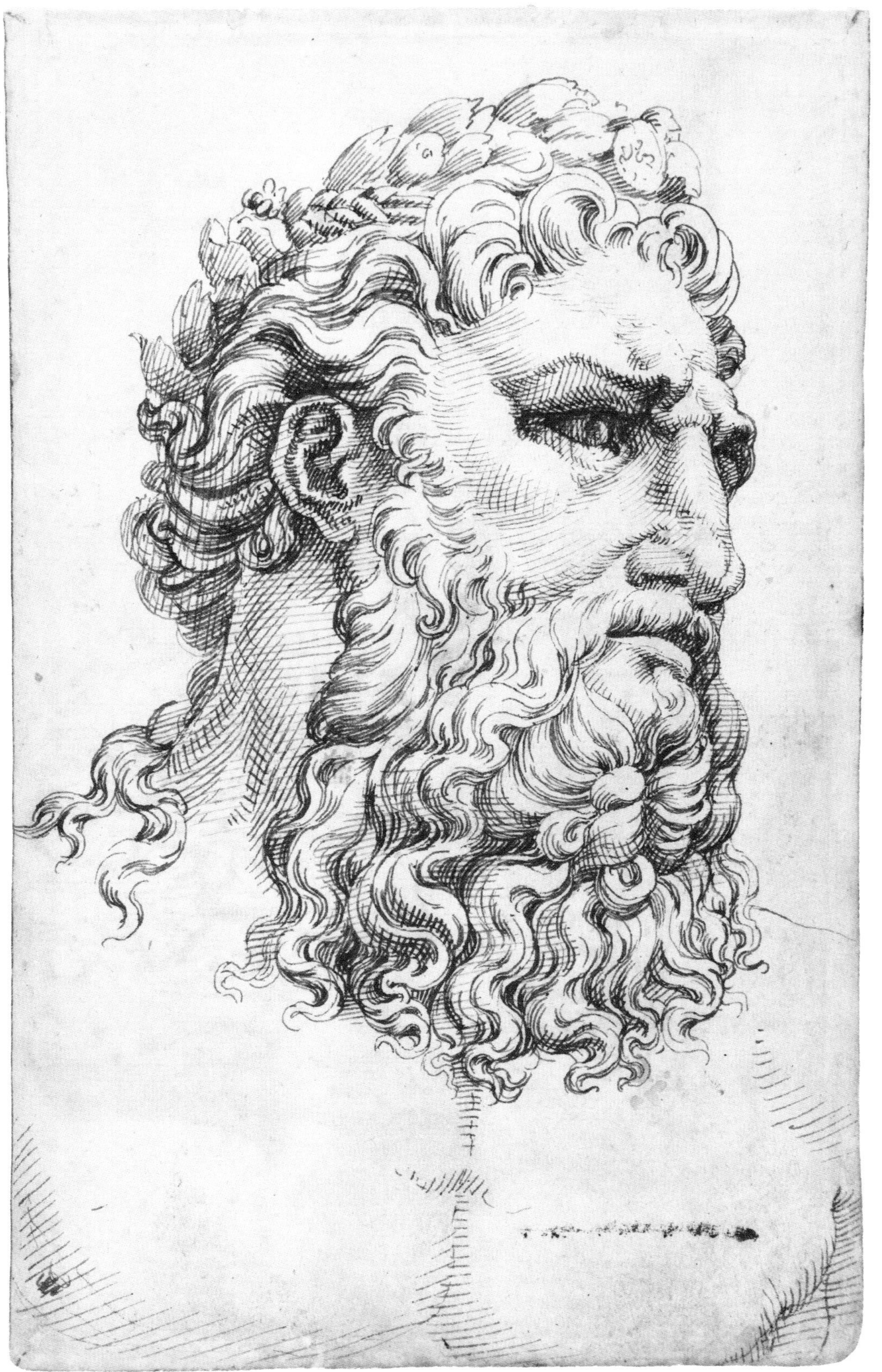

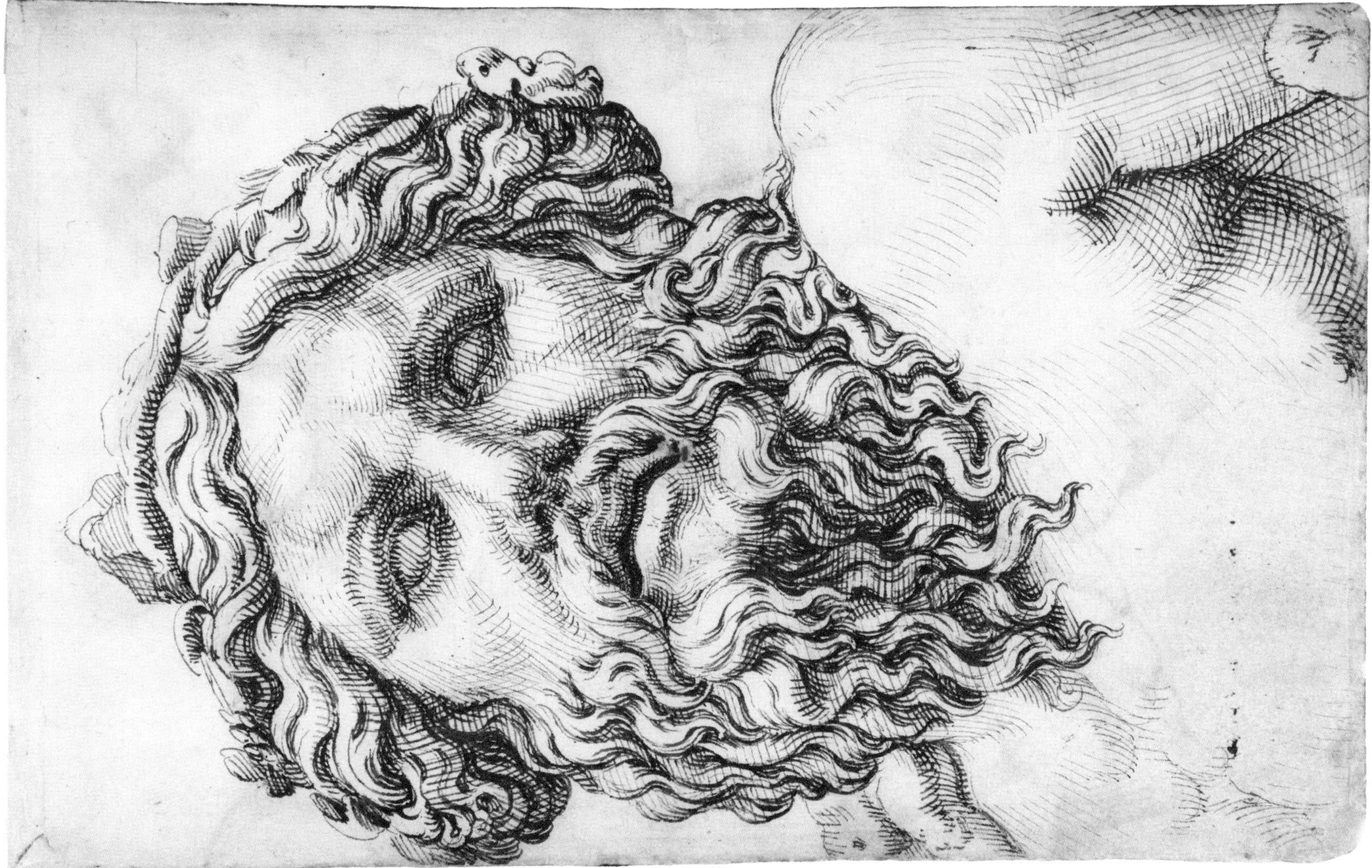

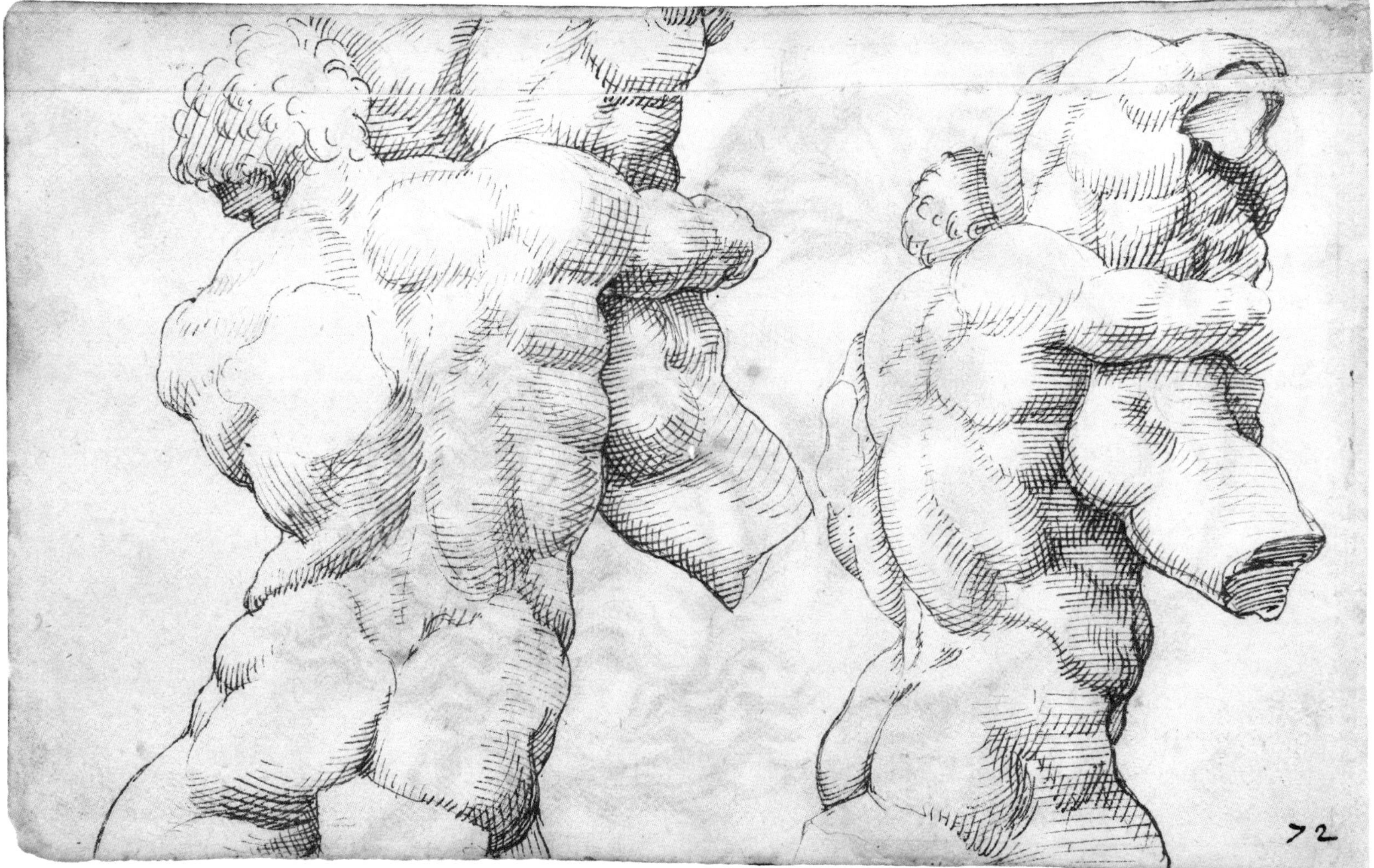
72

[TWO MISSING PAGES]

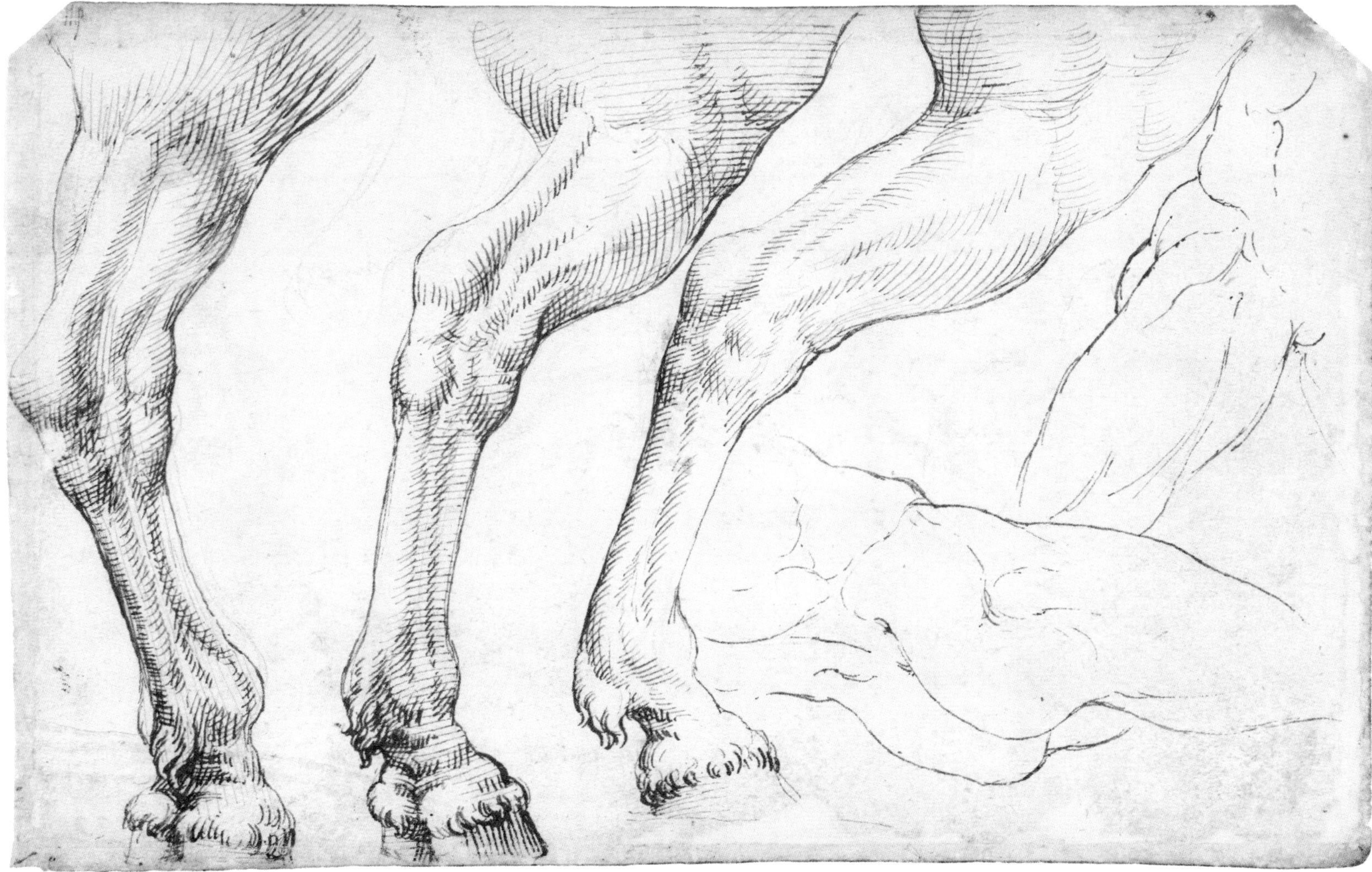

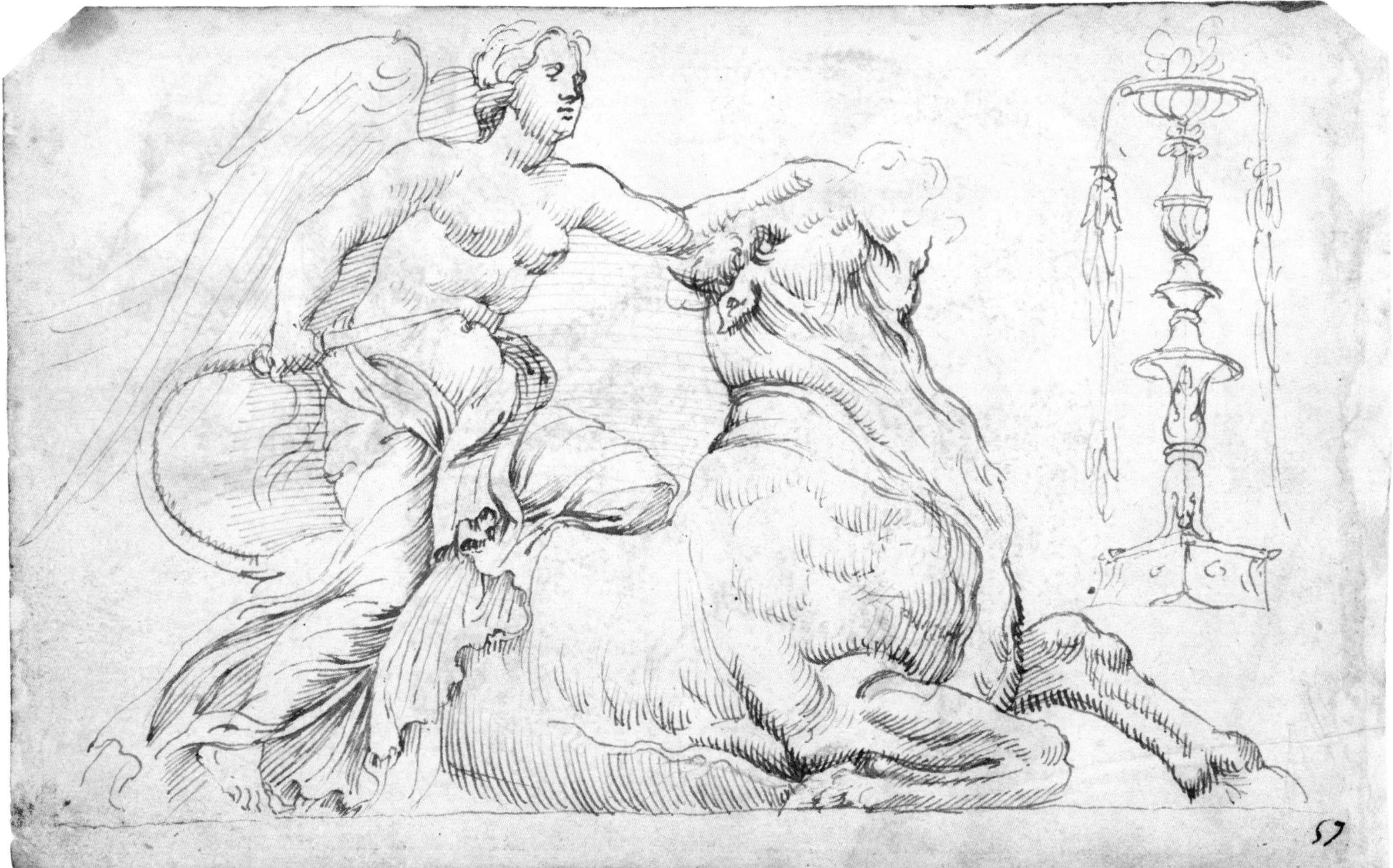

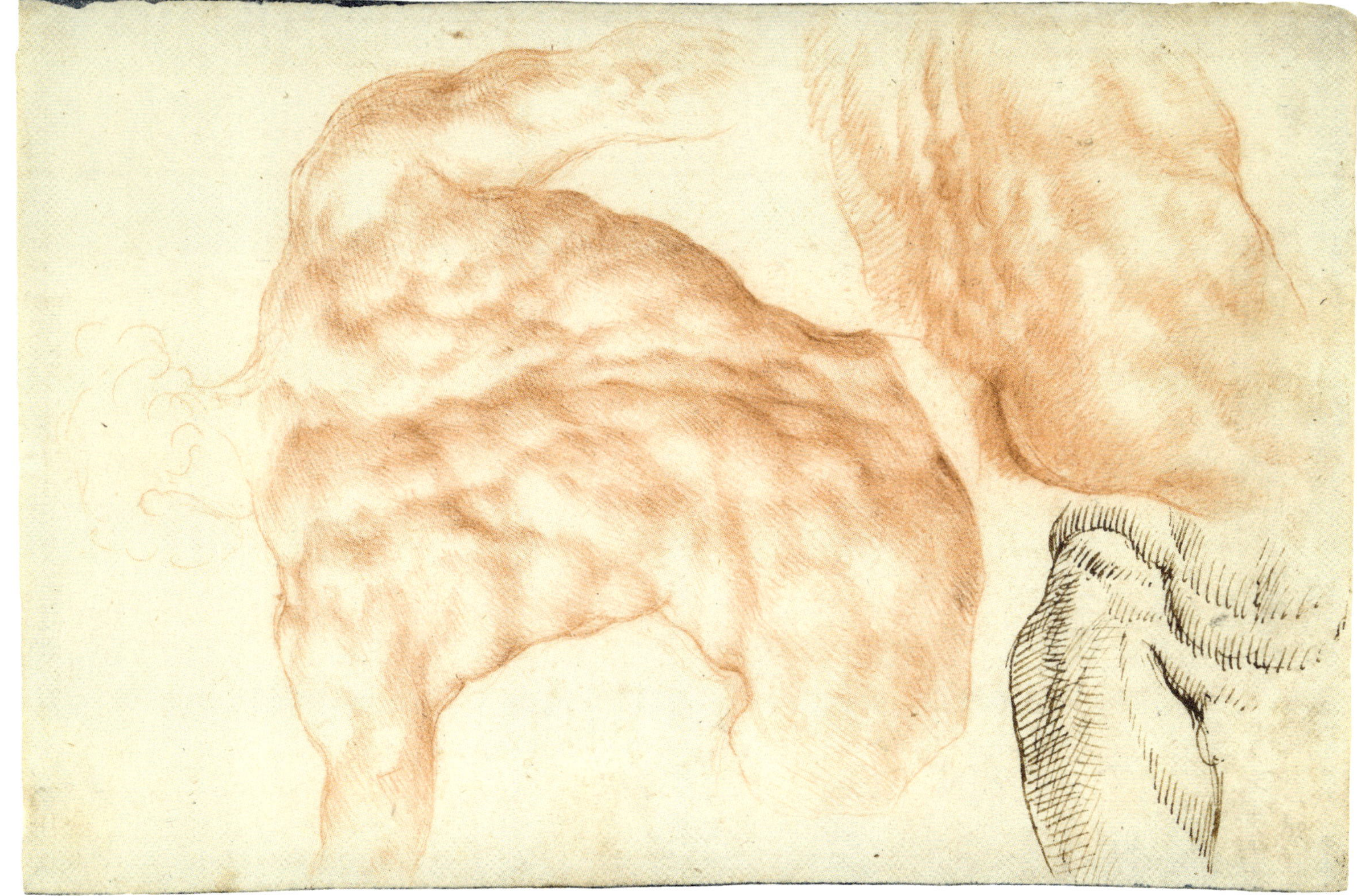

[TWO MISSING PAGES]

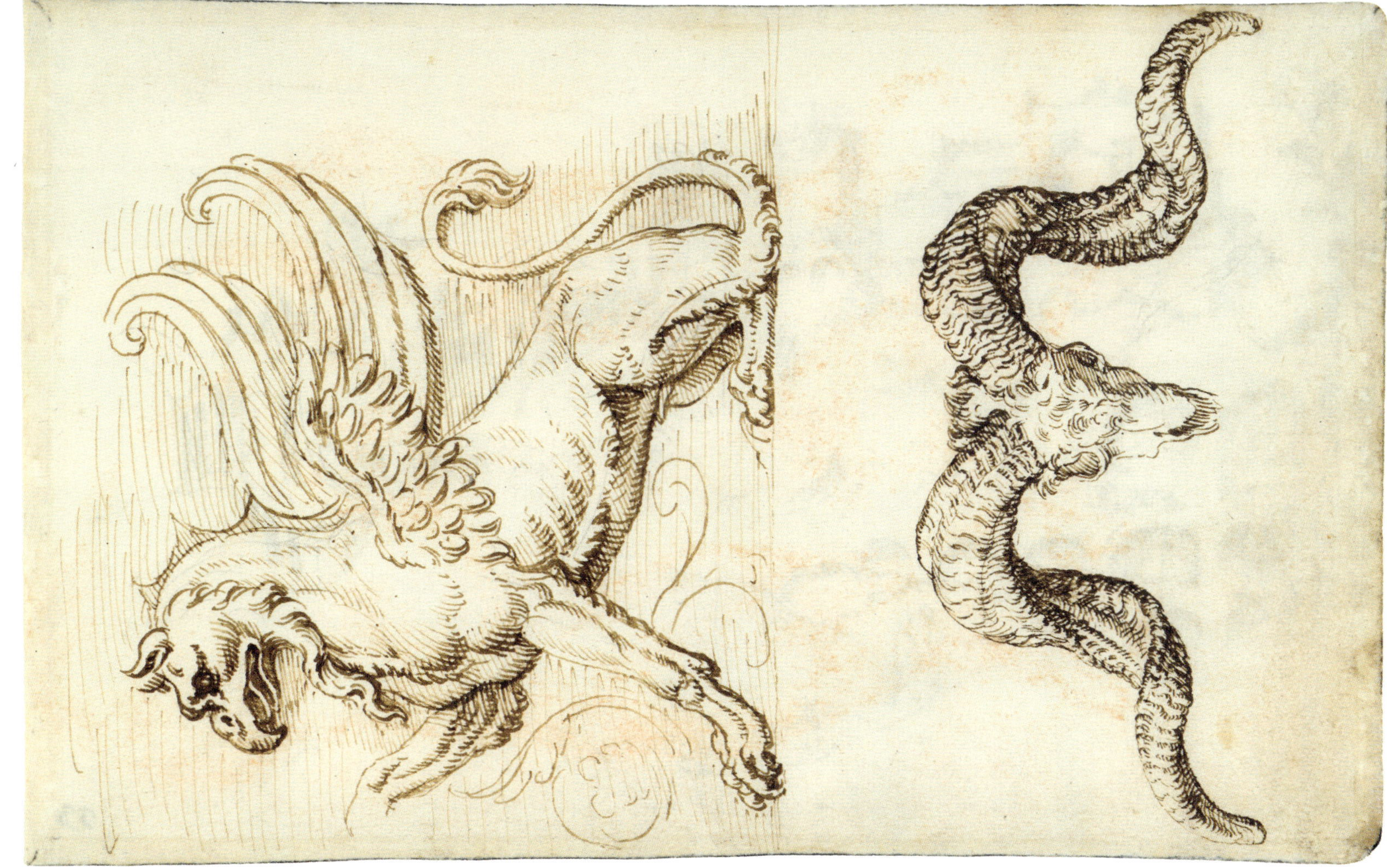

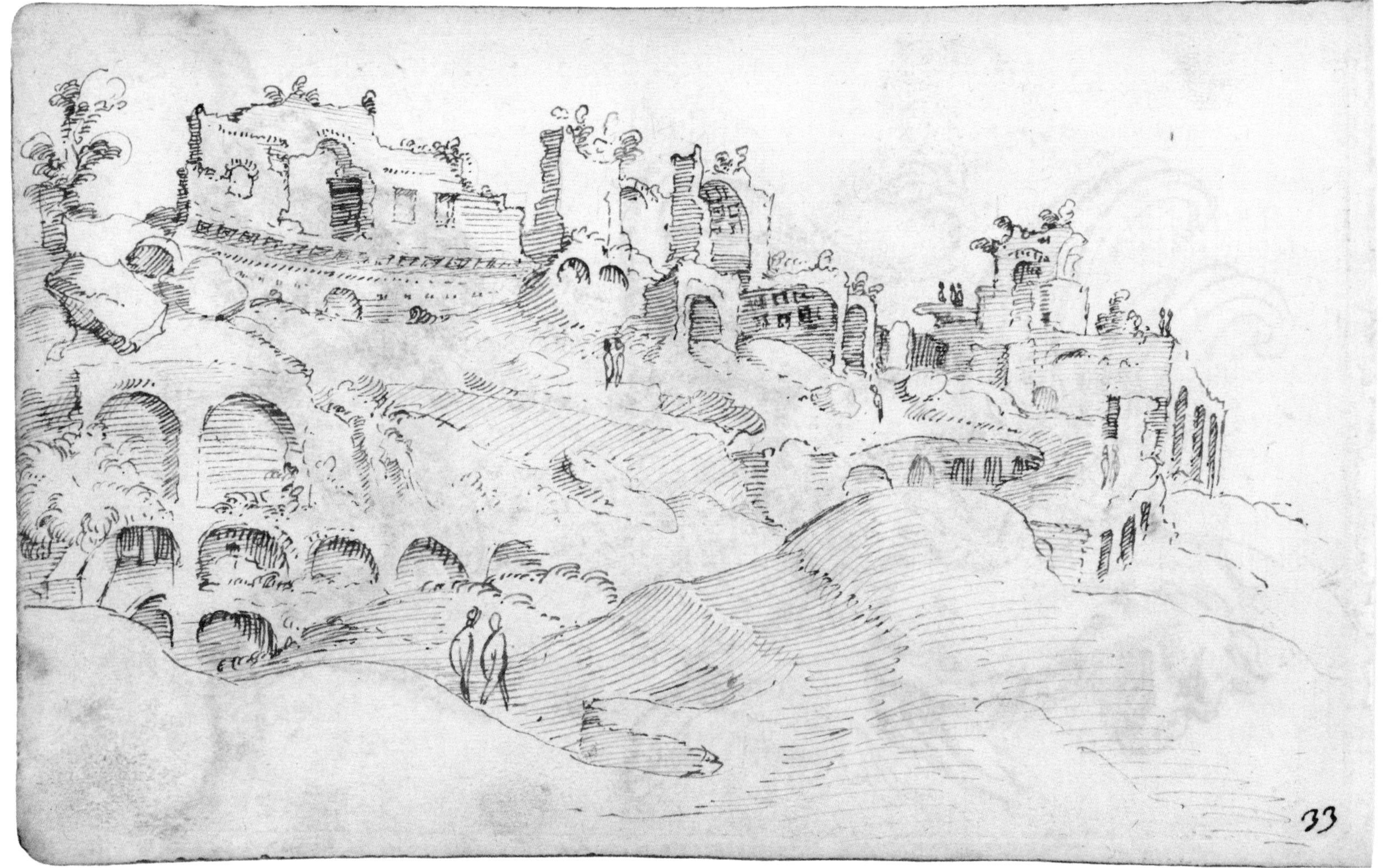

33

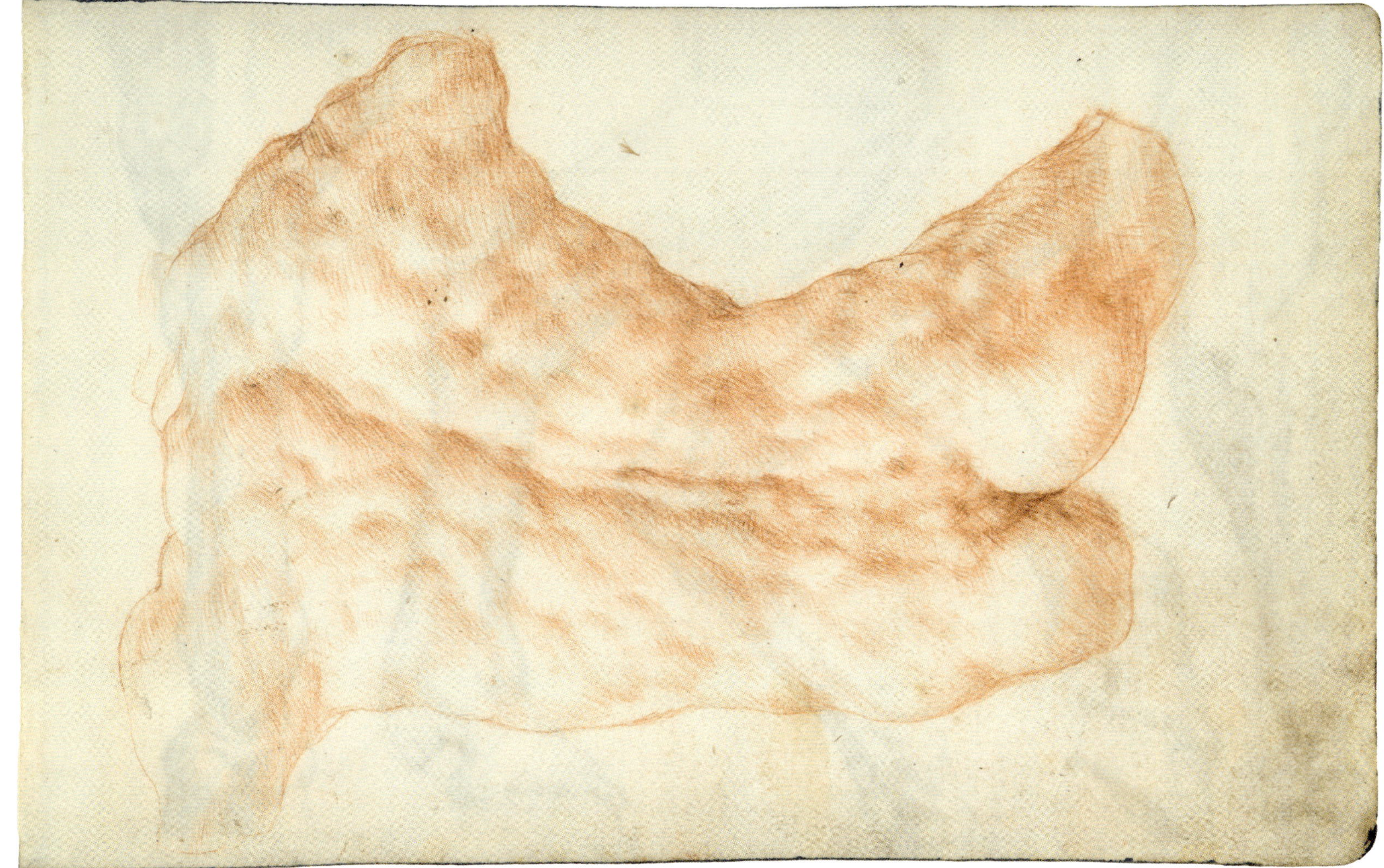

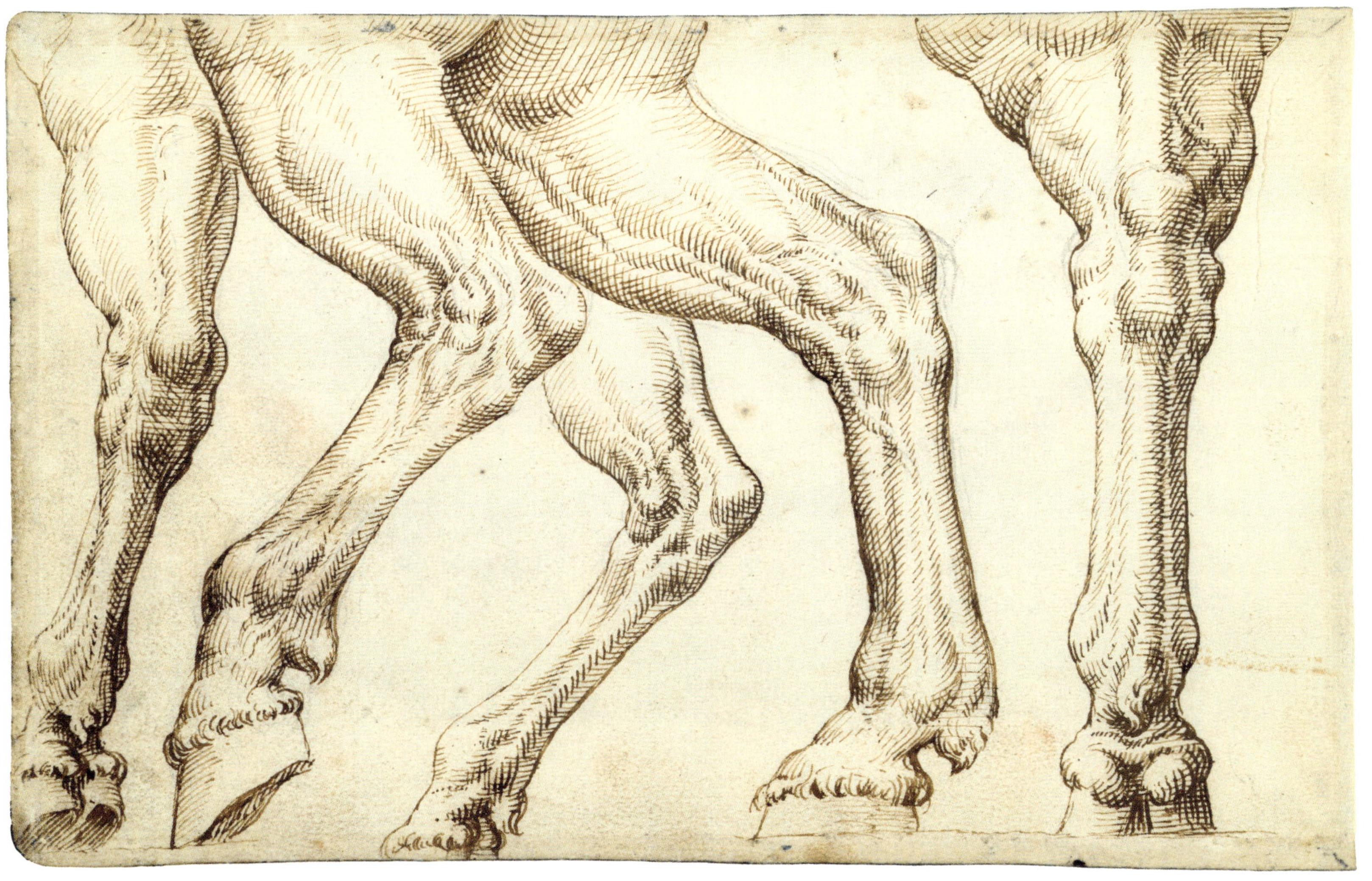

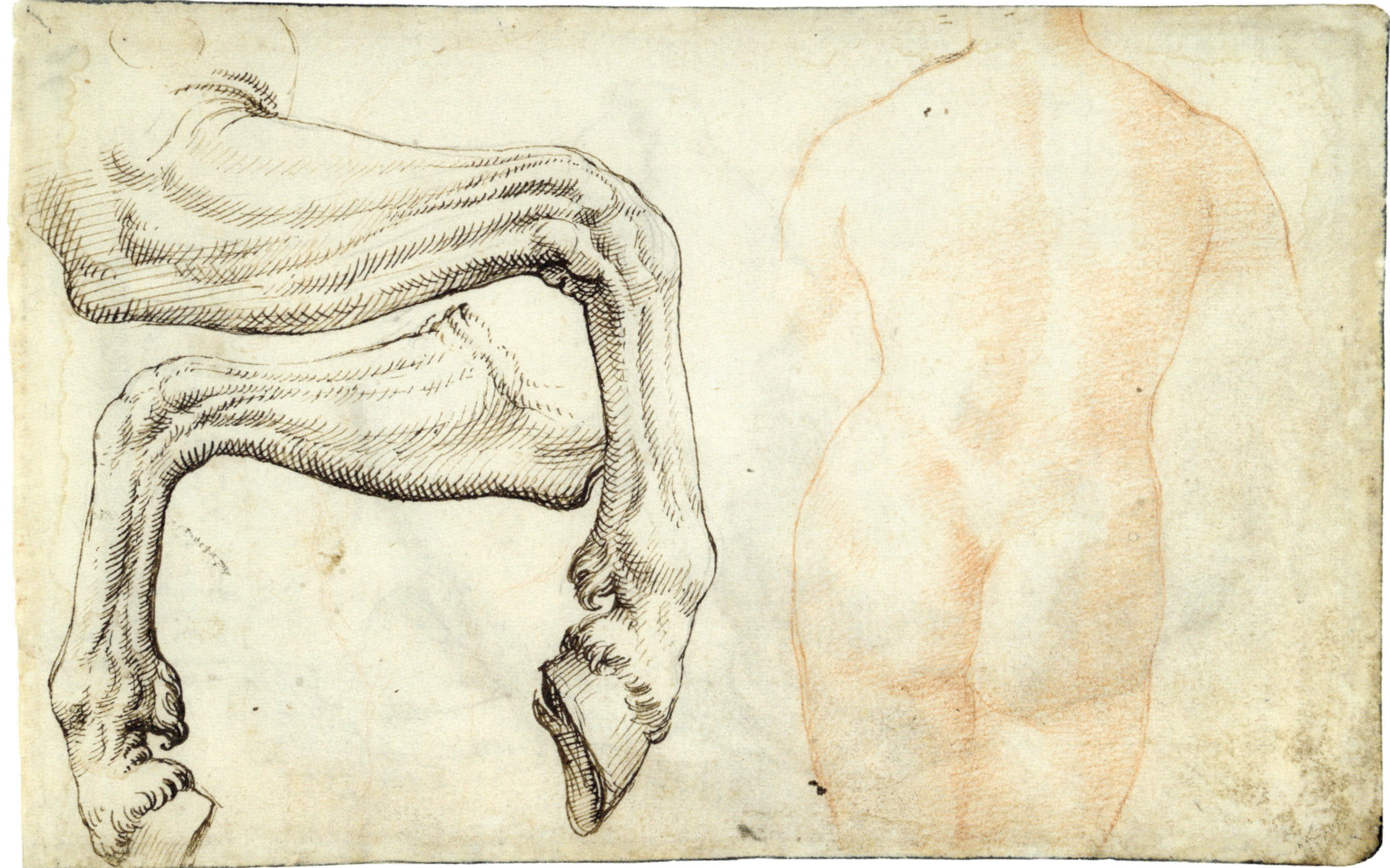

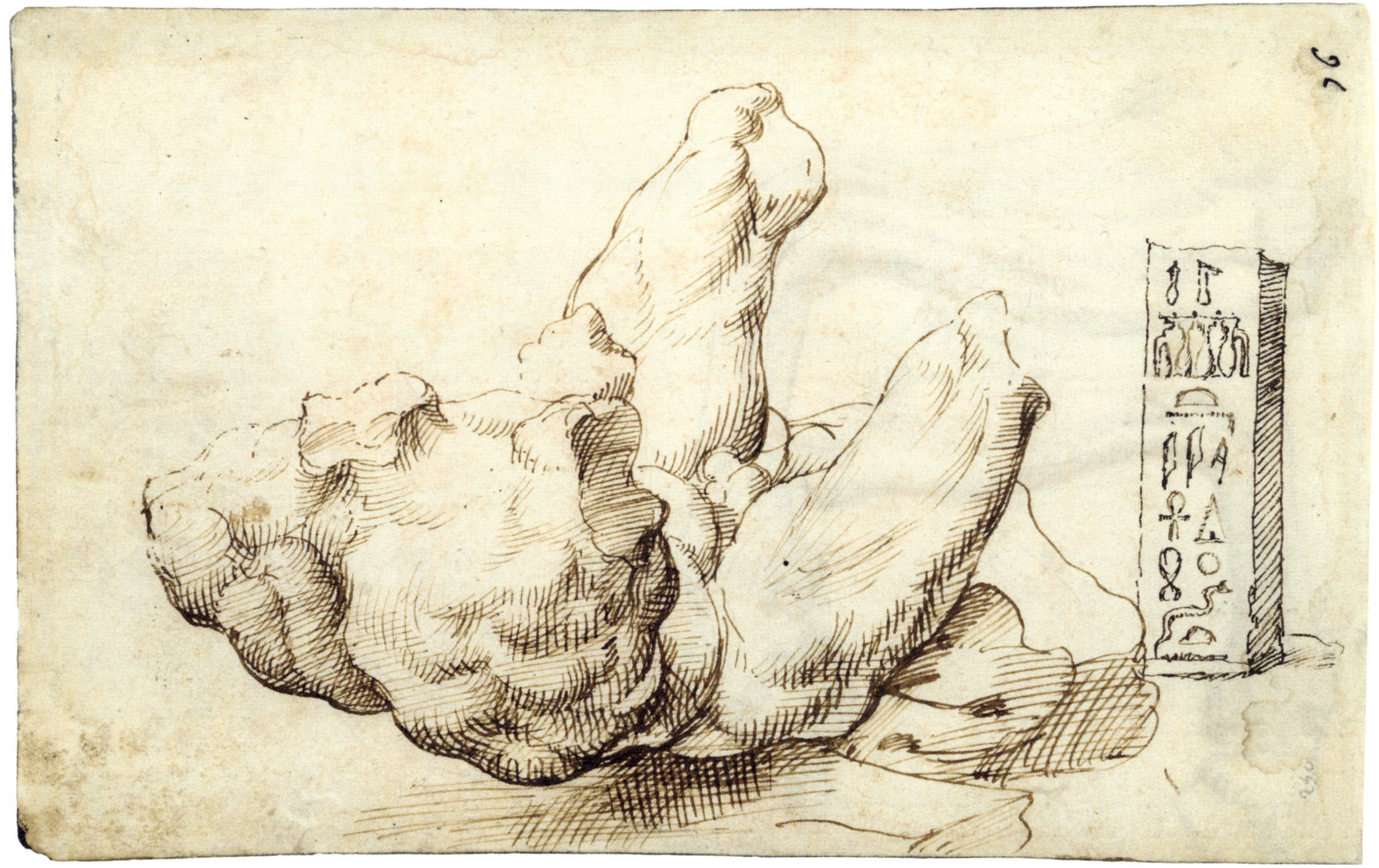

[ONE MISSING PAGE]

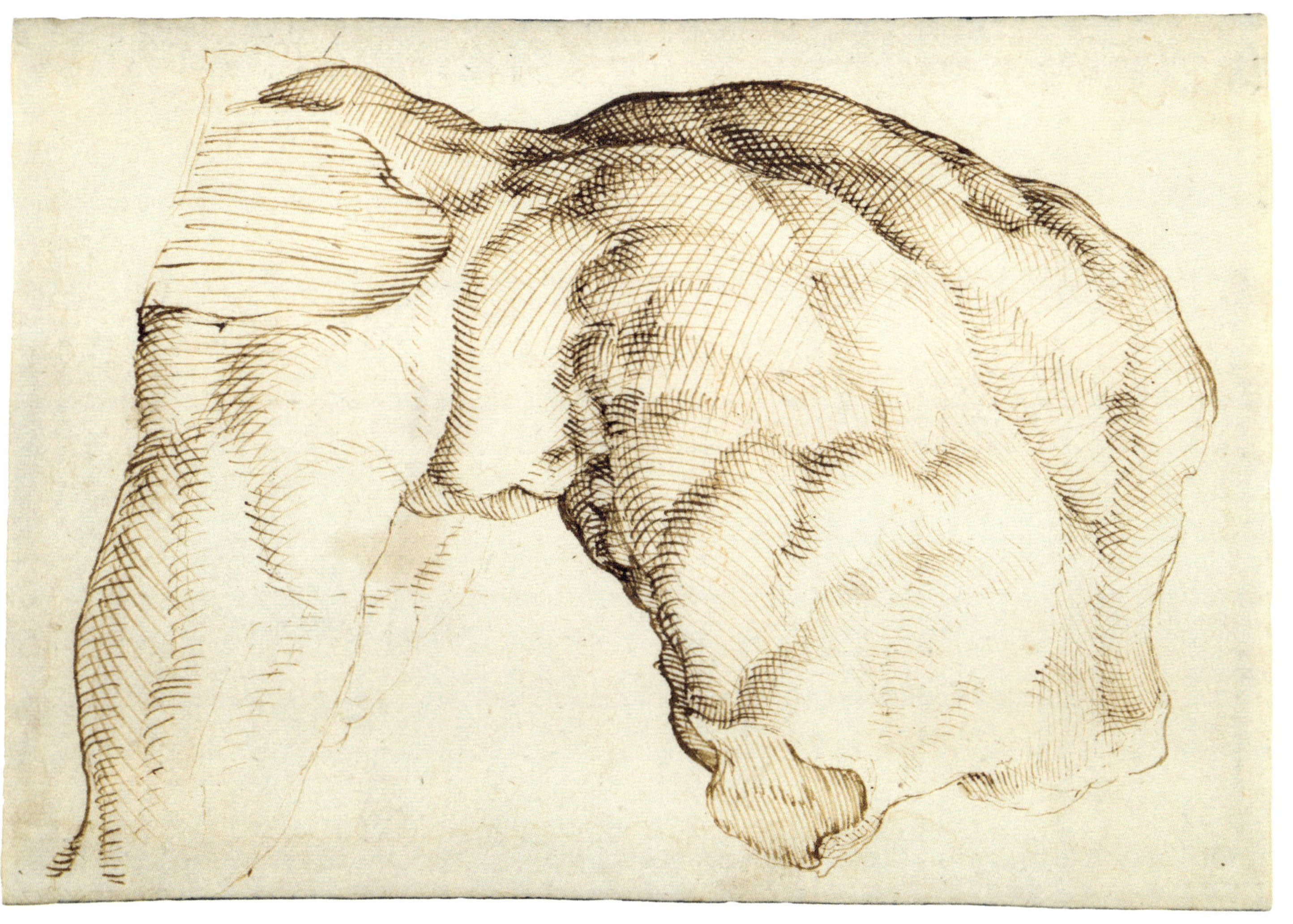

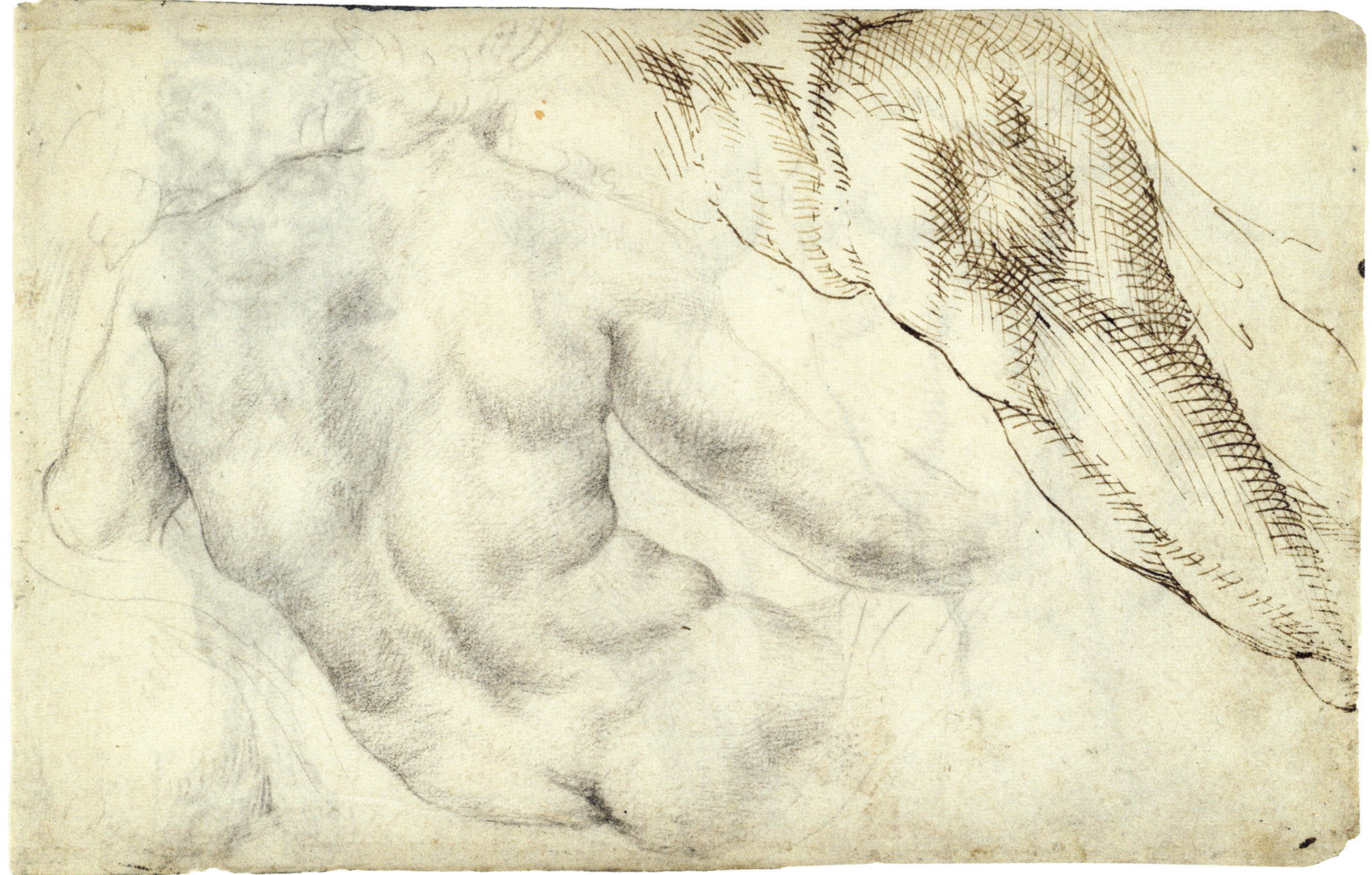

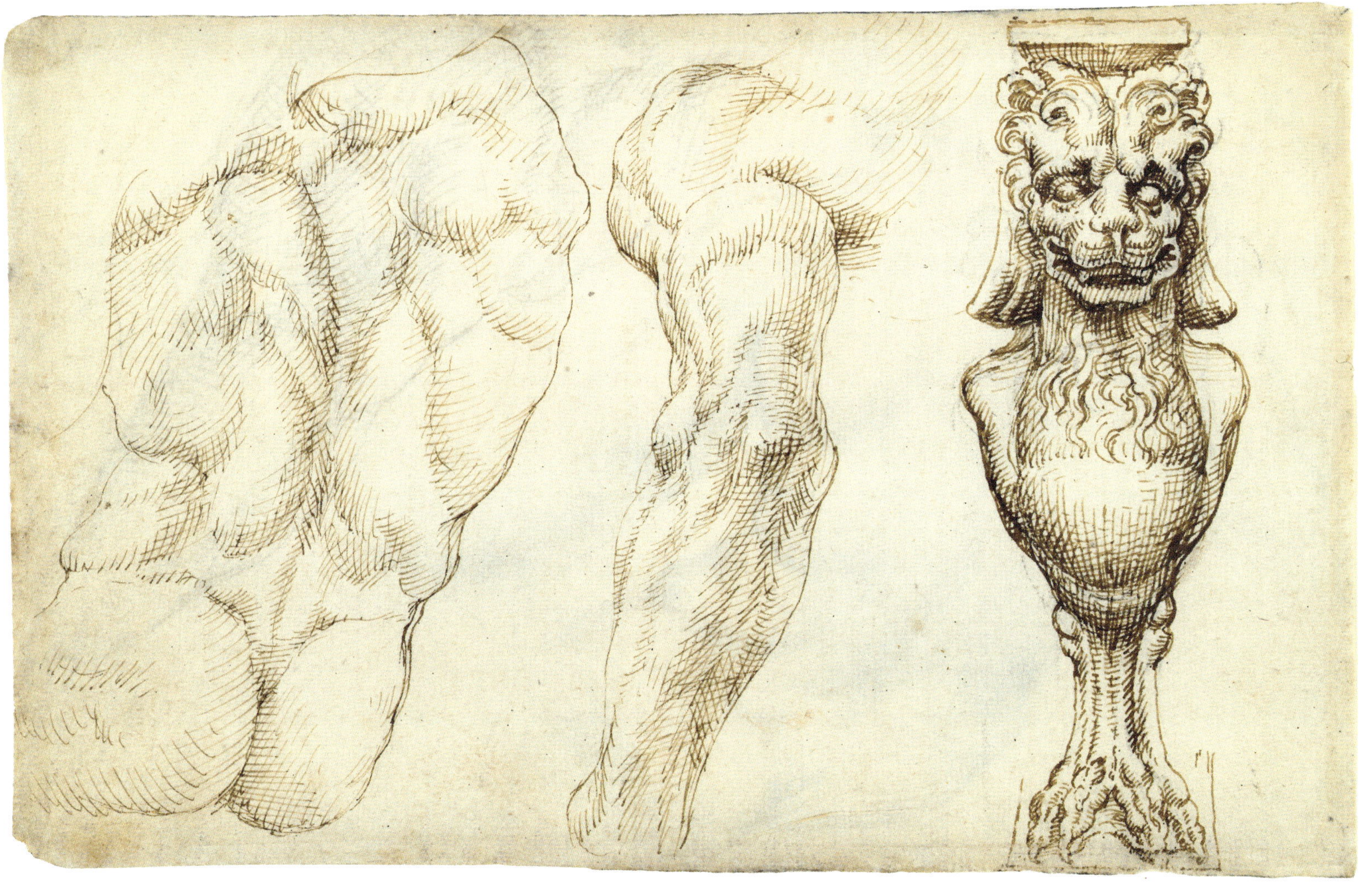

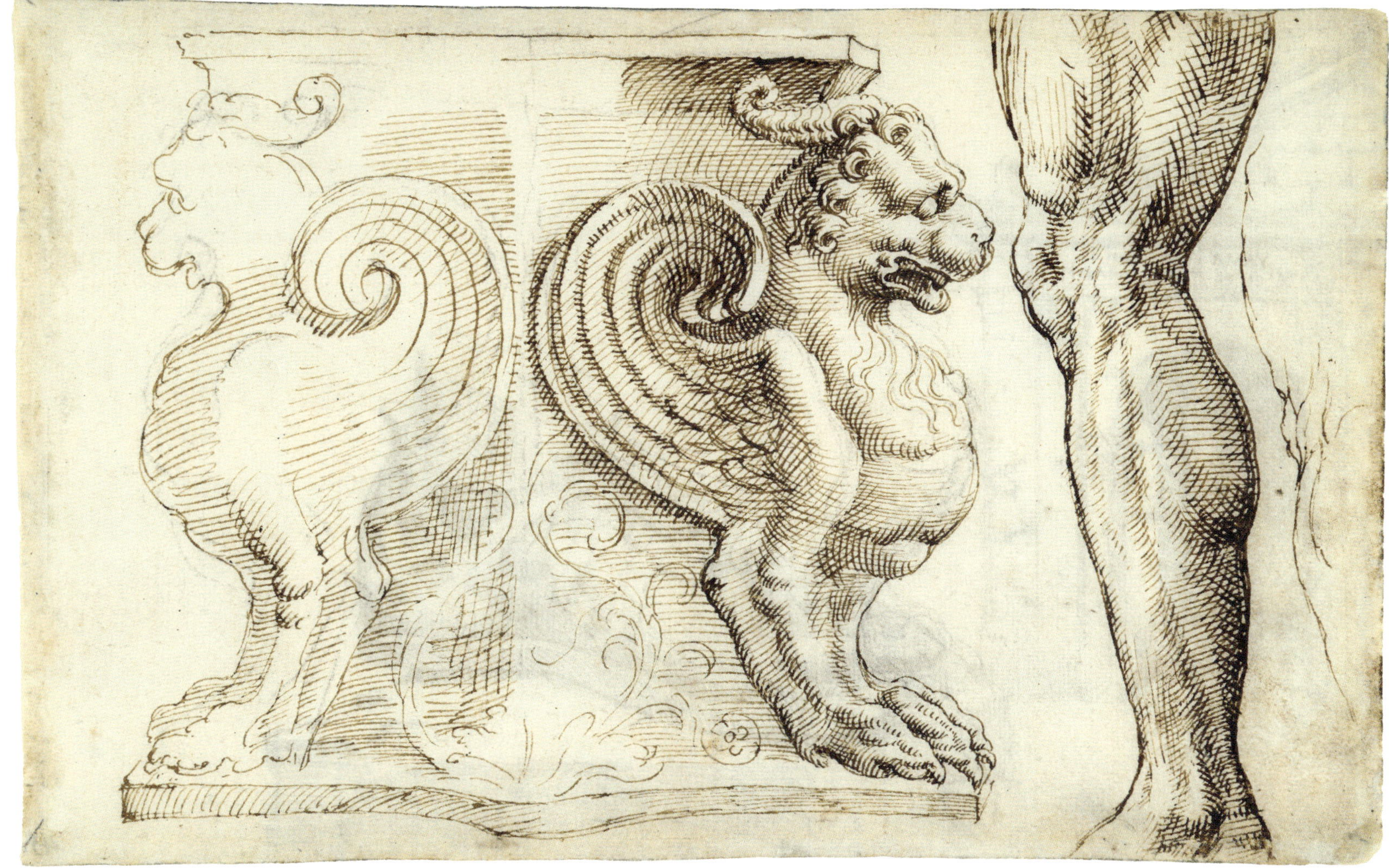

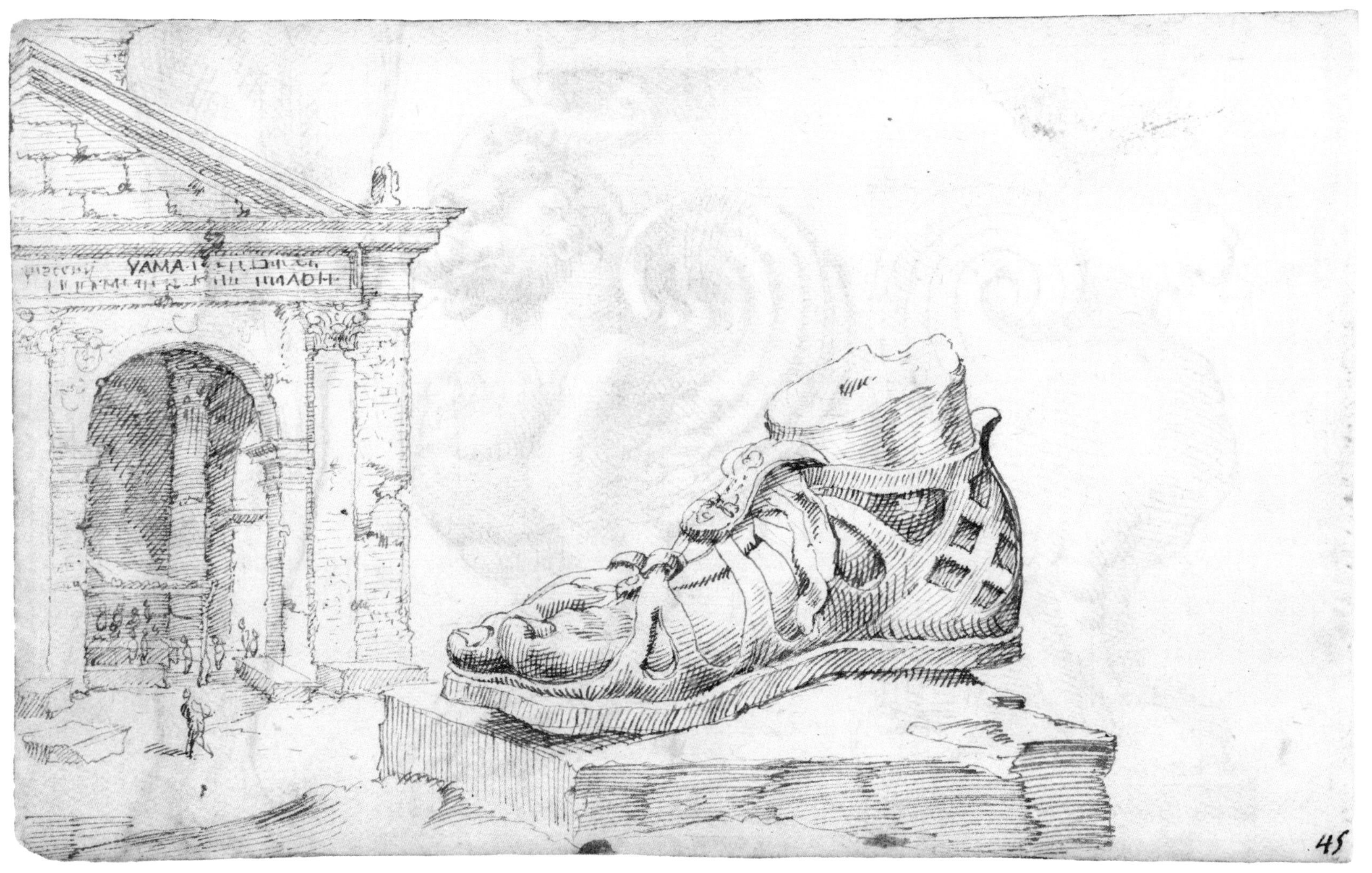
45

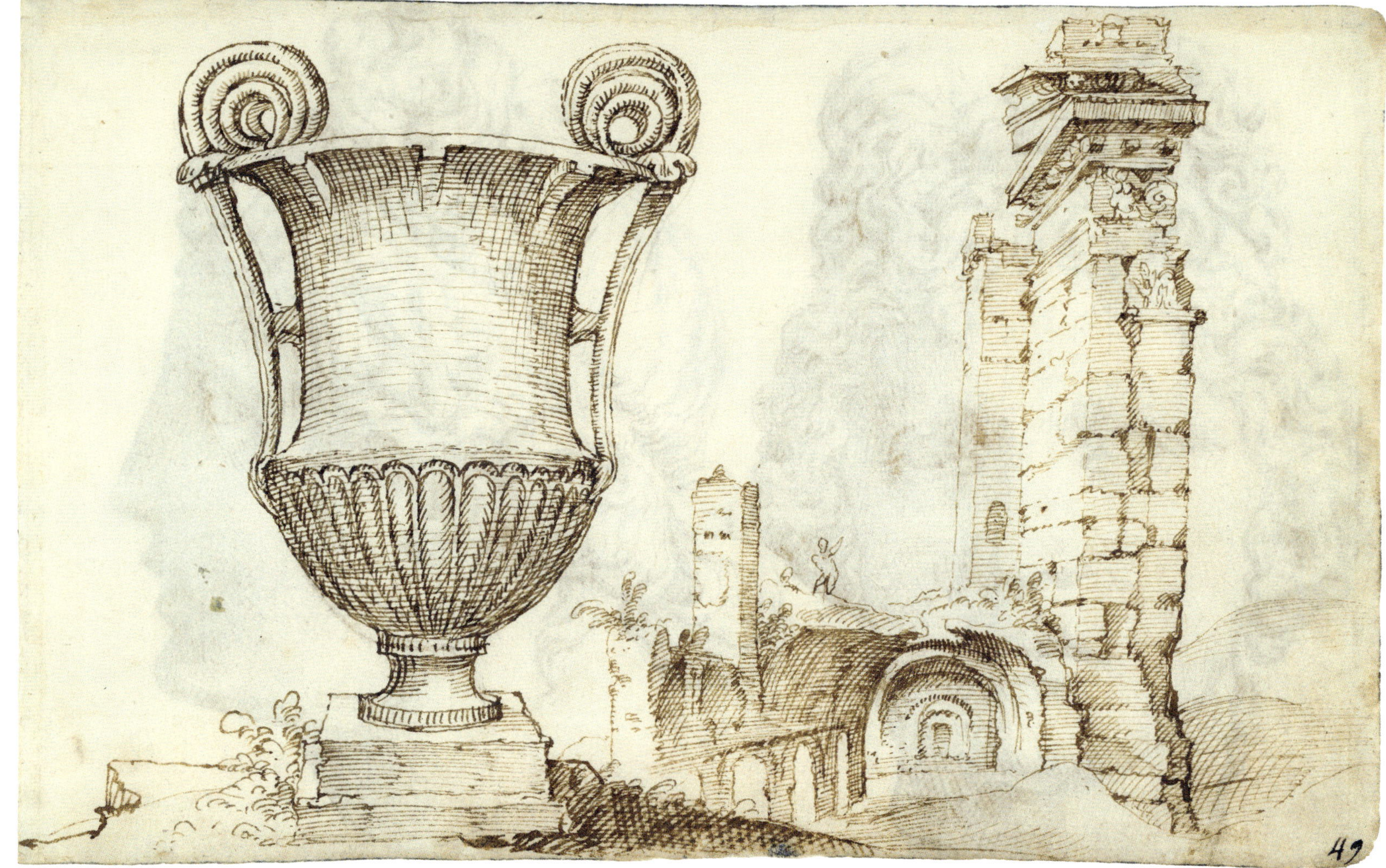

49

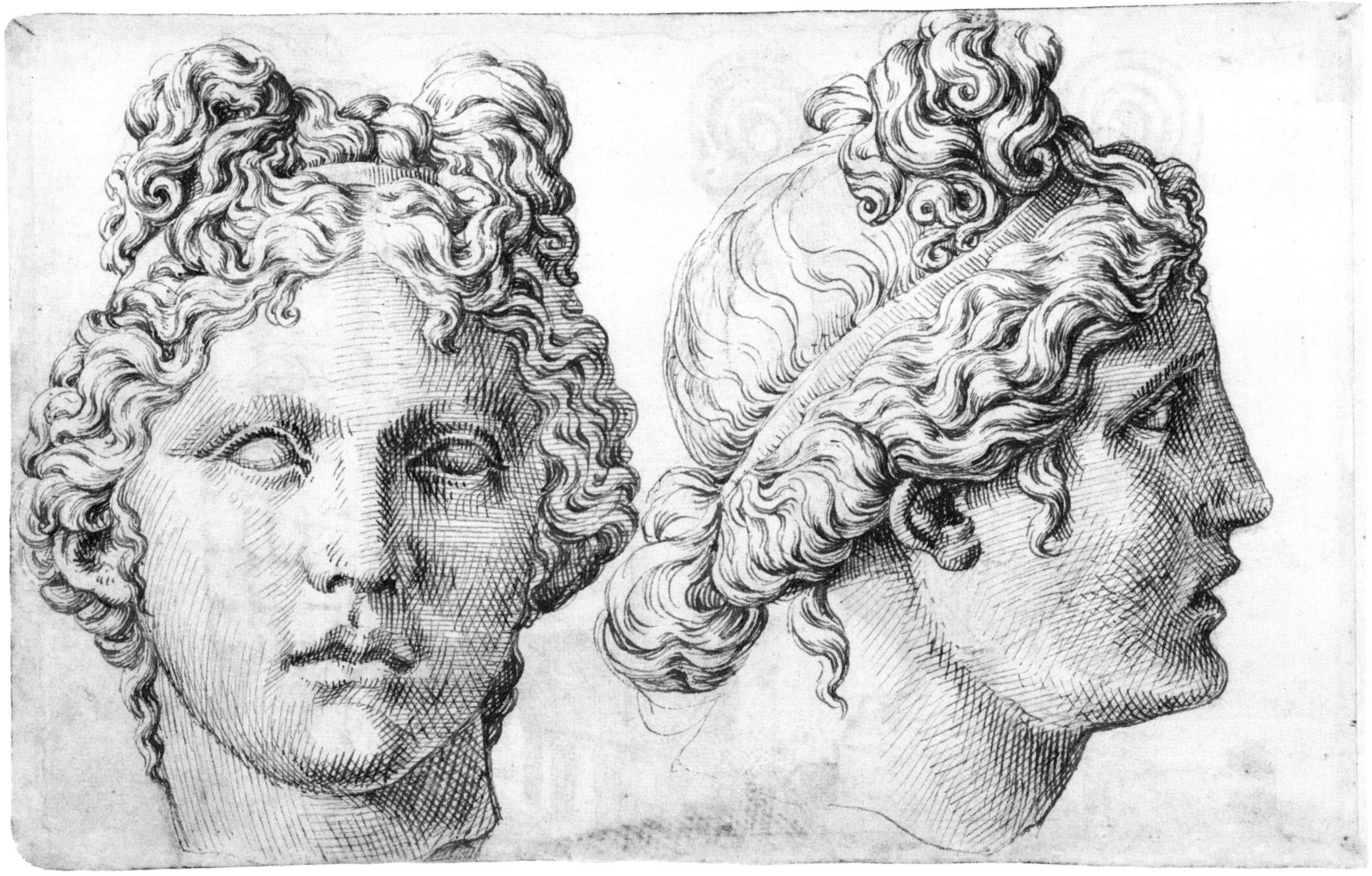

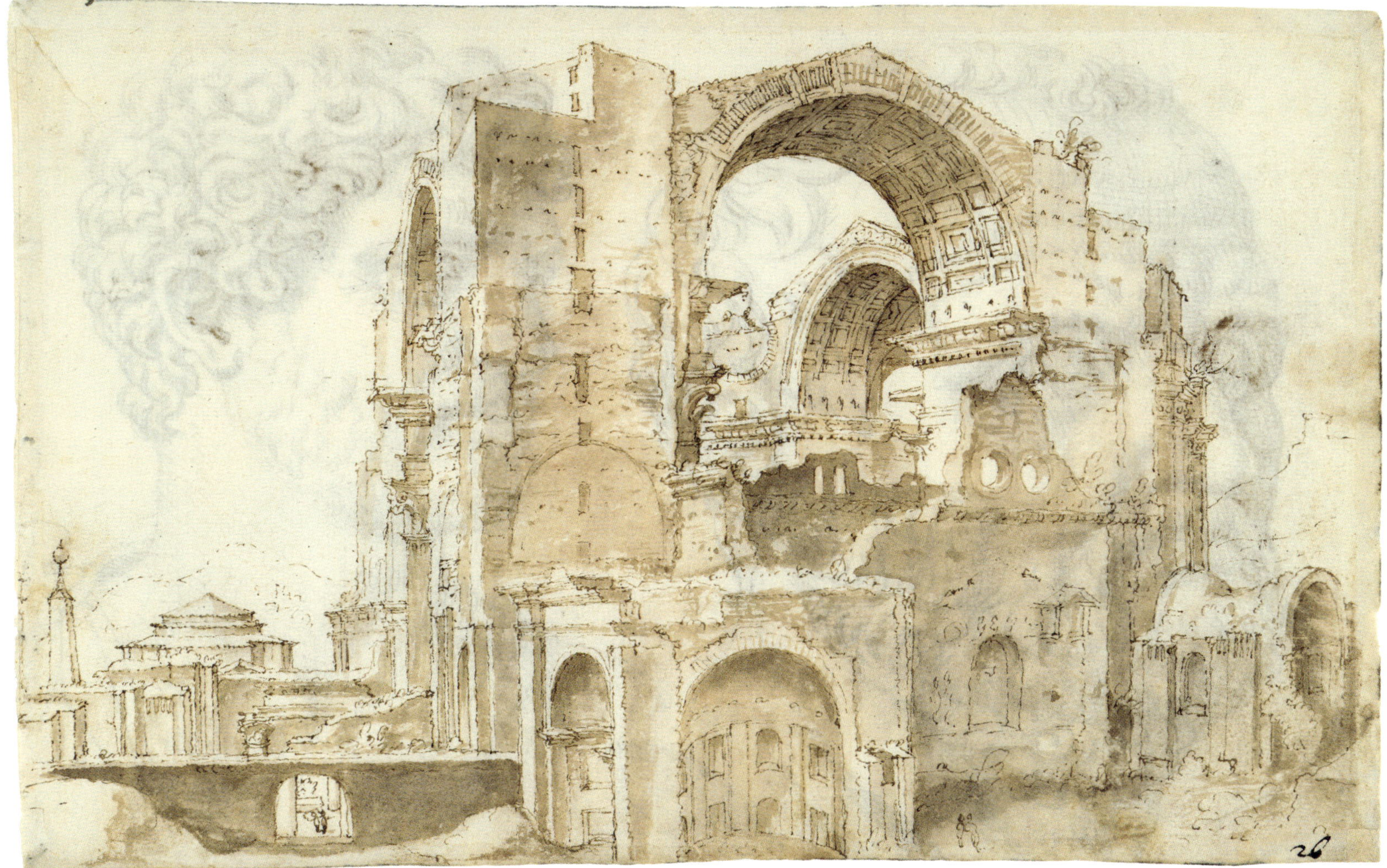

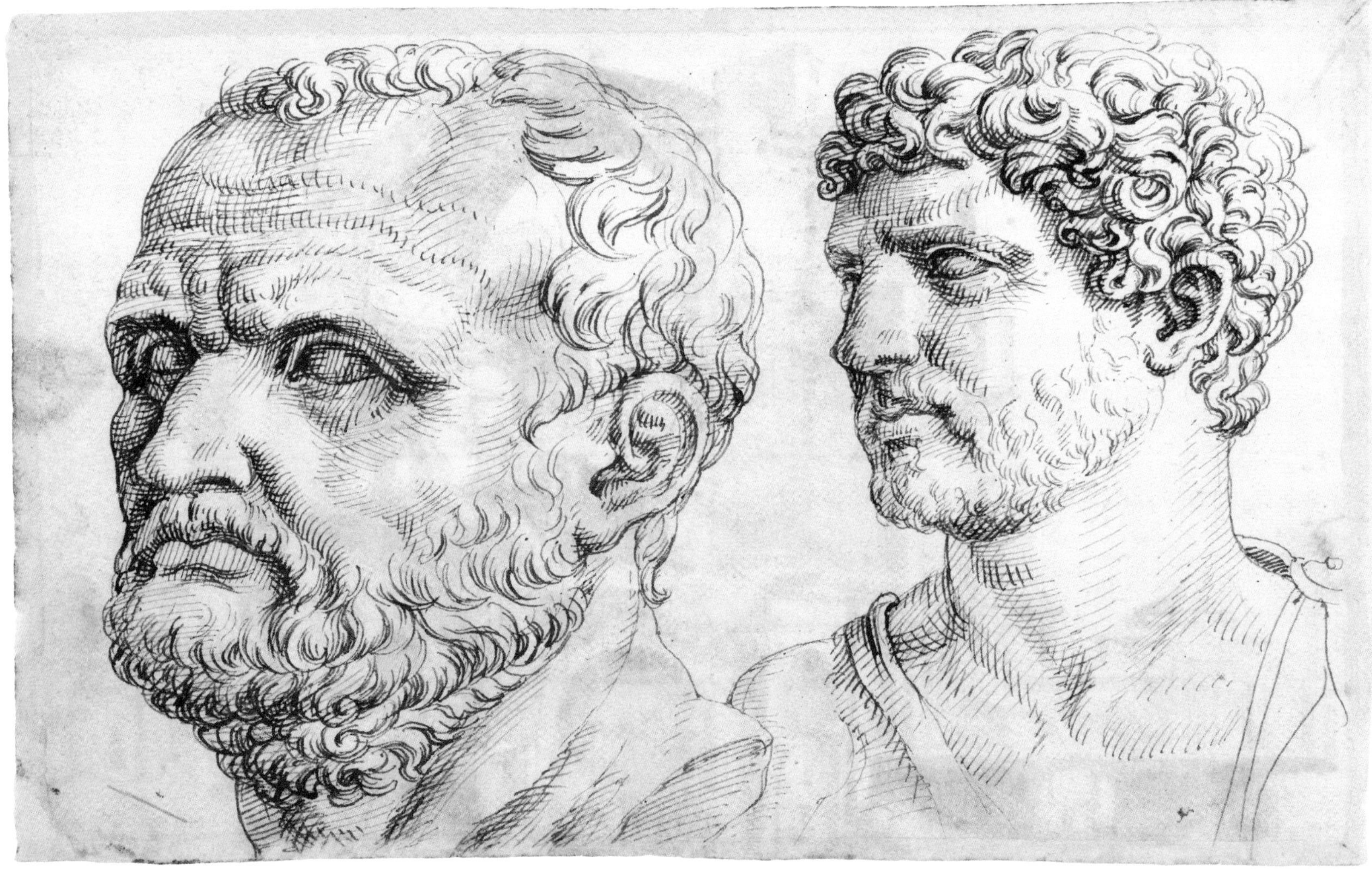

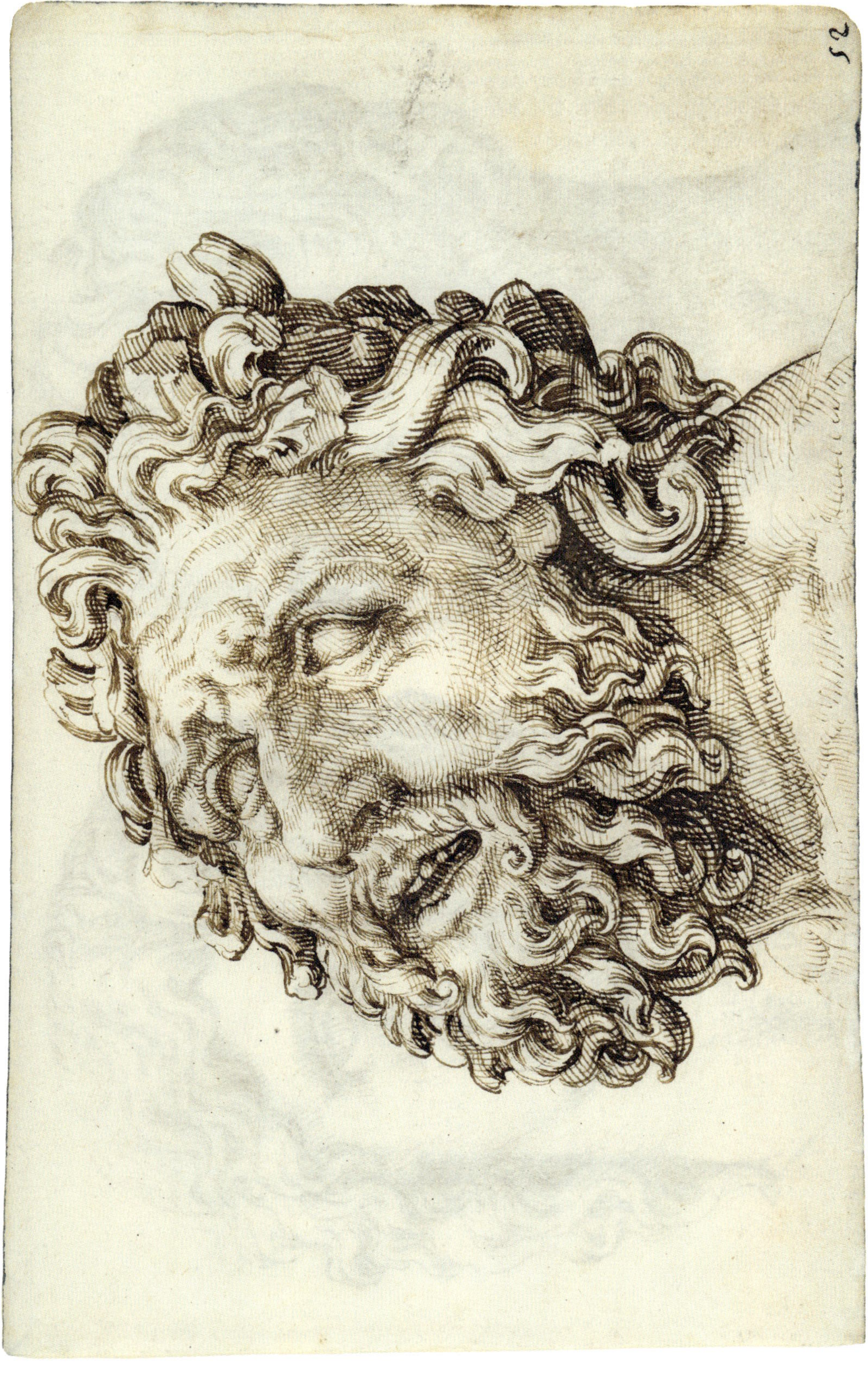

52

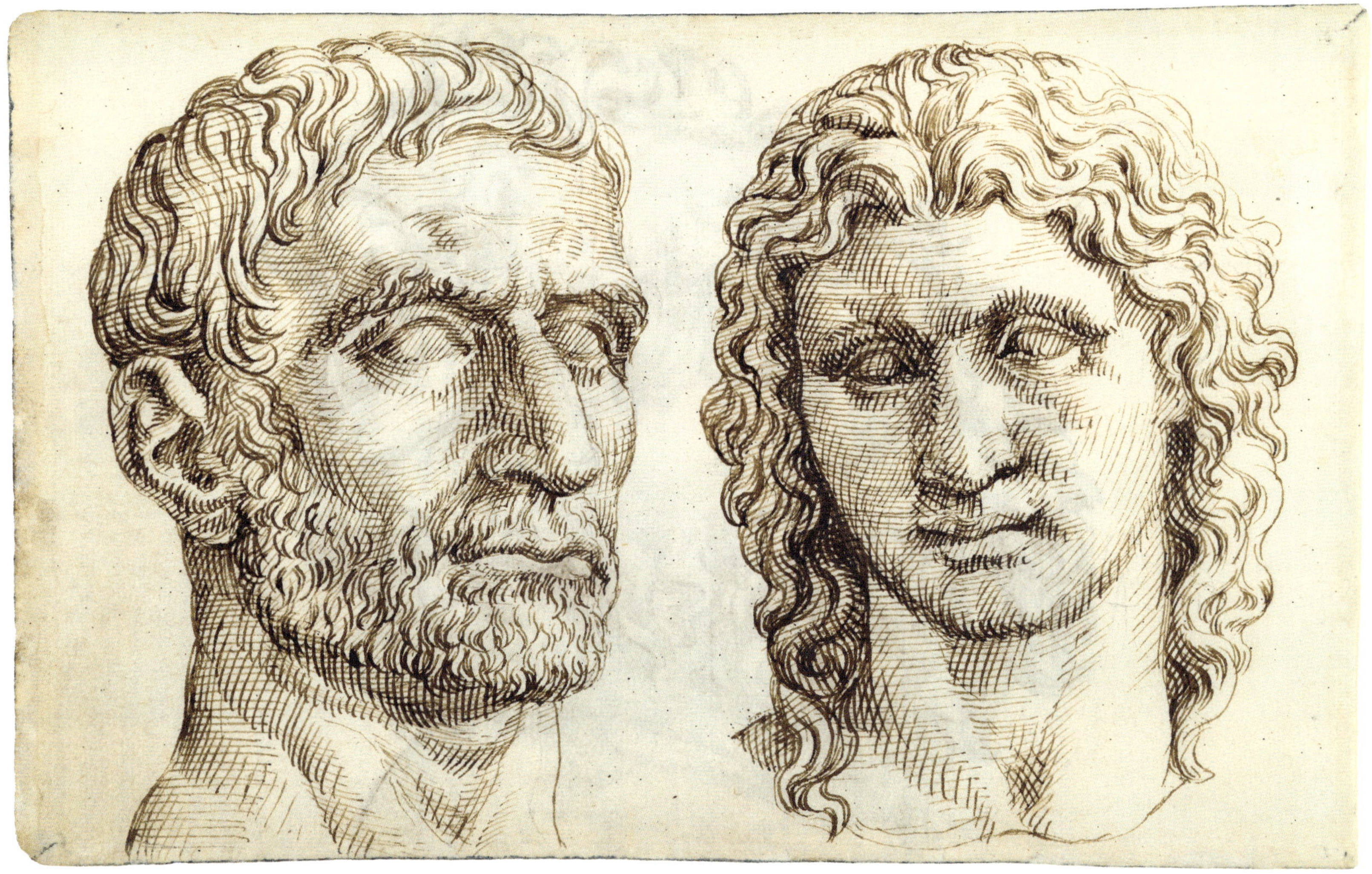

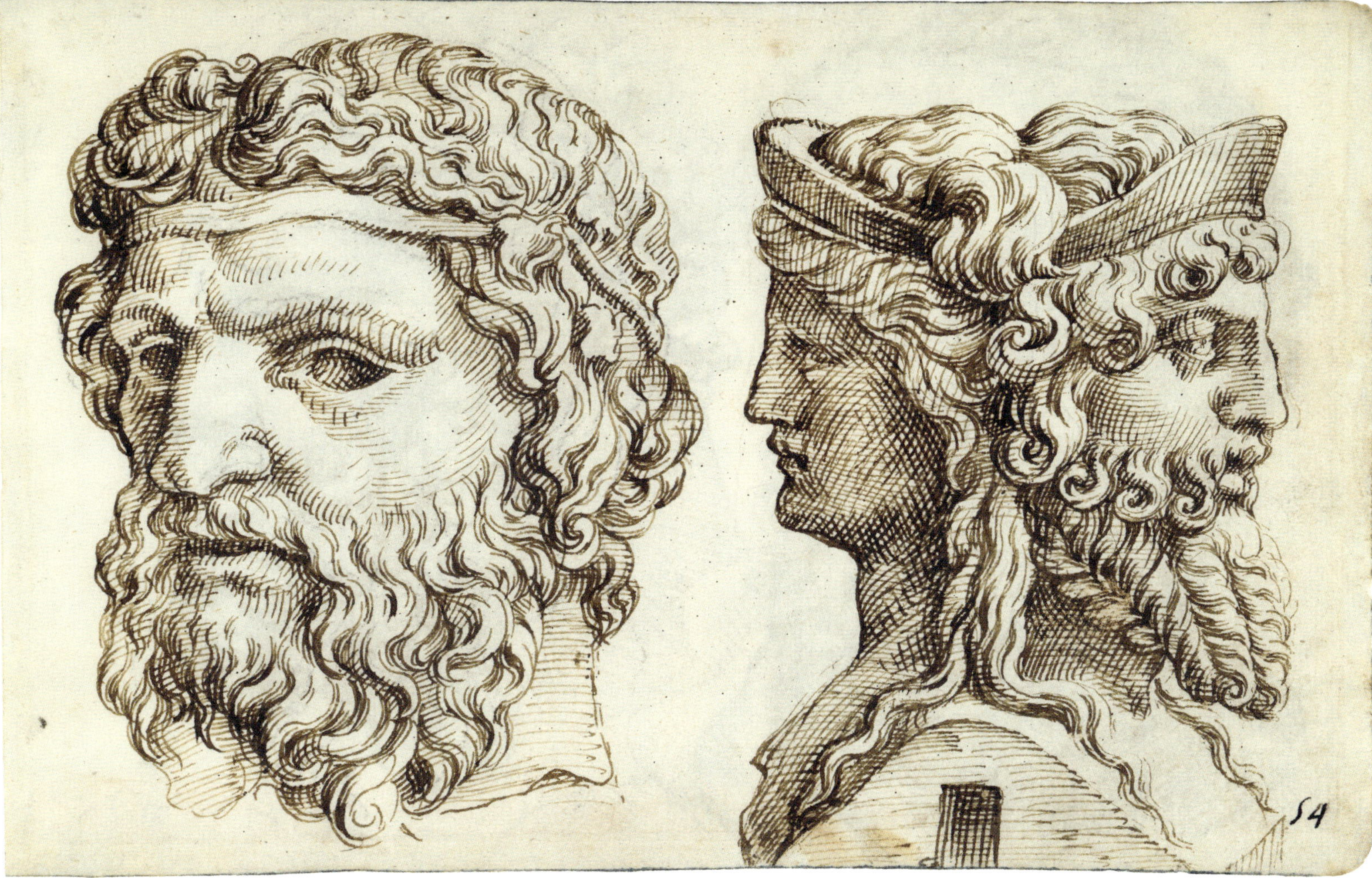
54

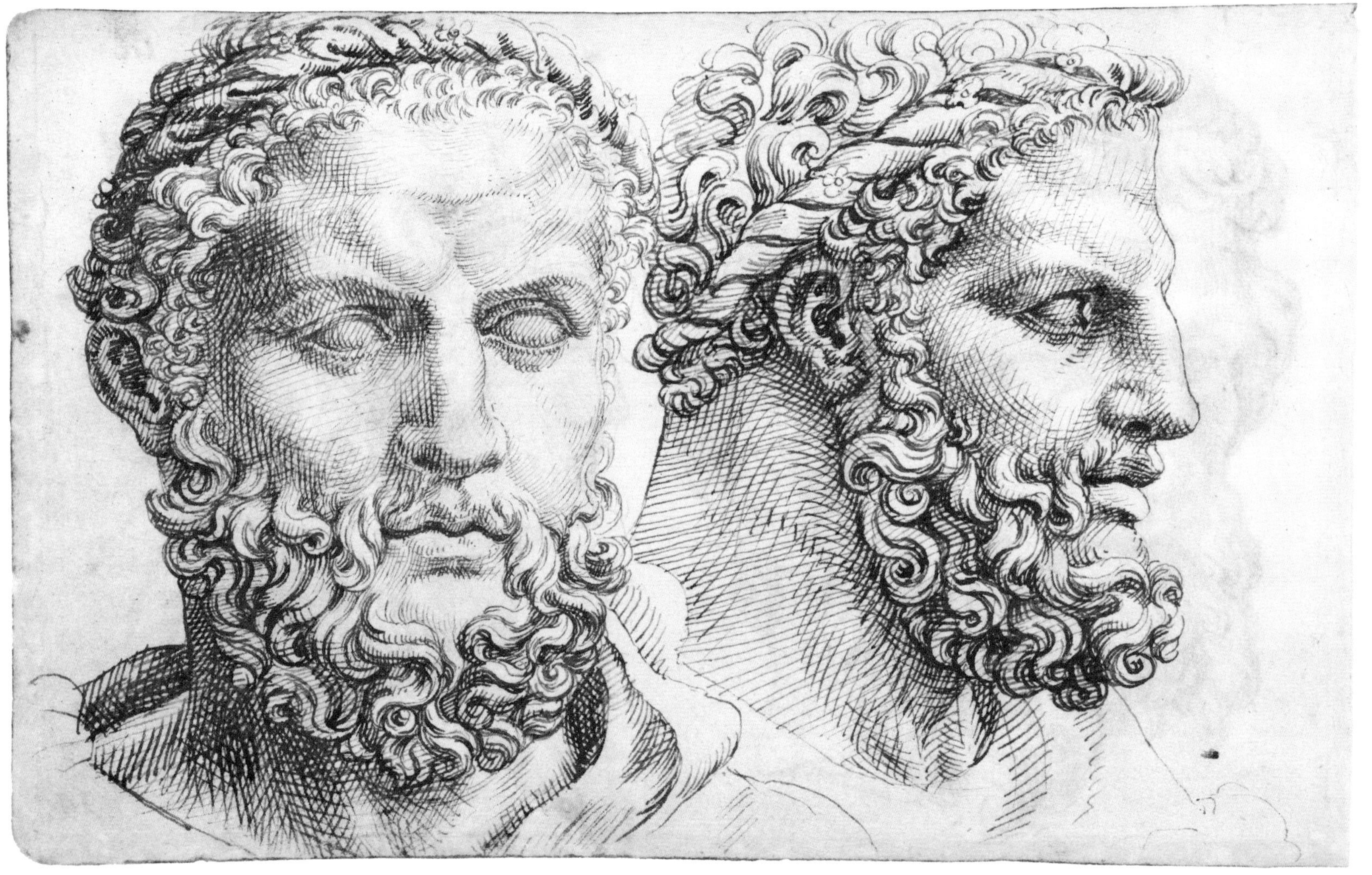

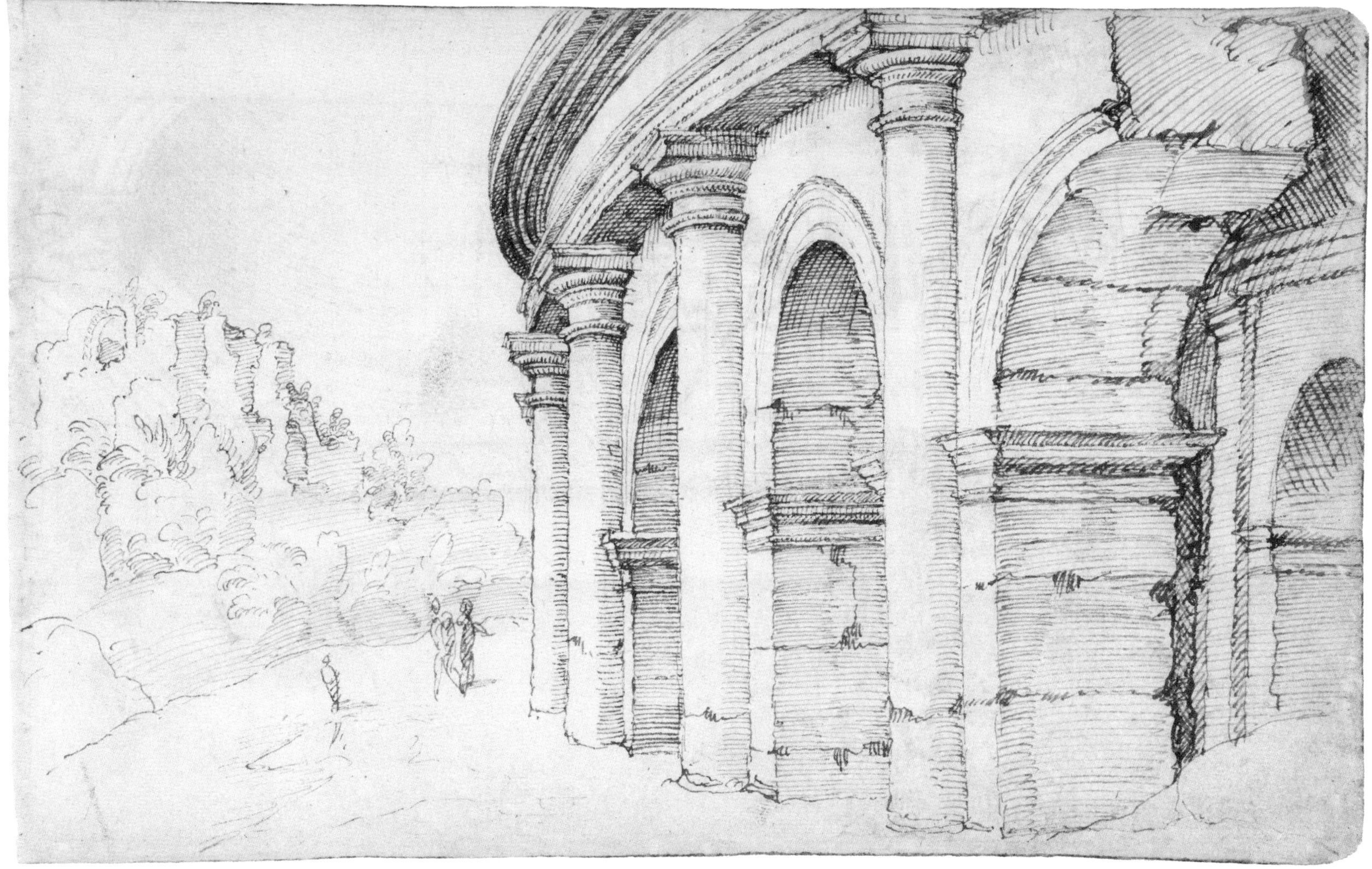

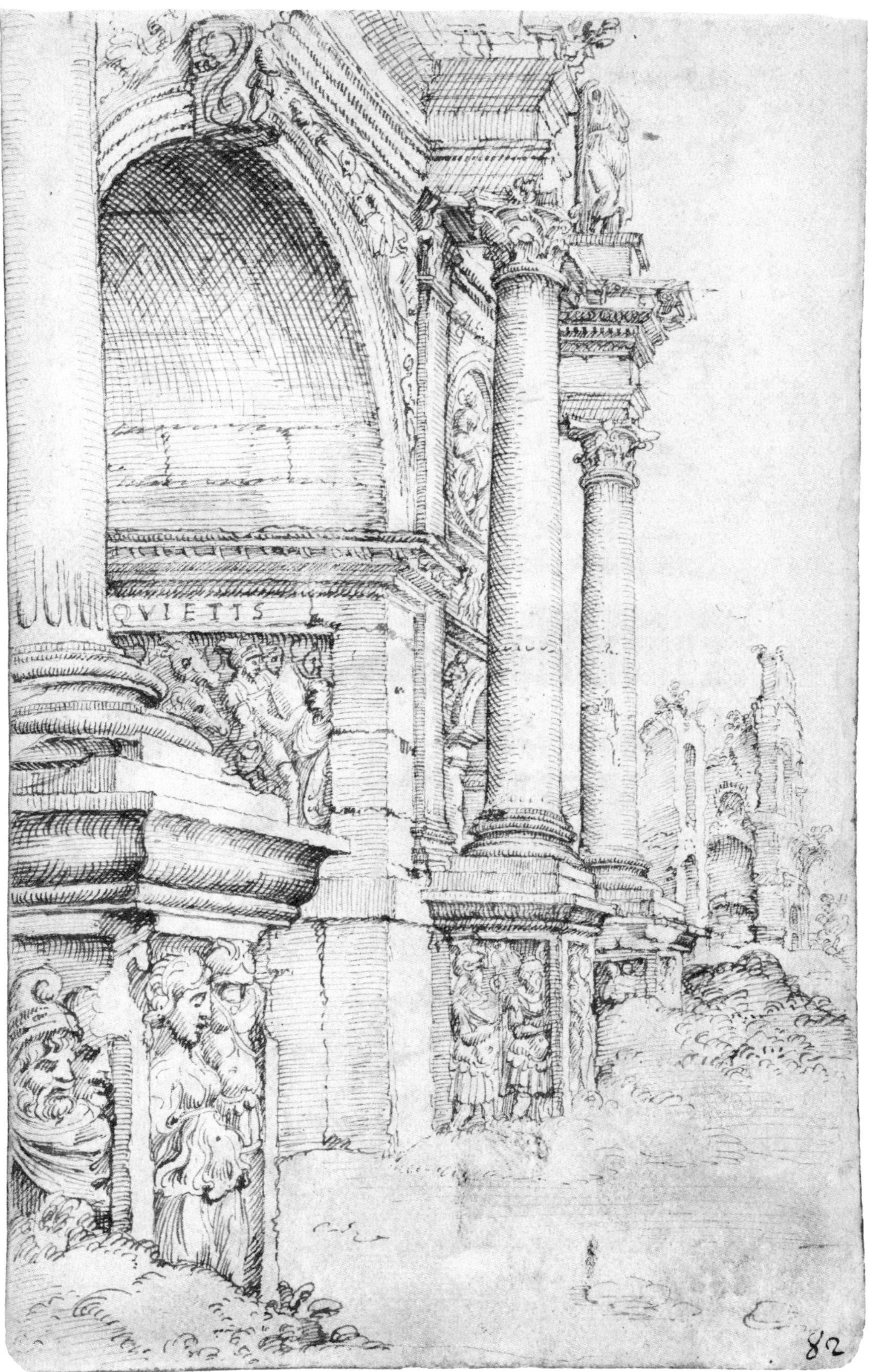
QVIETIS

[ONE MISSING PAGE]

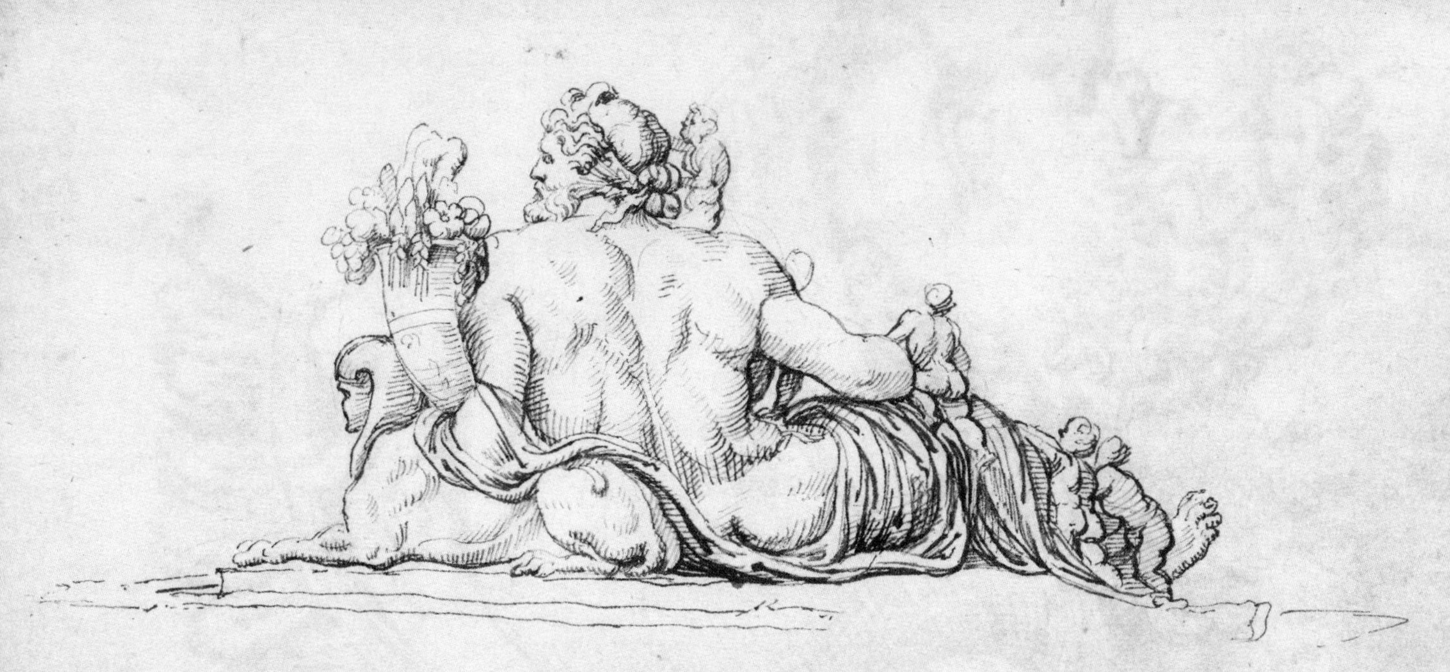

67

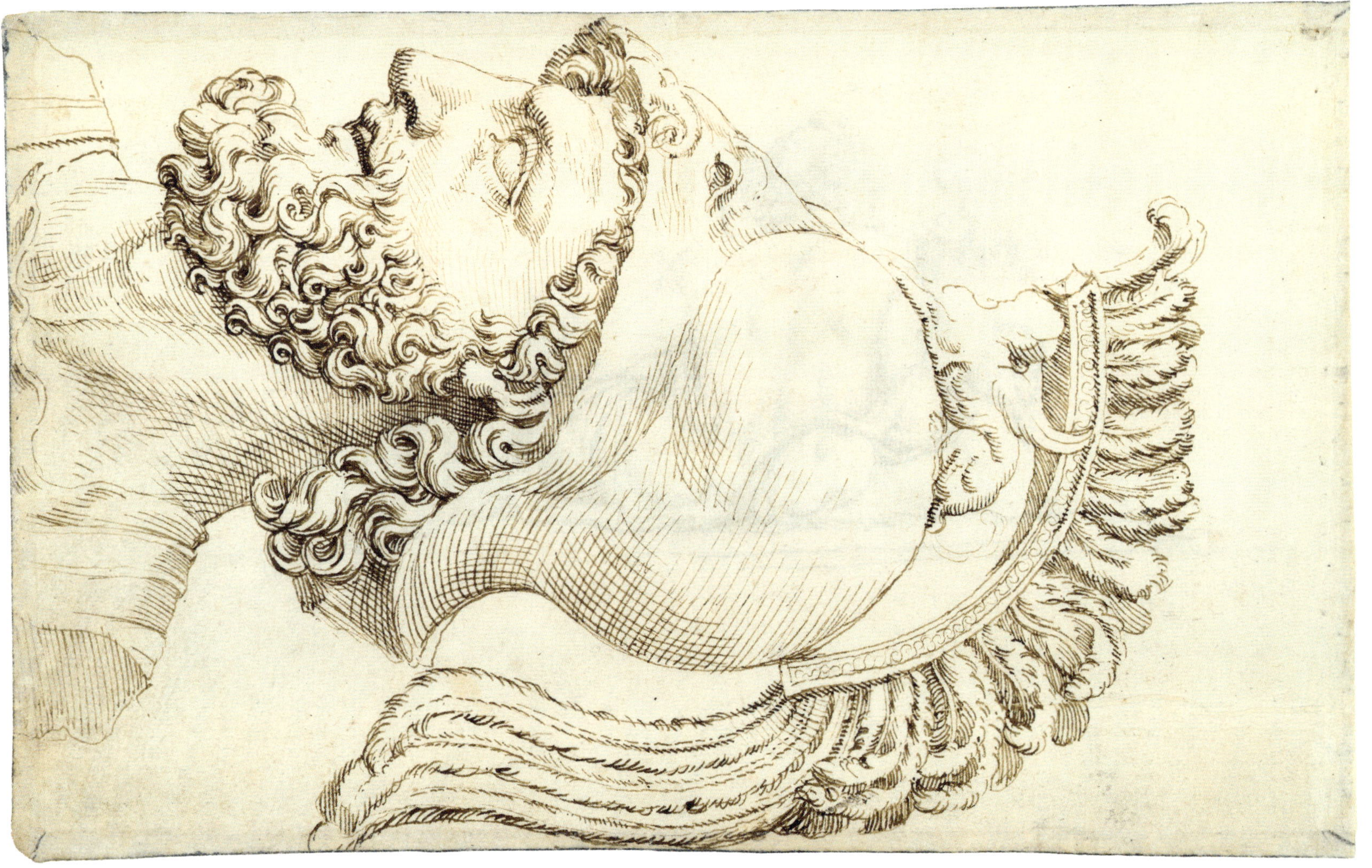

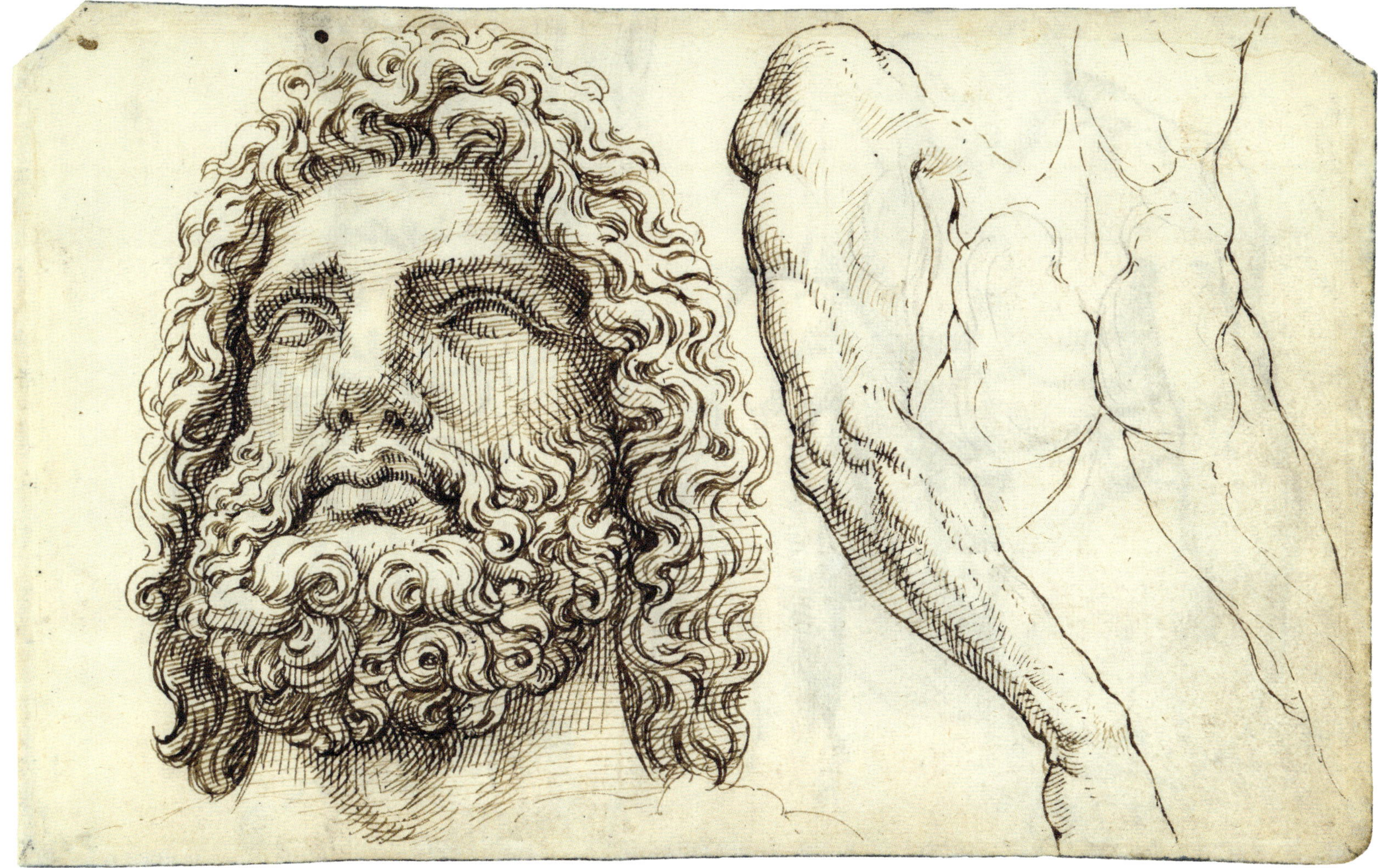

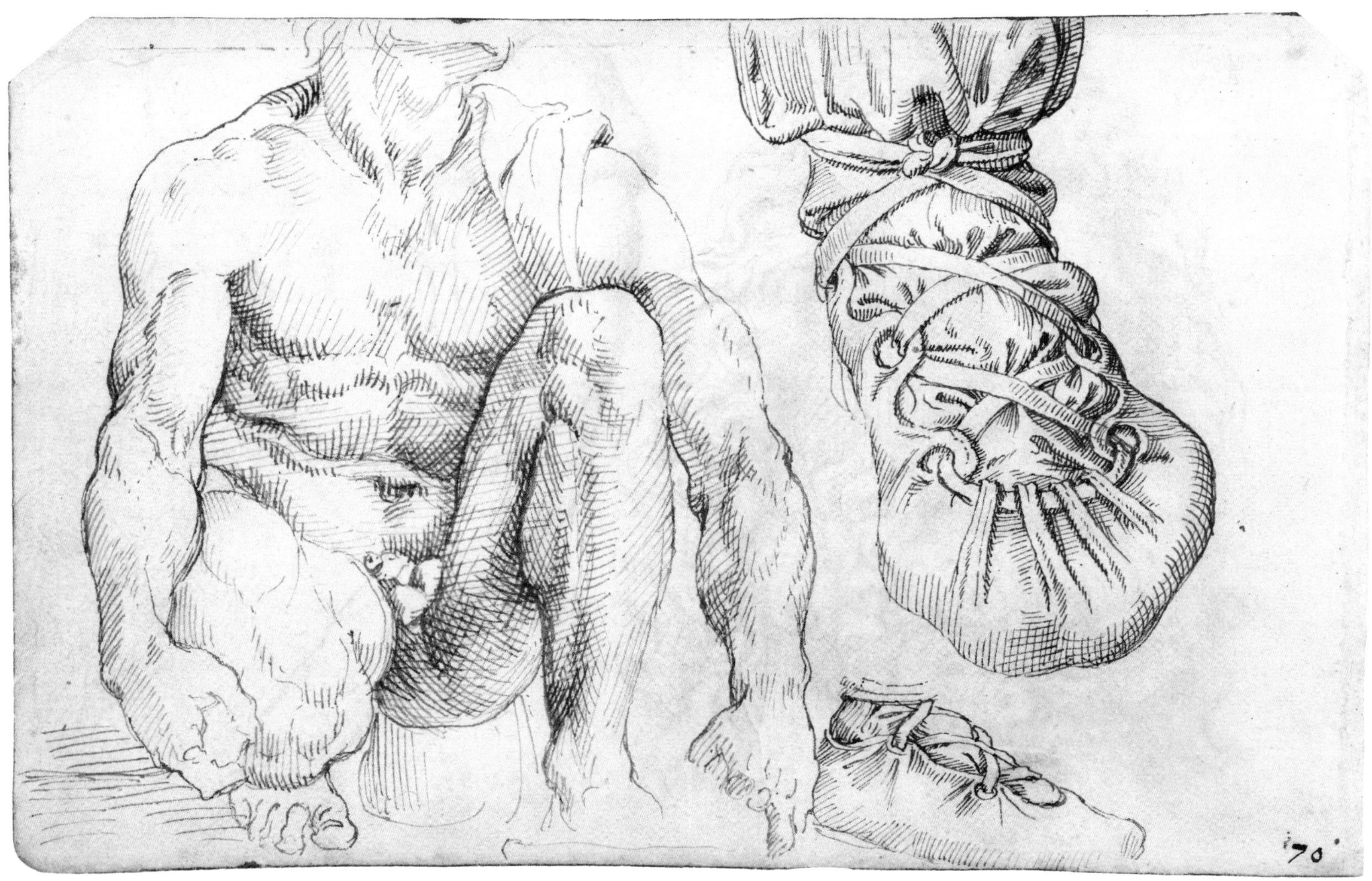

'70'

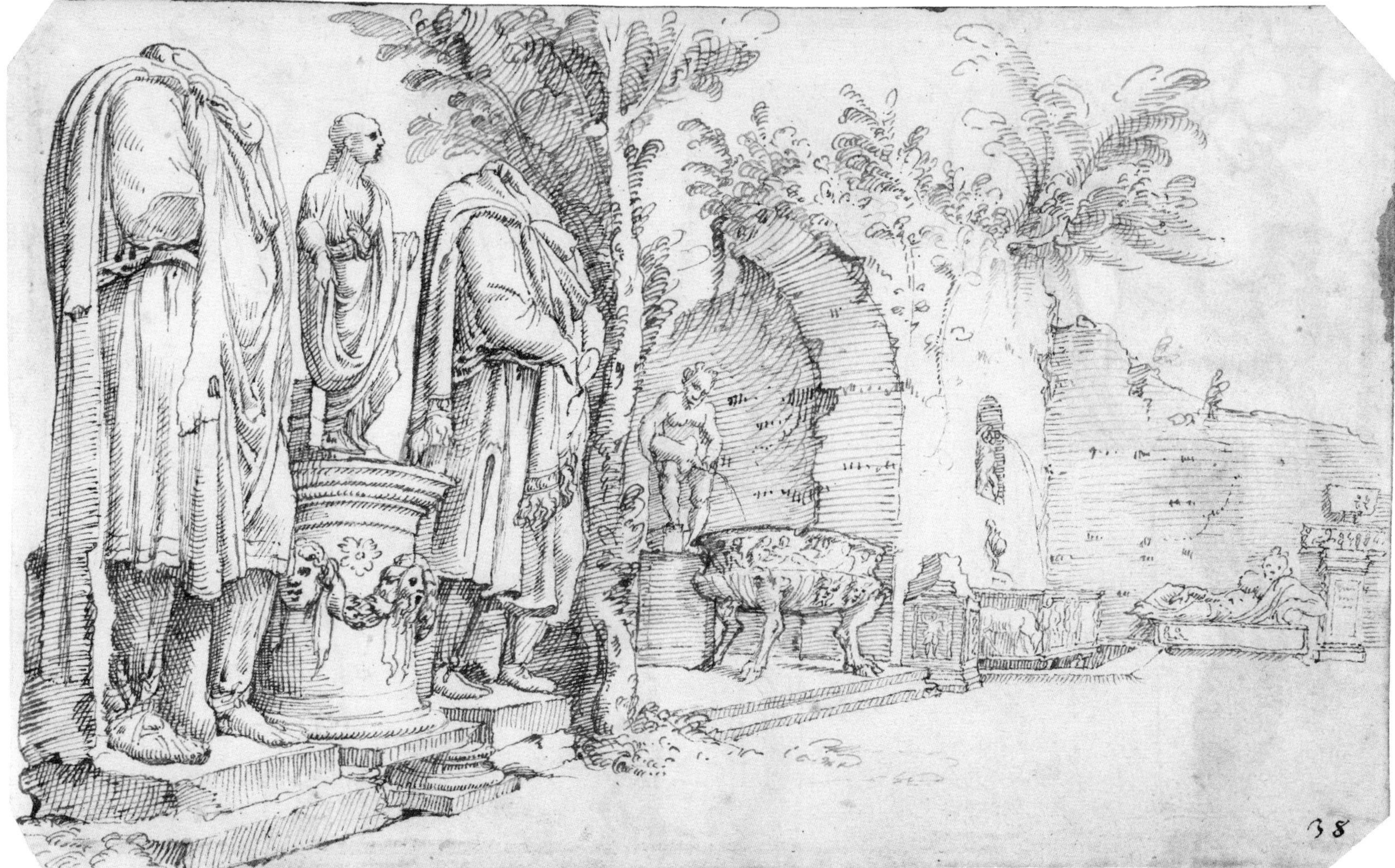

38

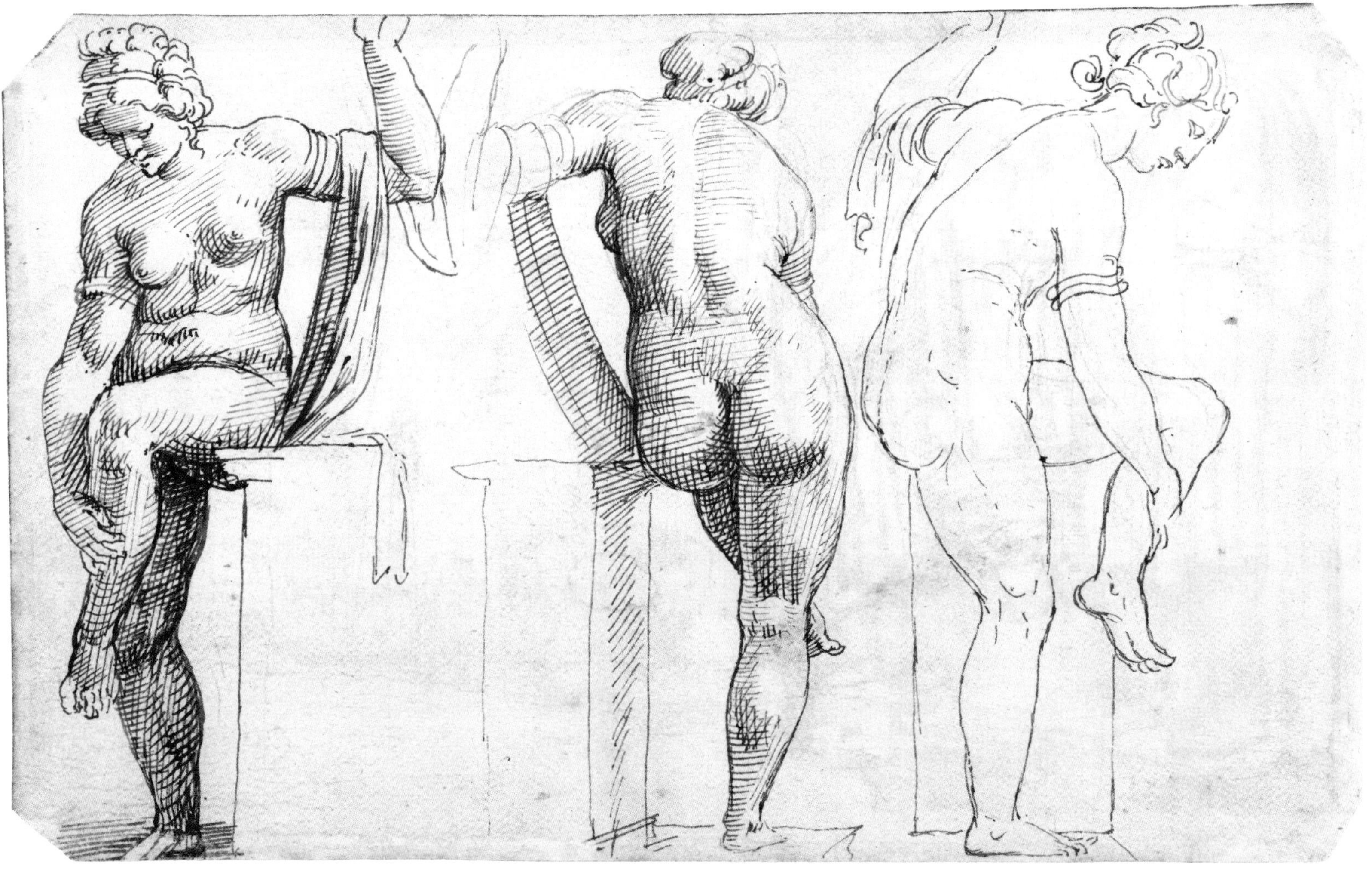

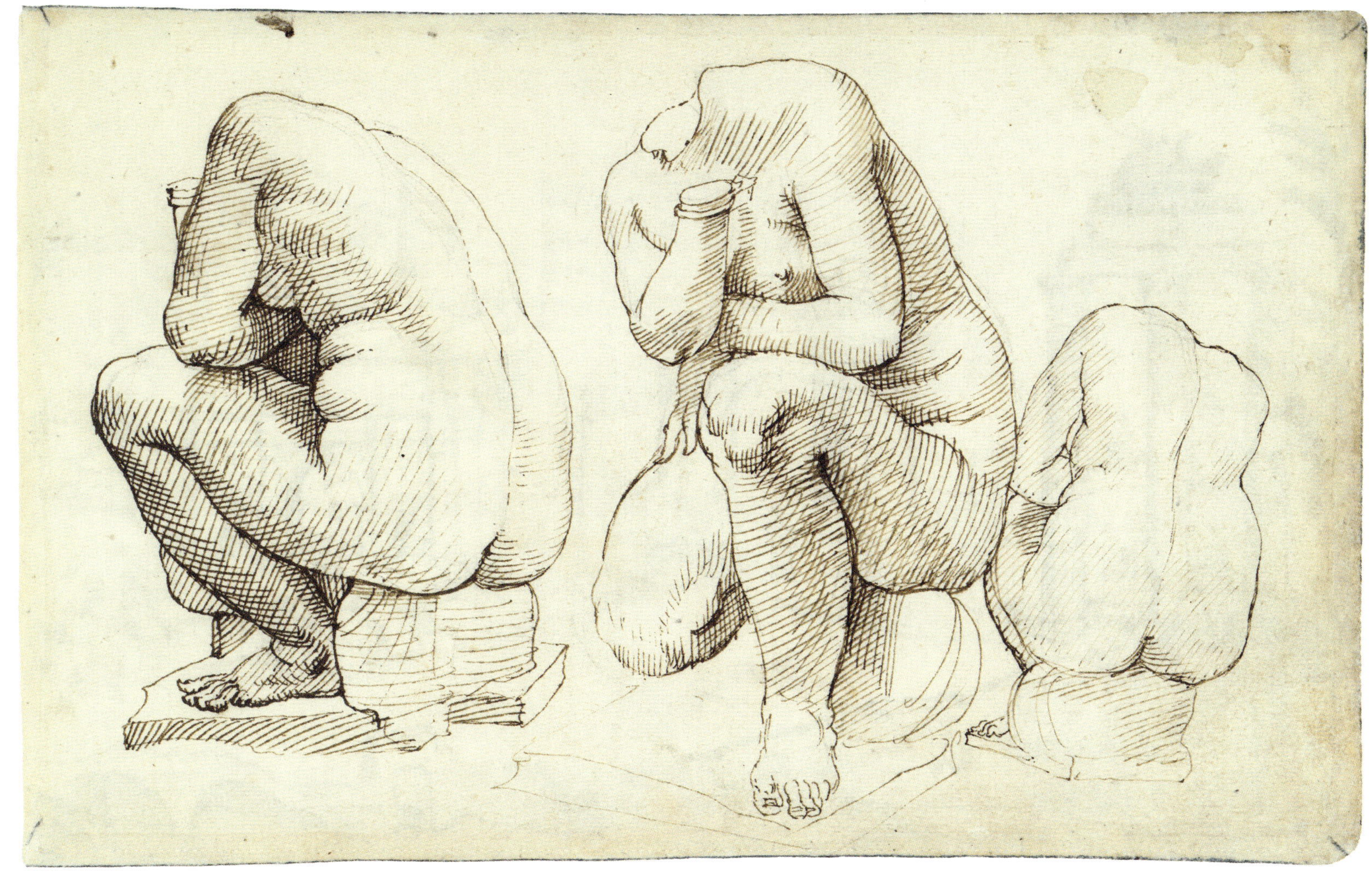

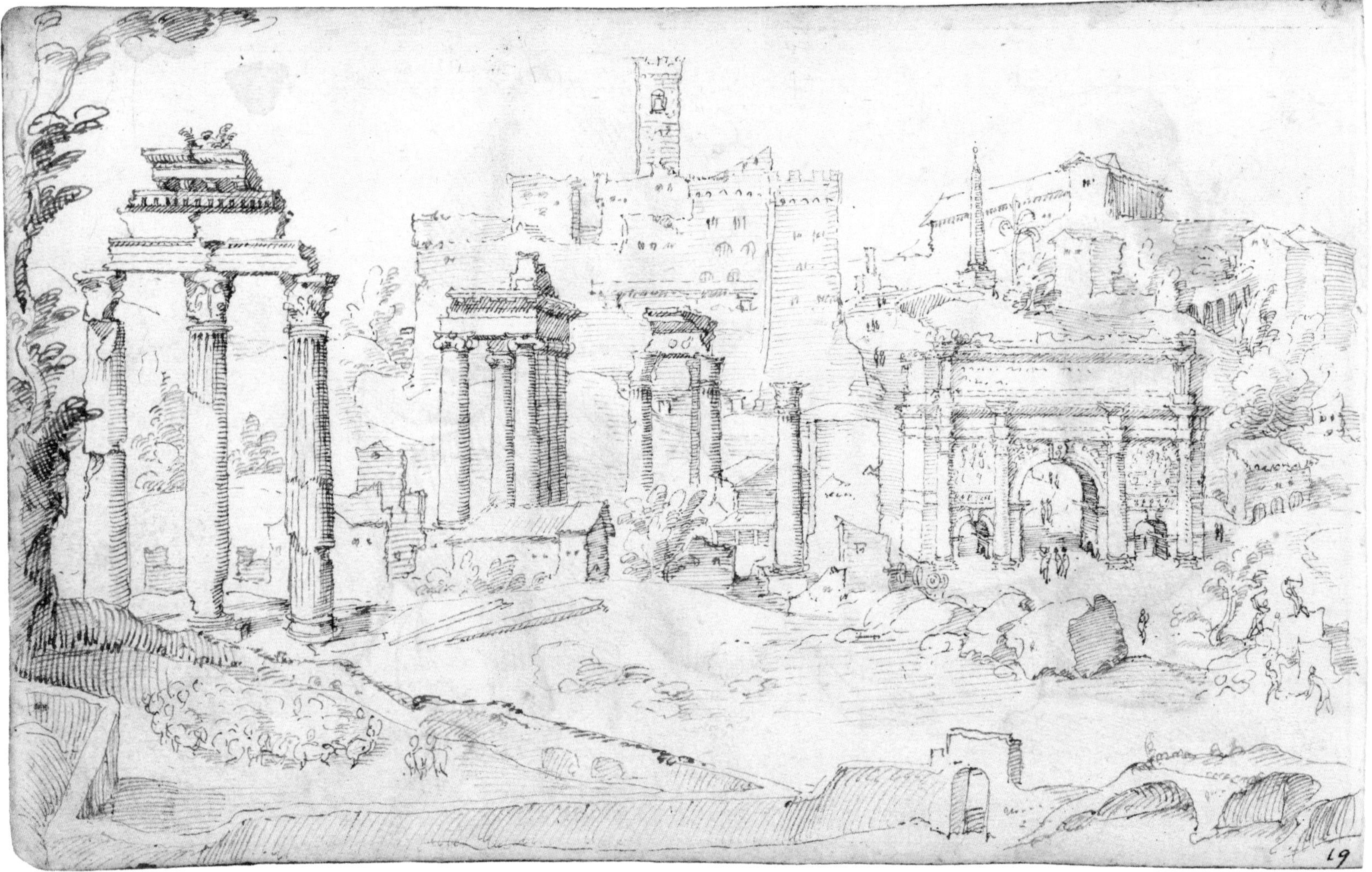

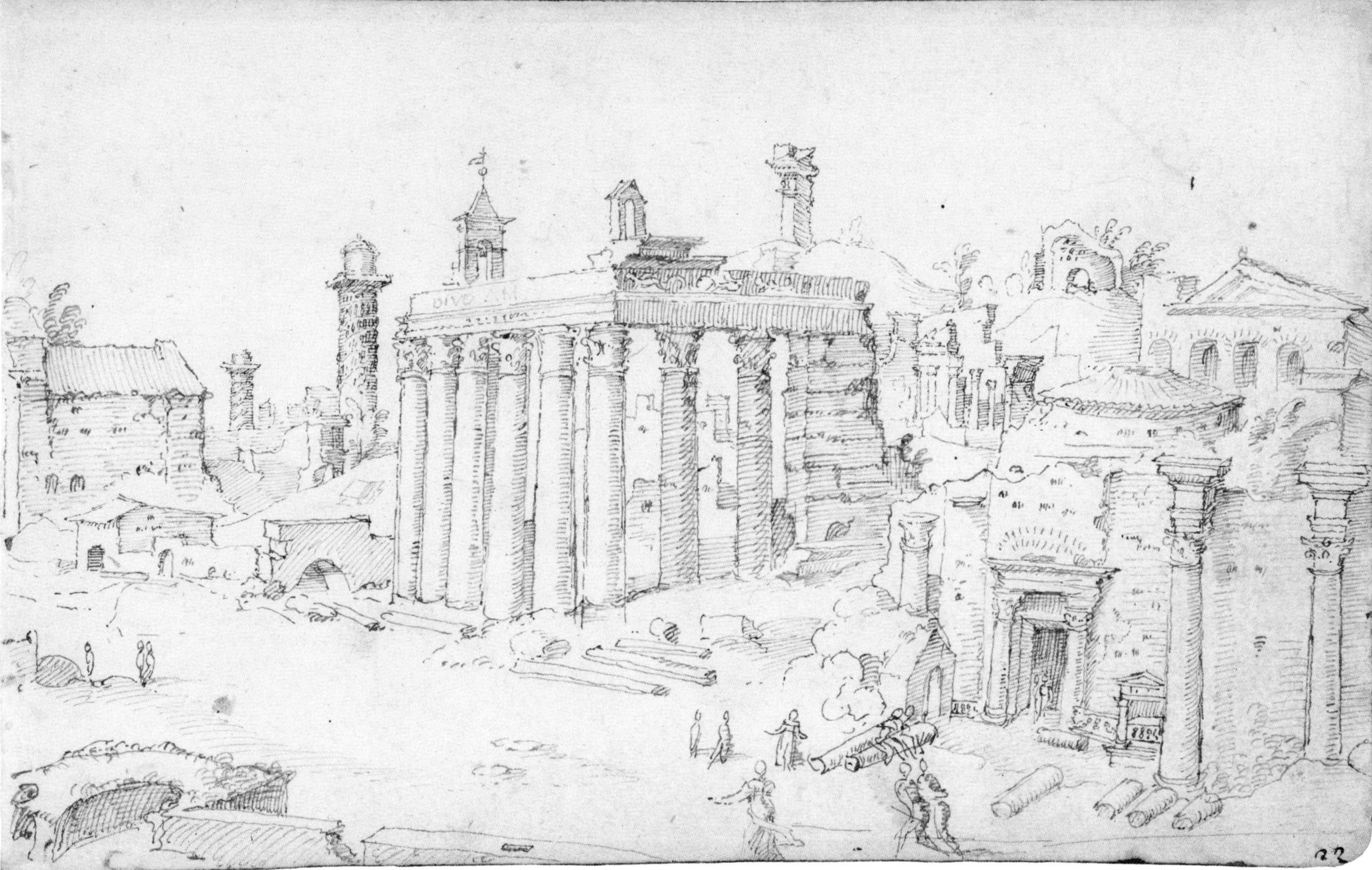

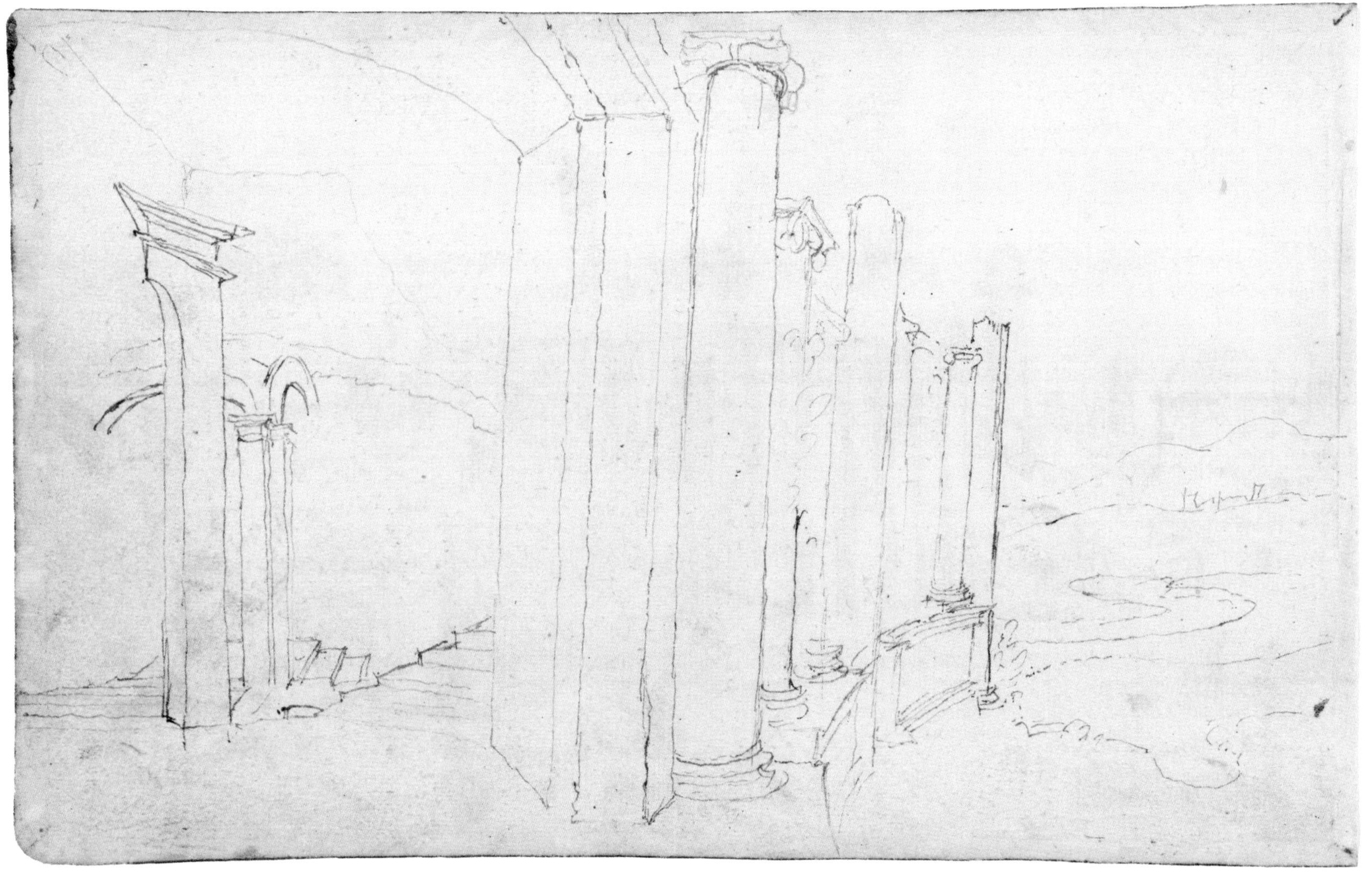

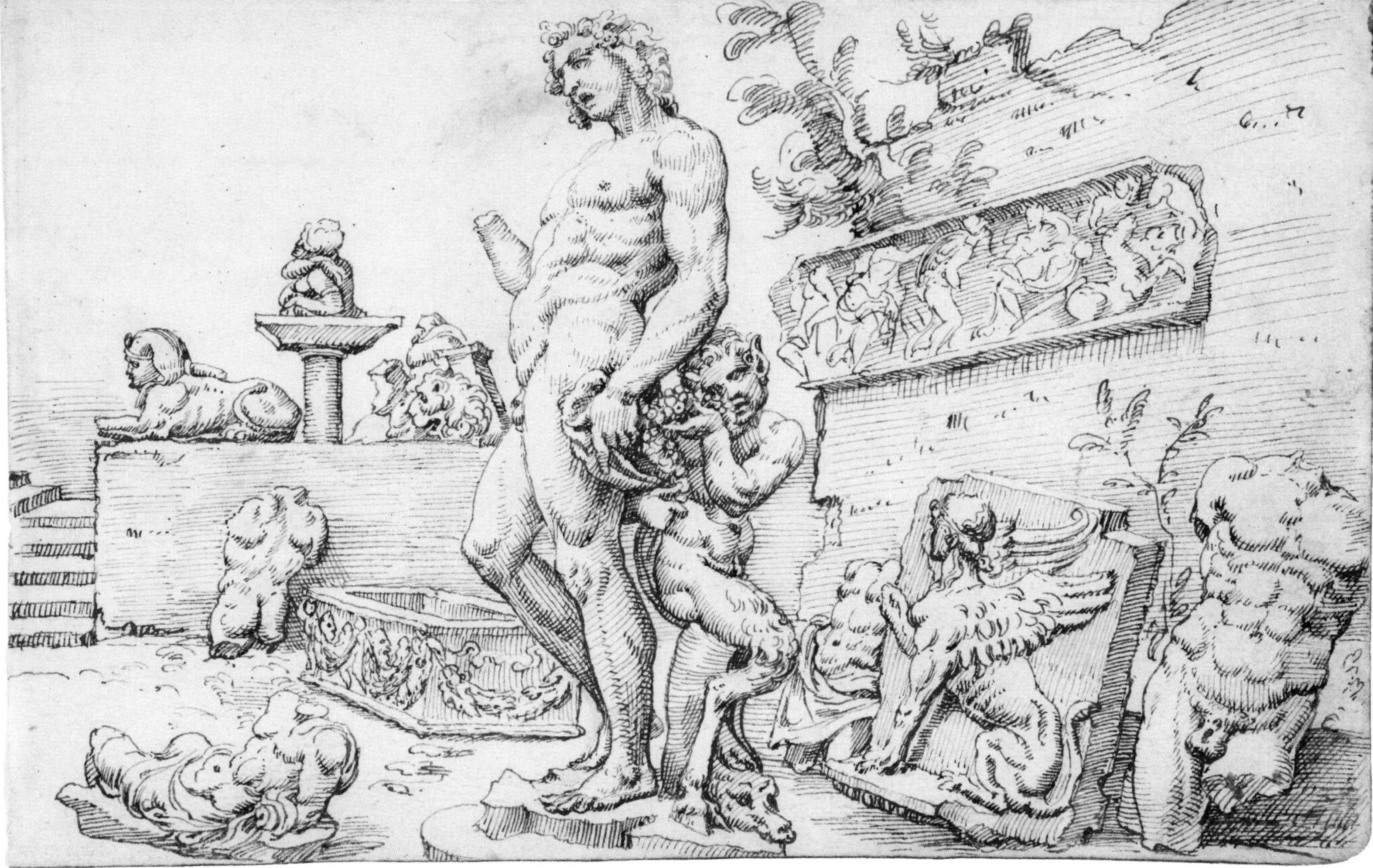

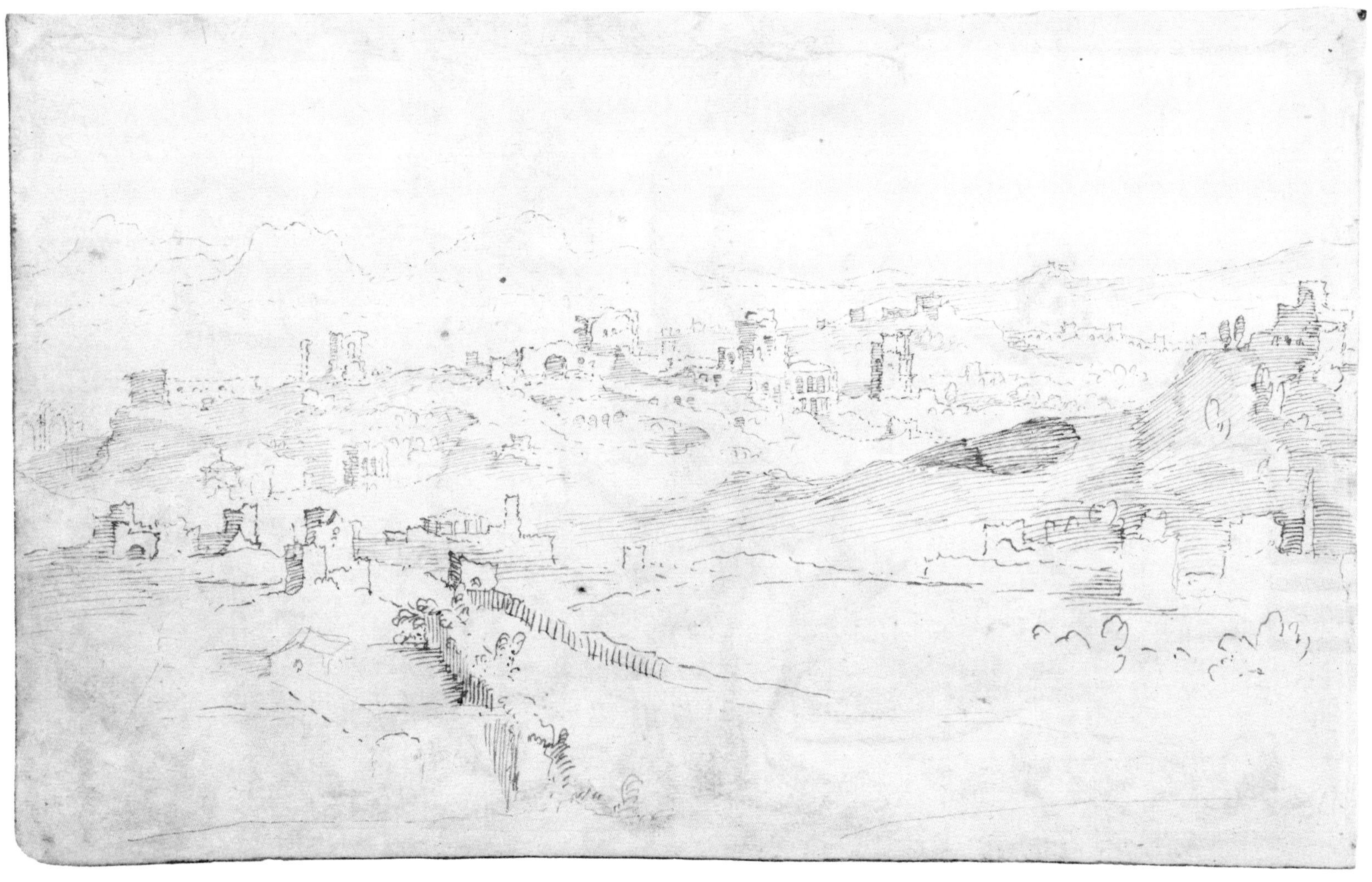

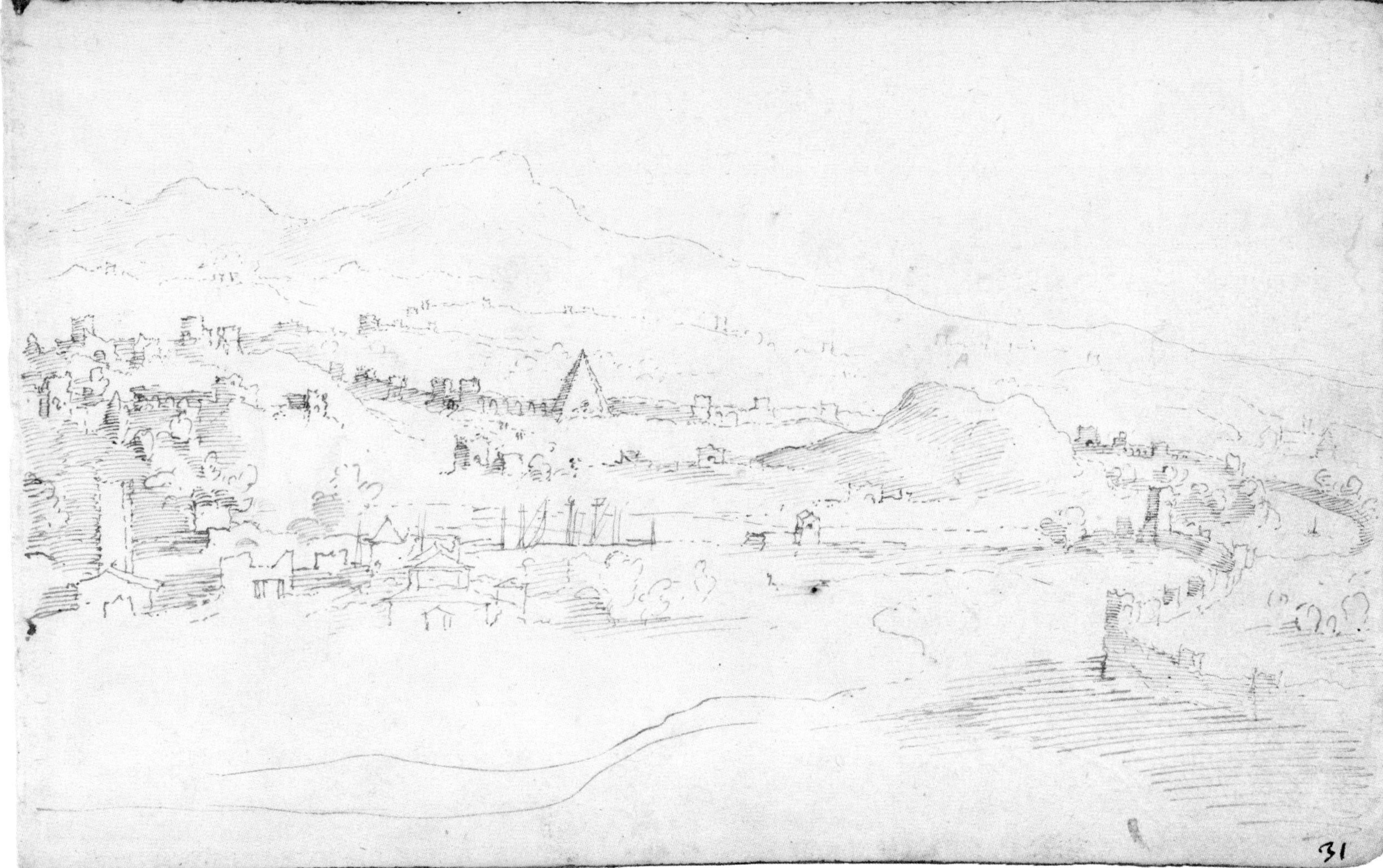

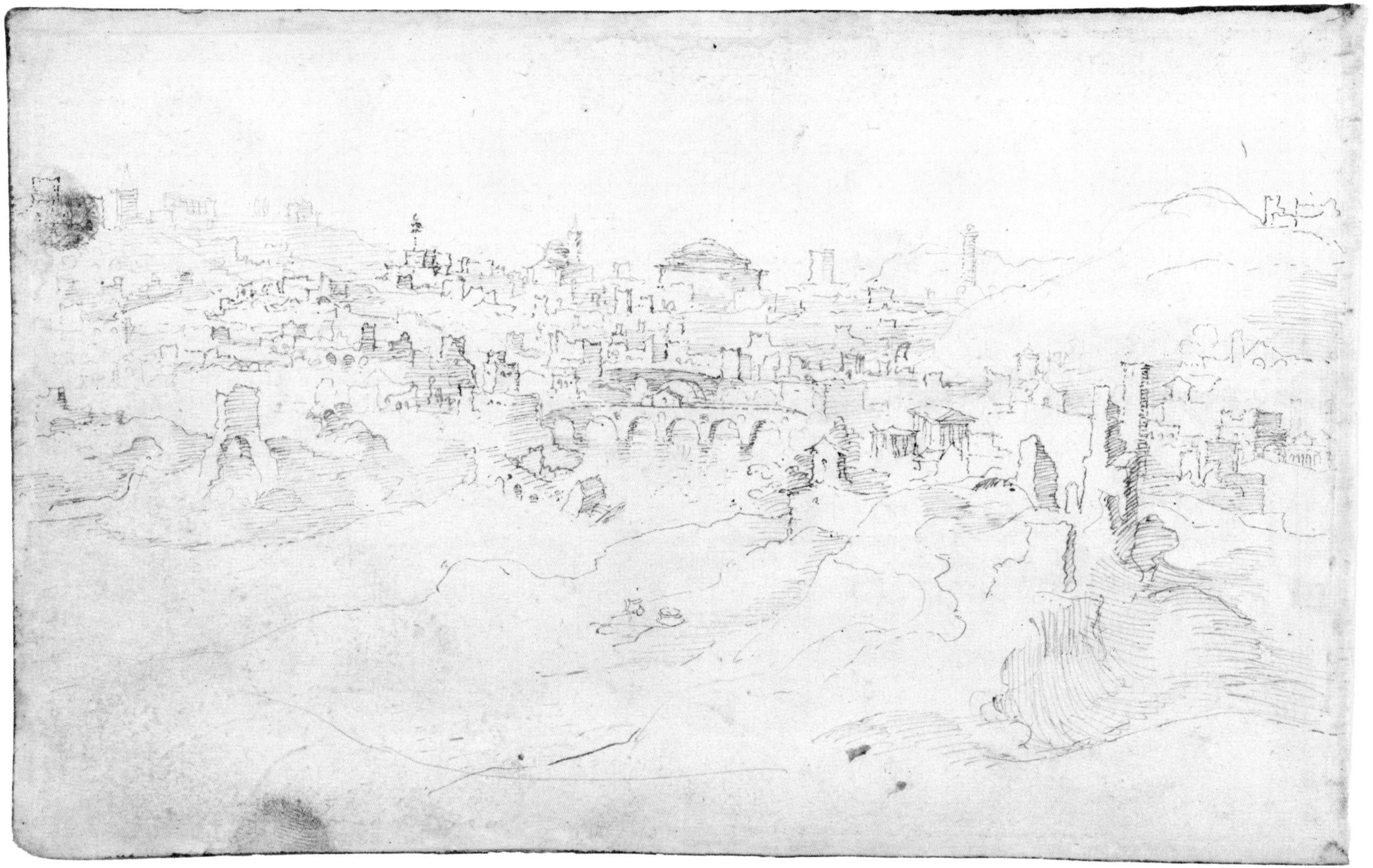

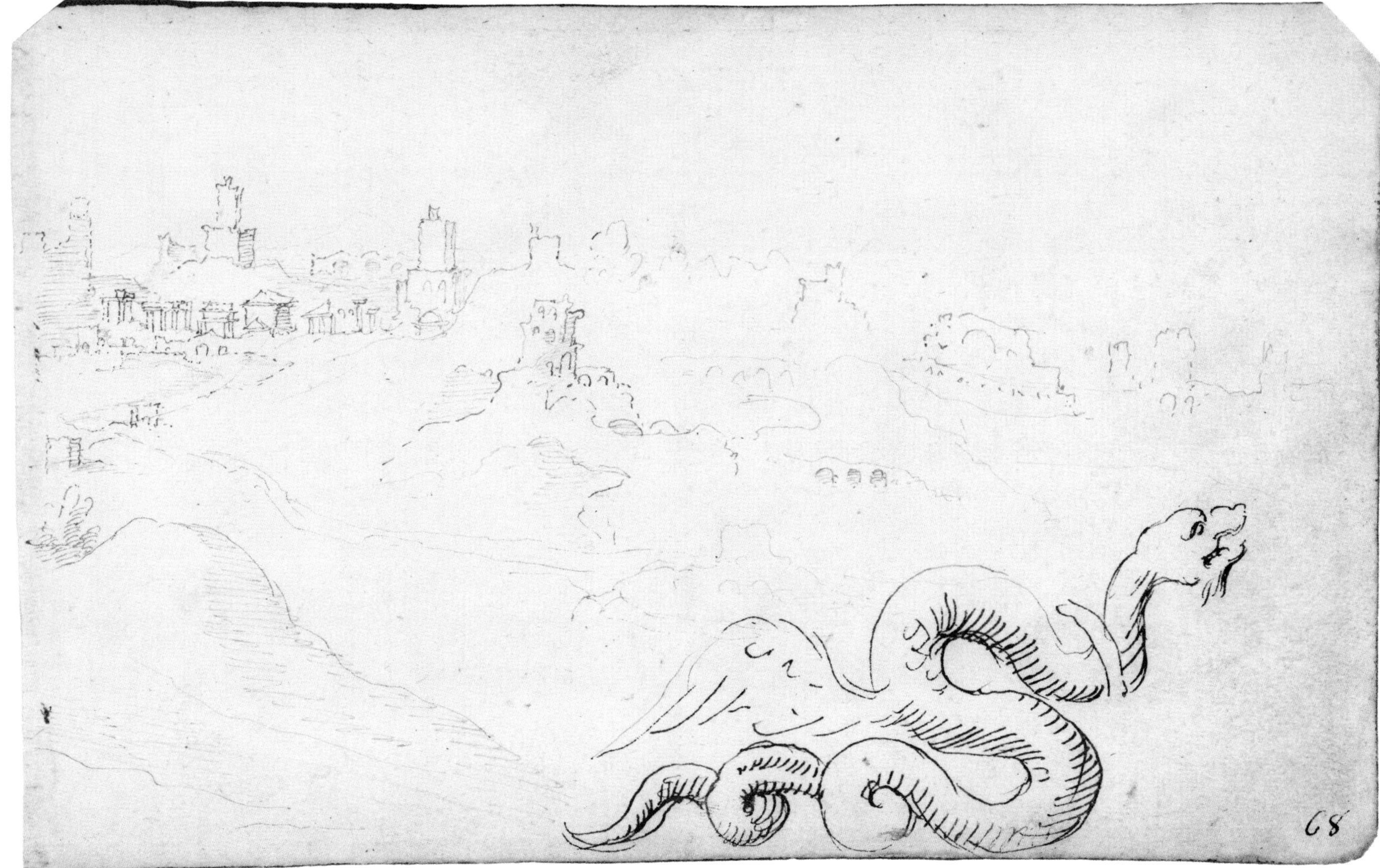

68

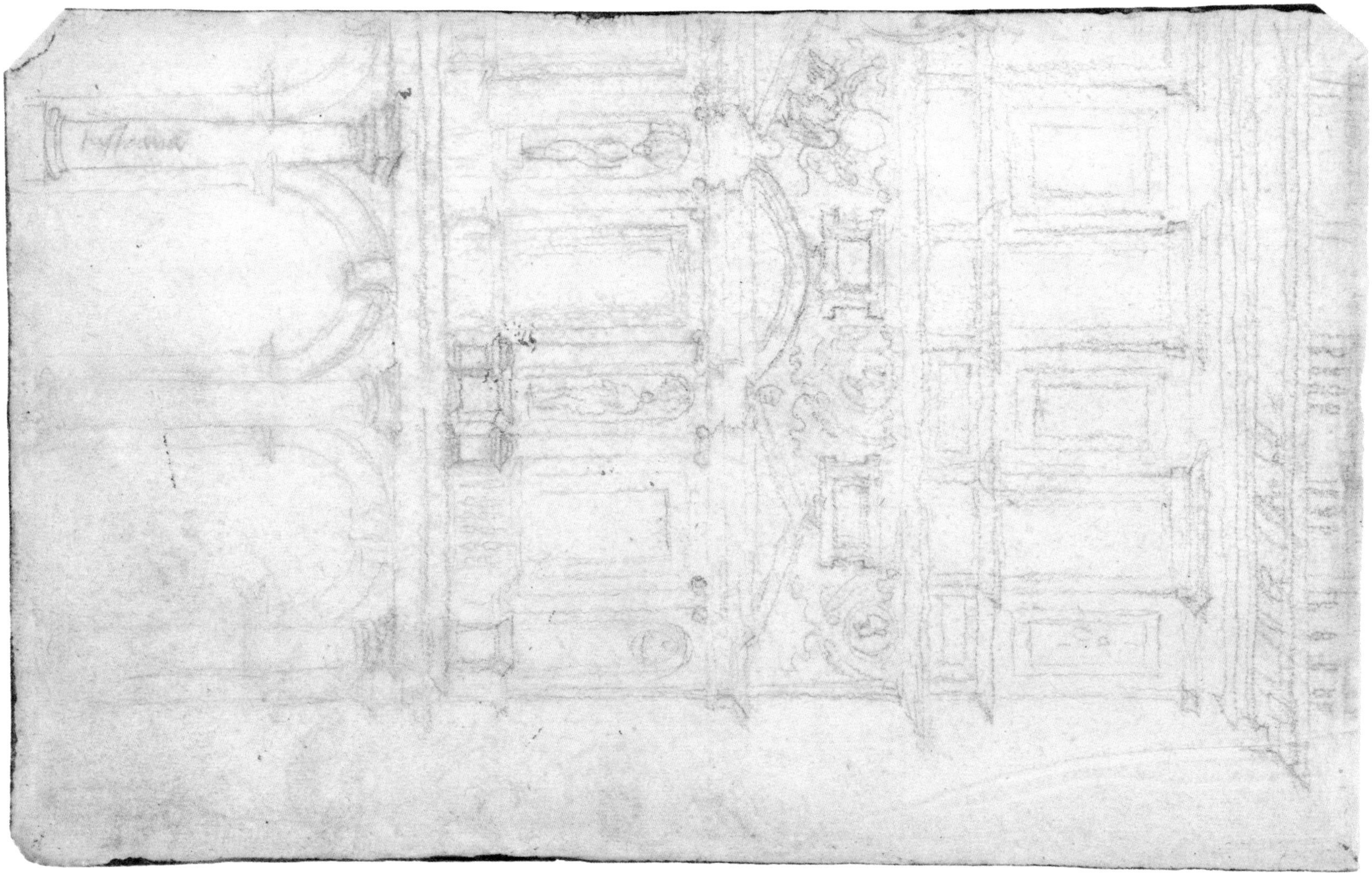

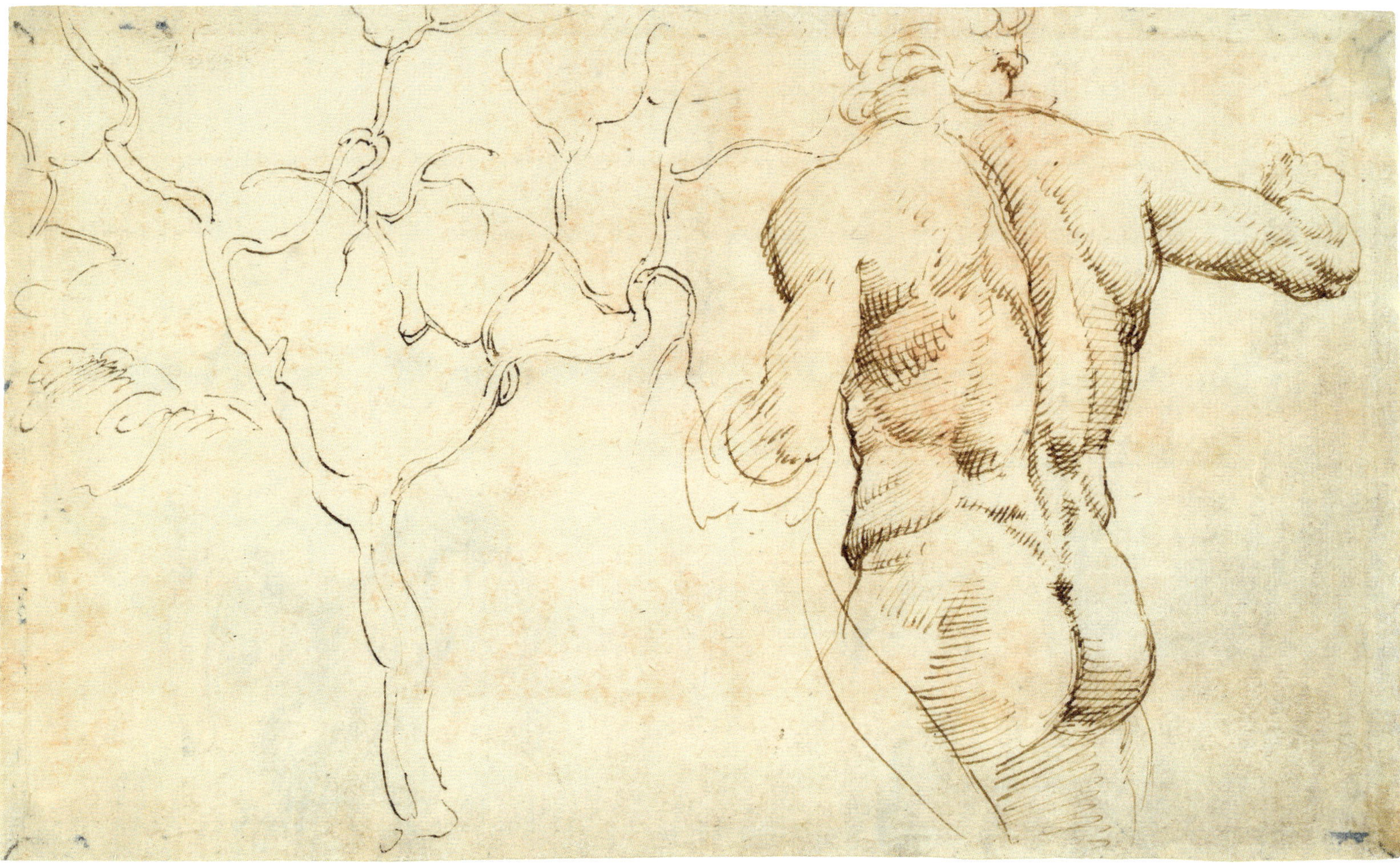

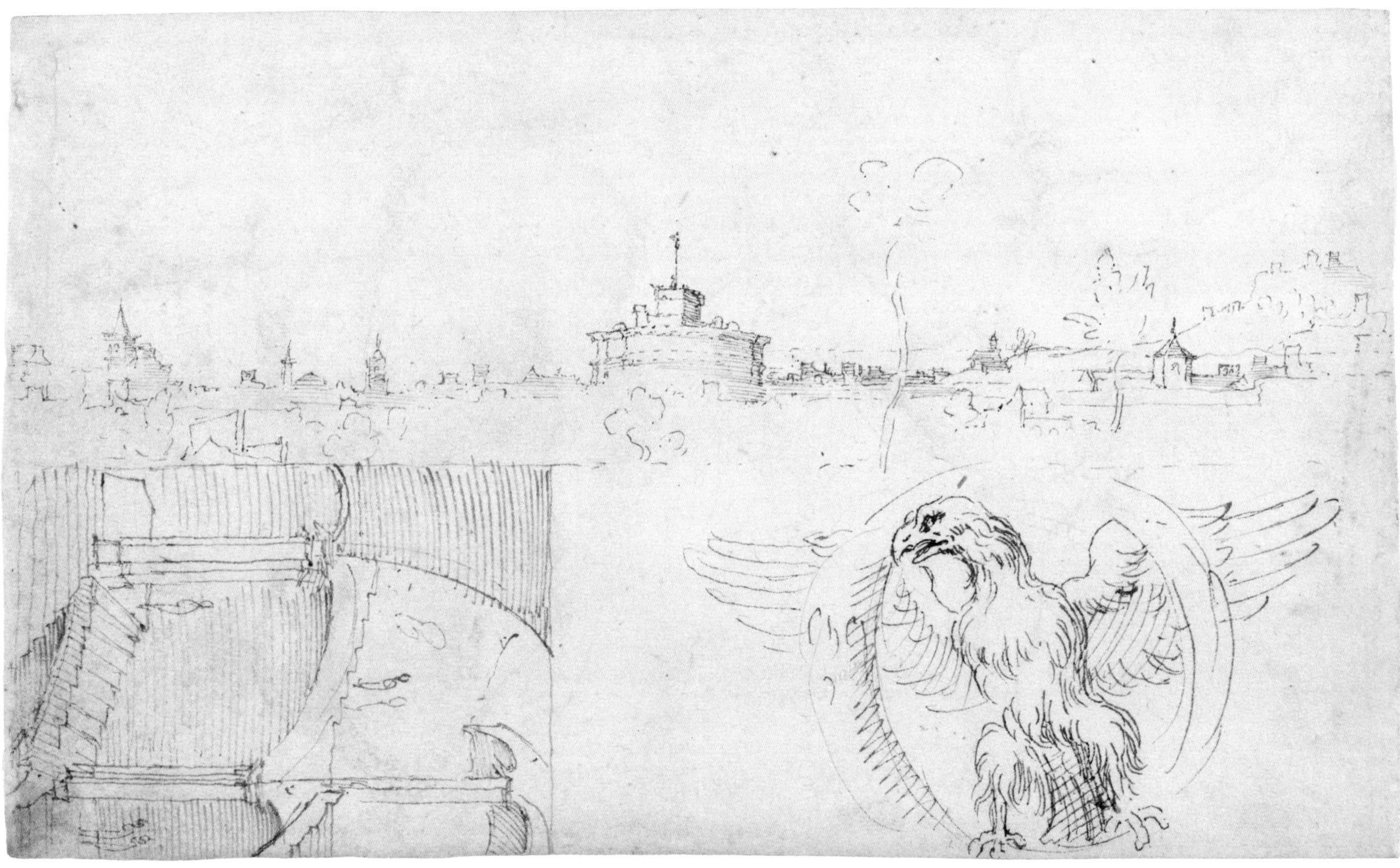

[ONE MISSING PAGE]

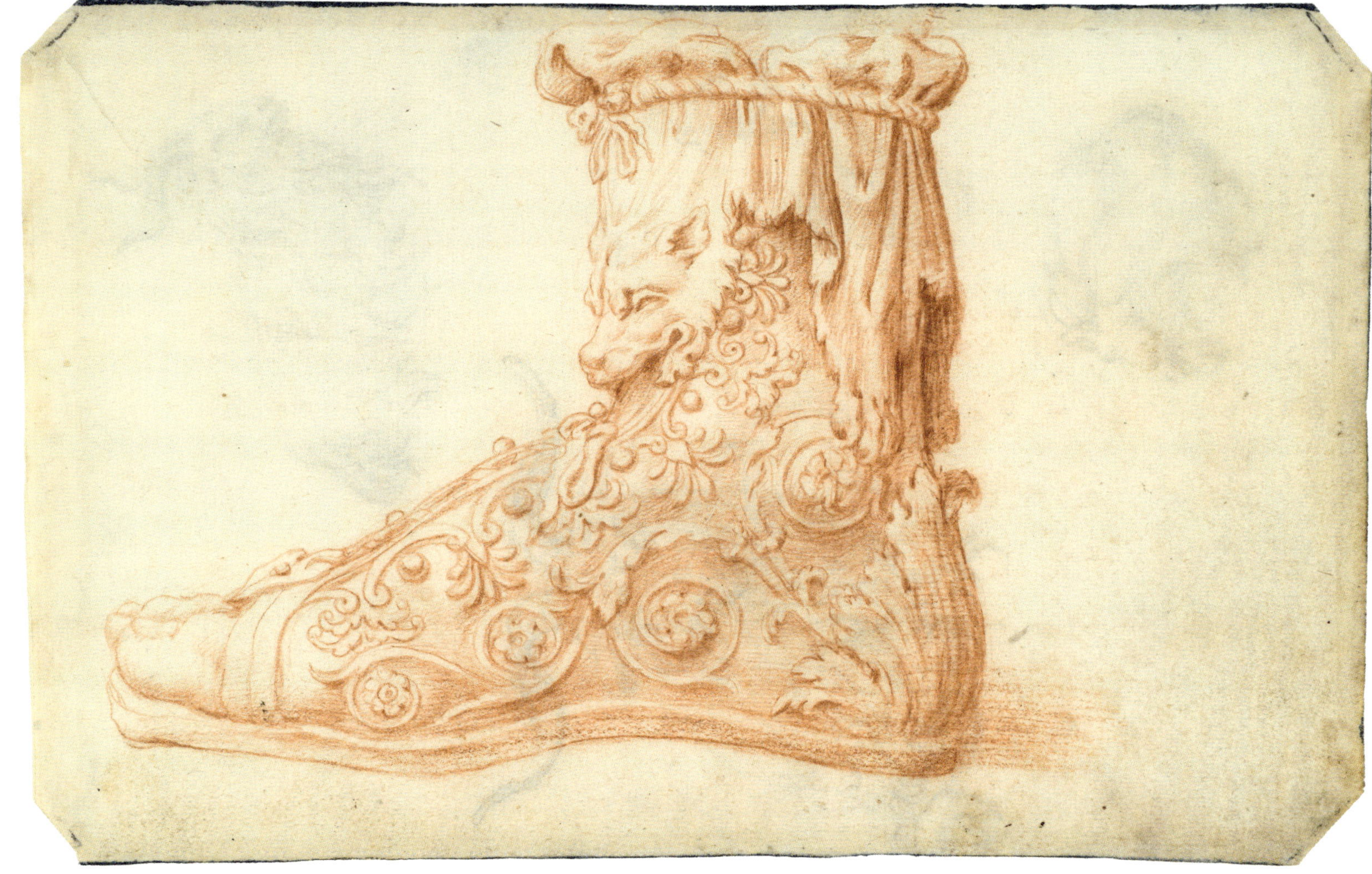

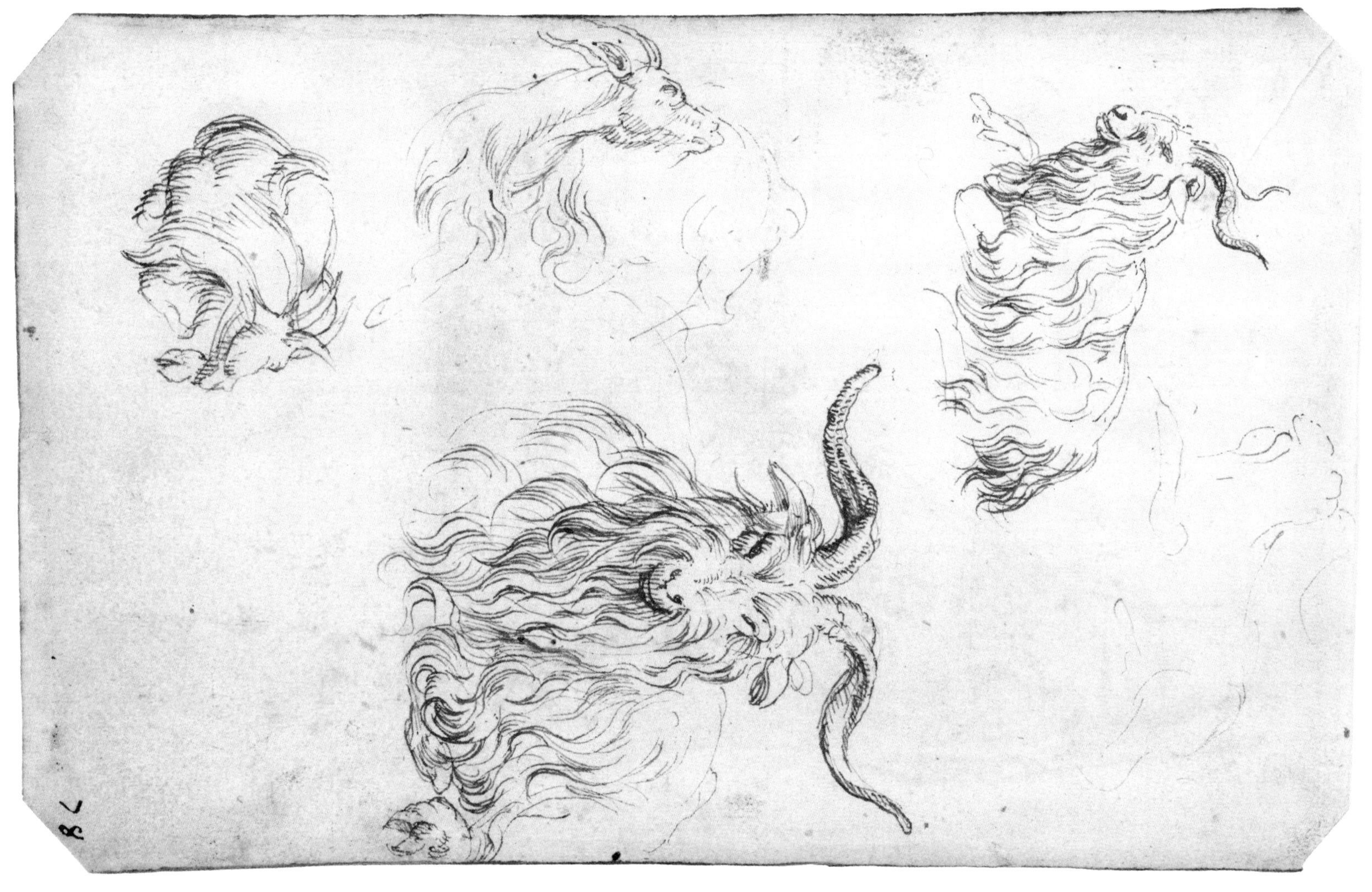

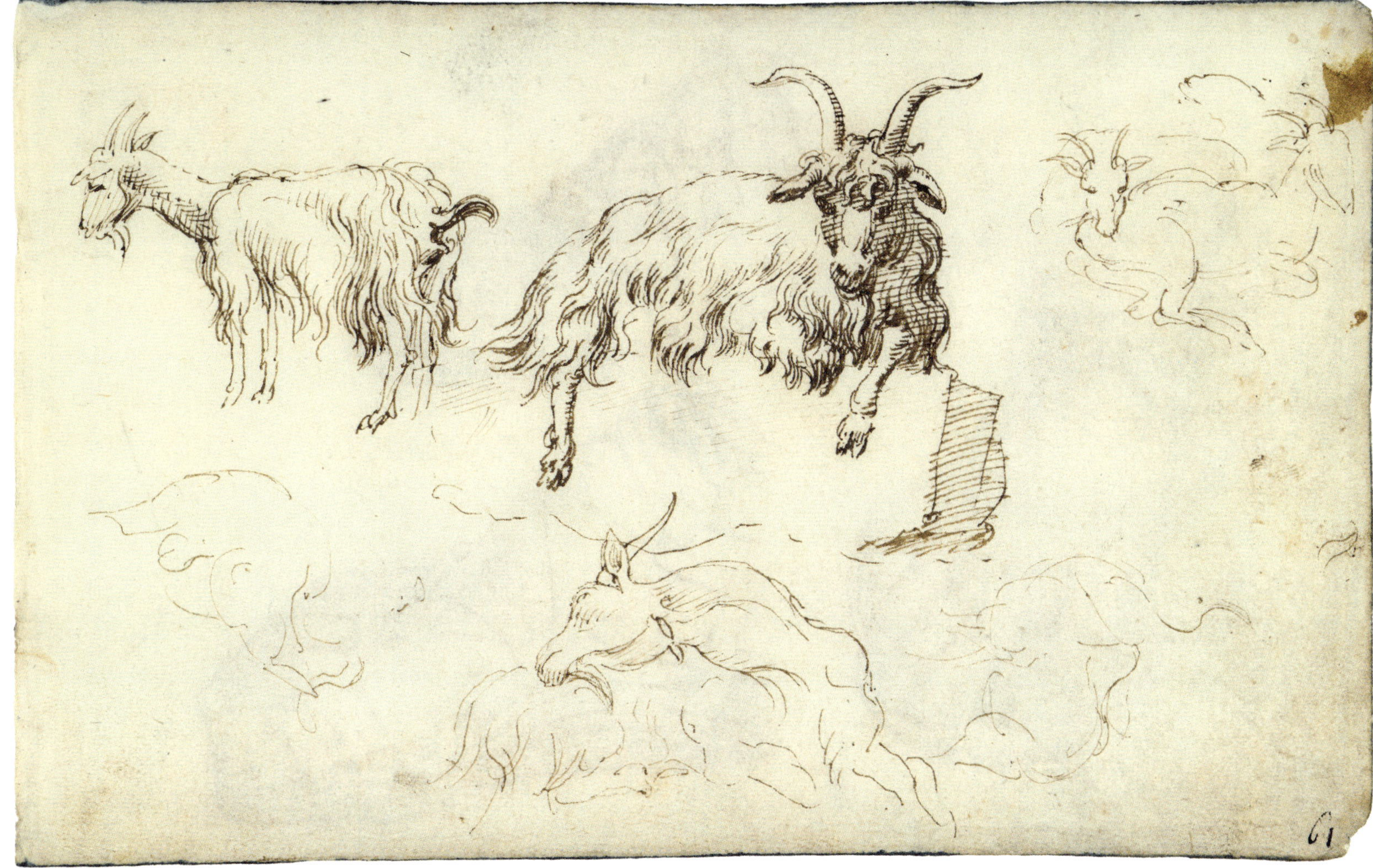

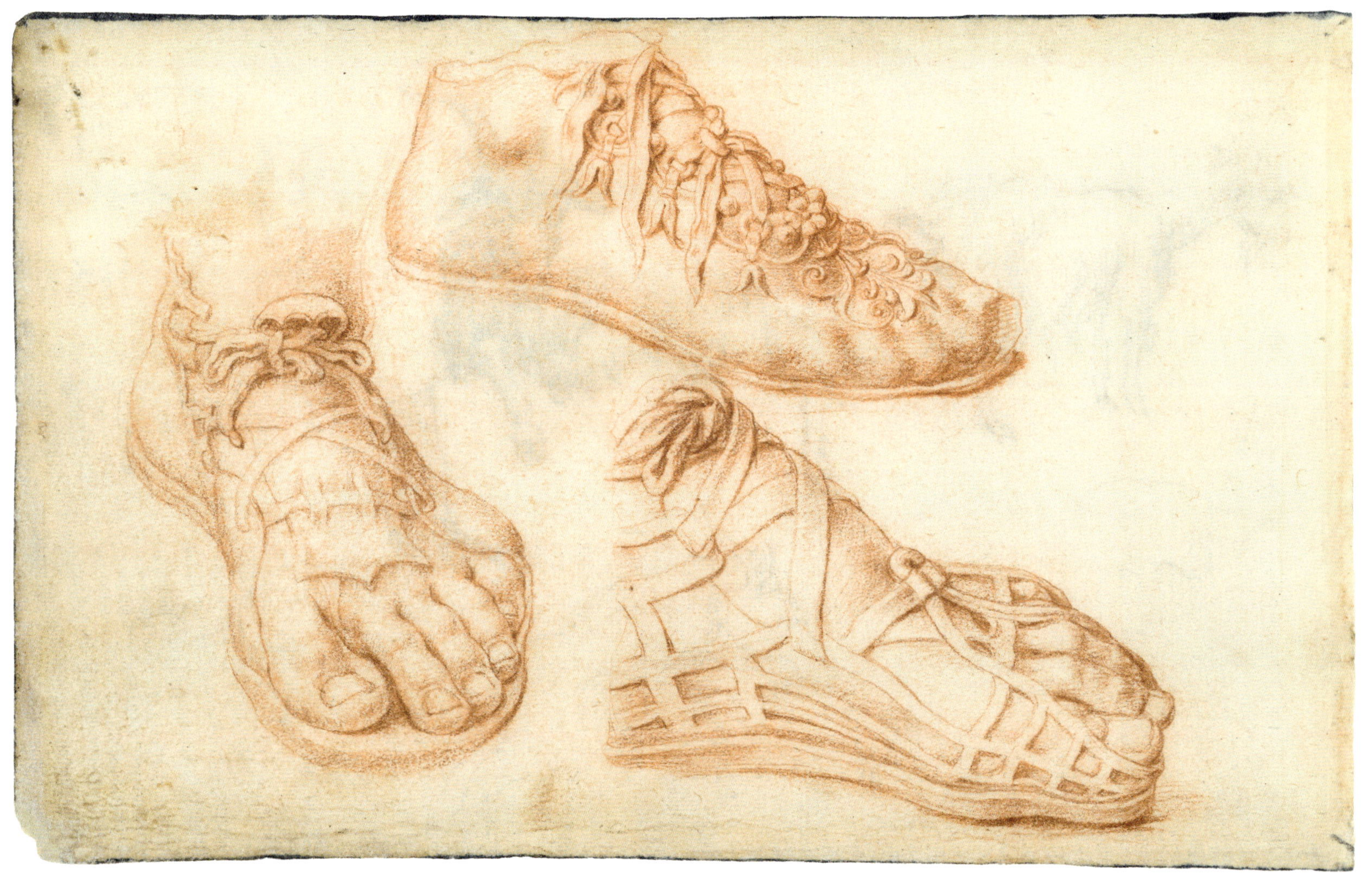

[INDETERMINATE NUMBER OF MISSING PAGES]

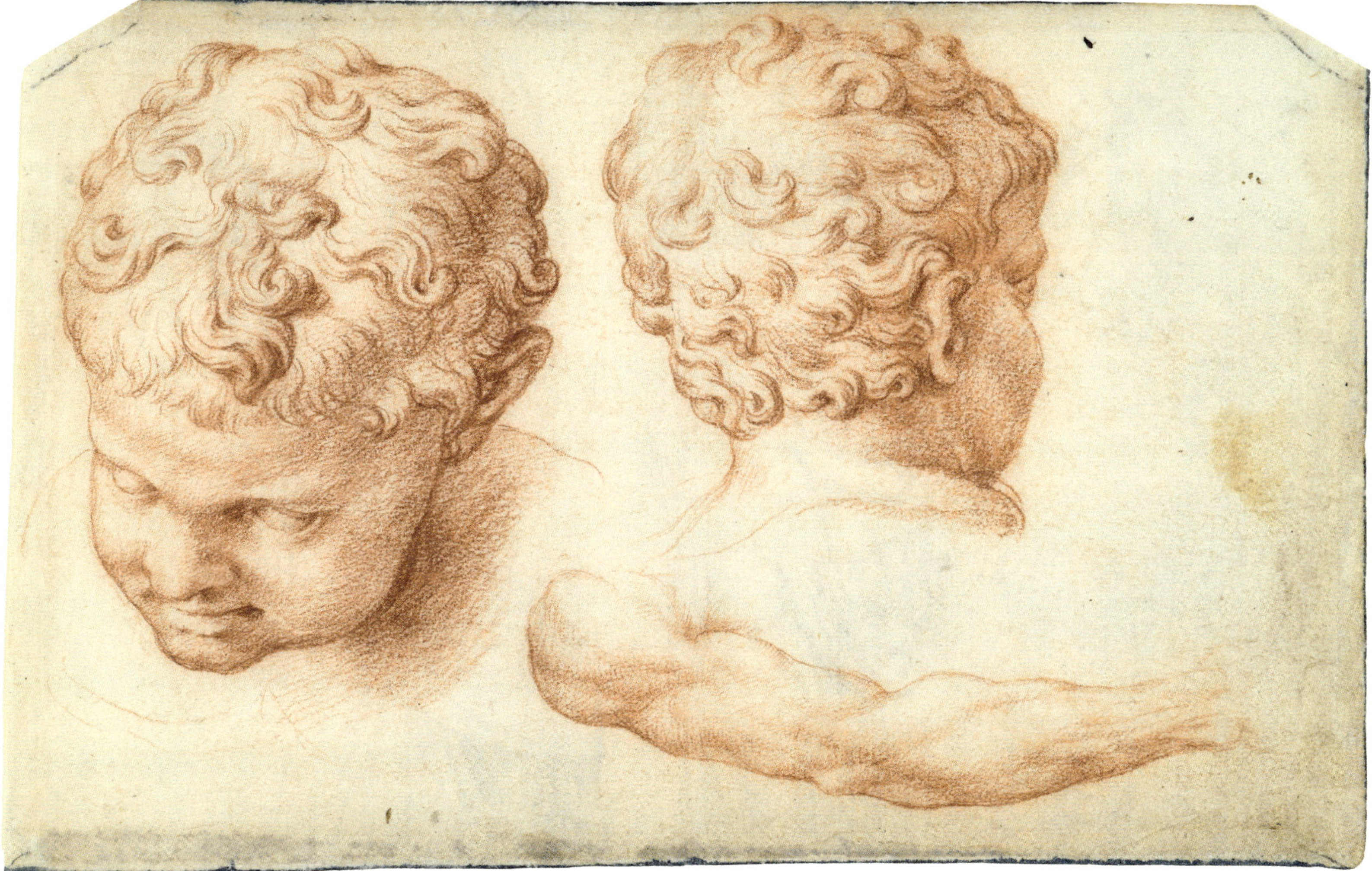

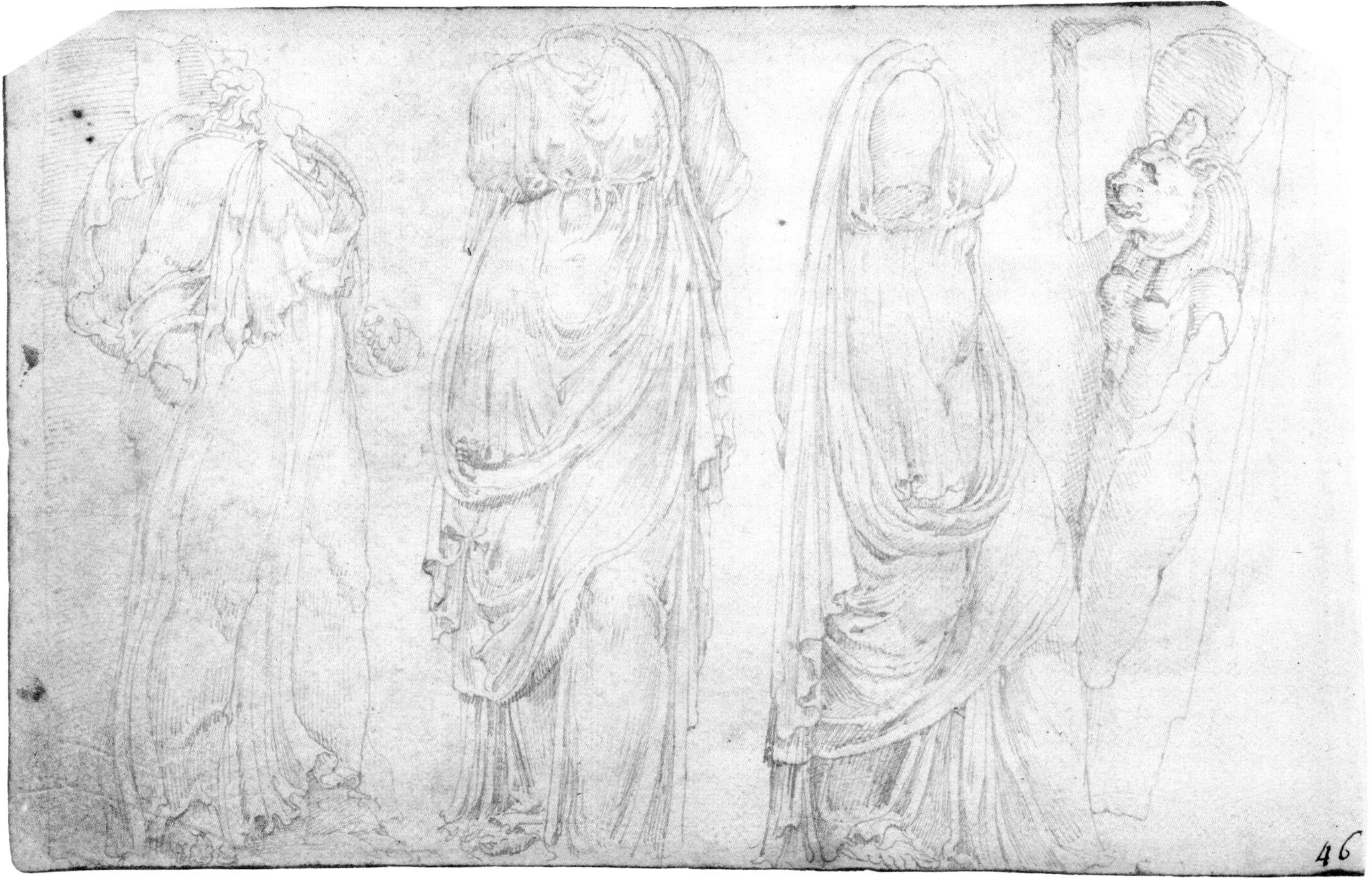
46

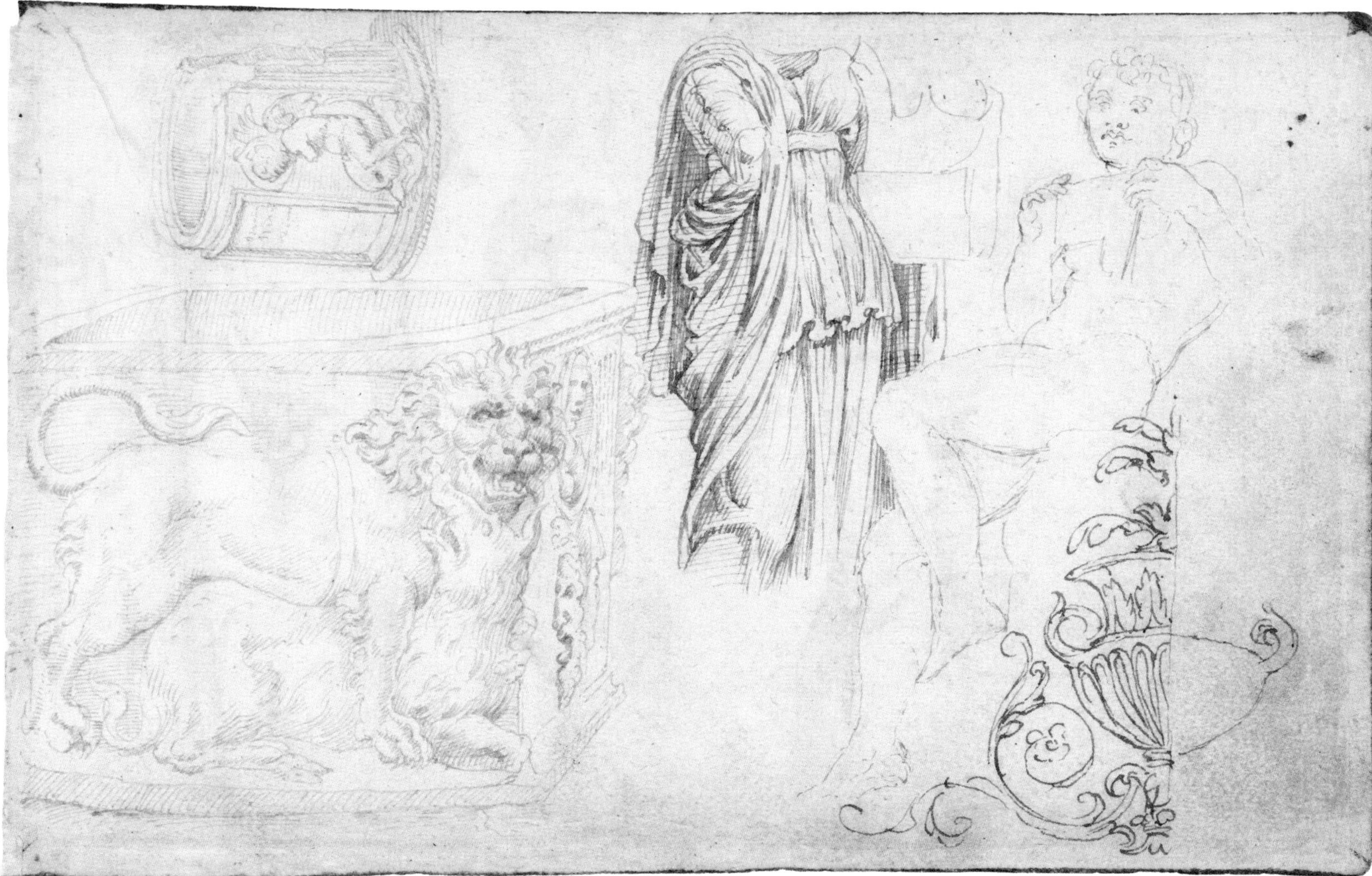

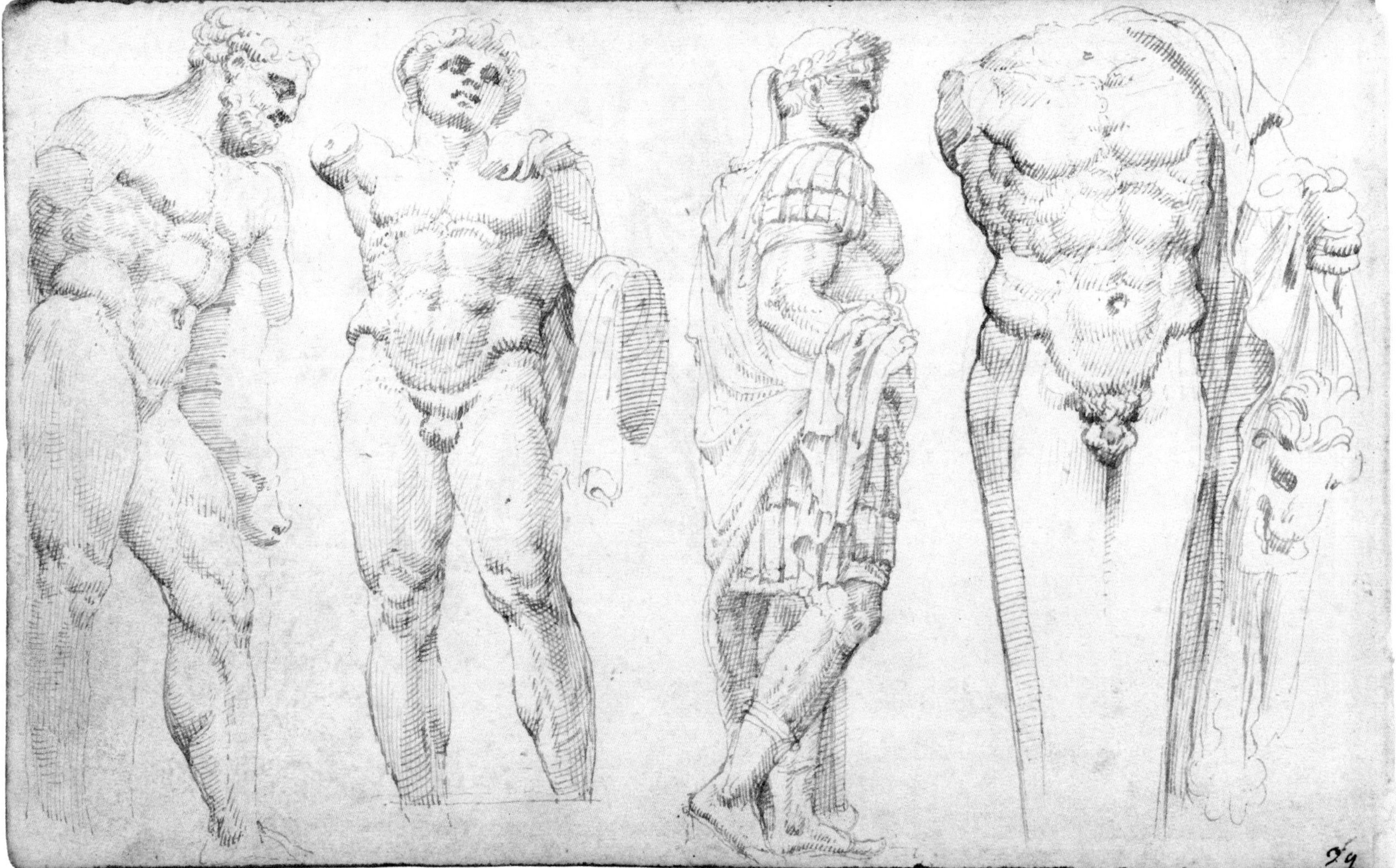

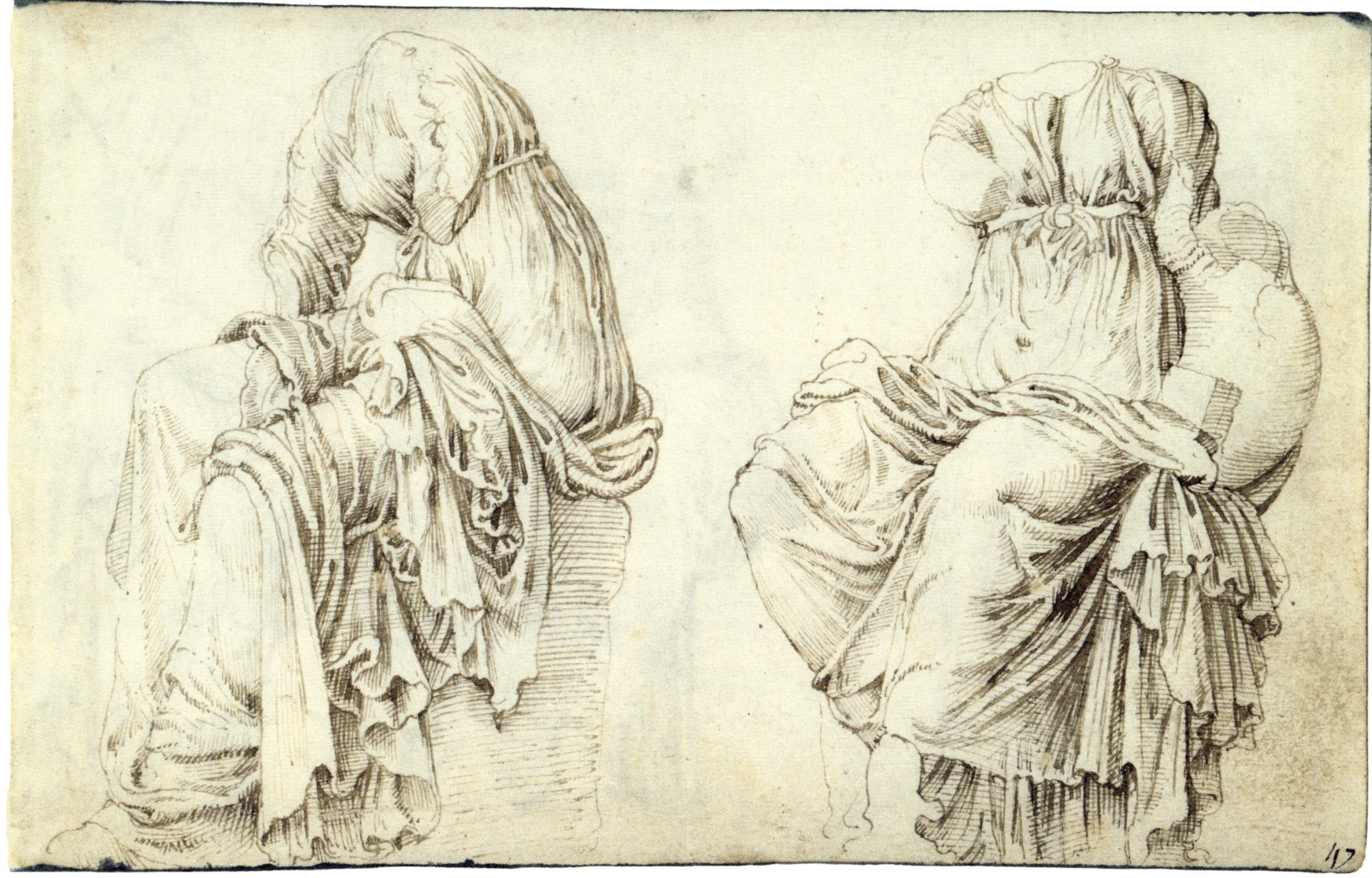

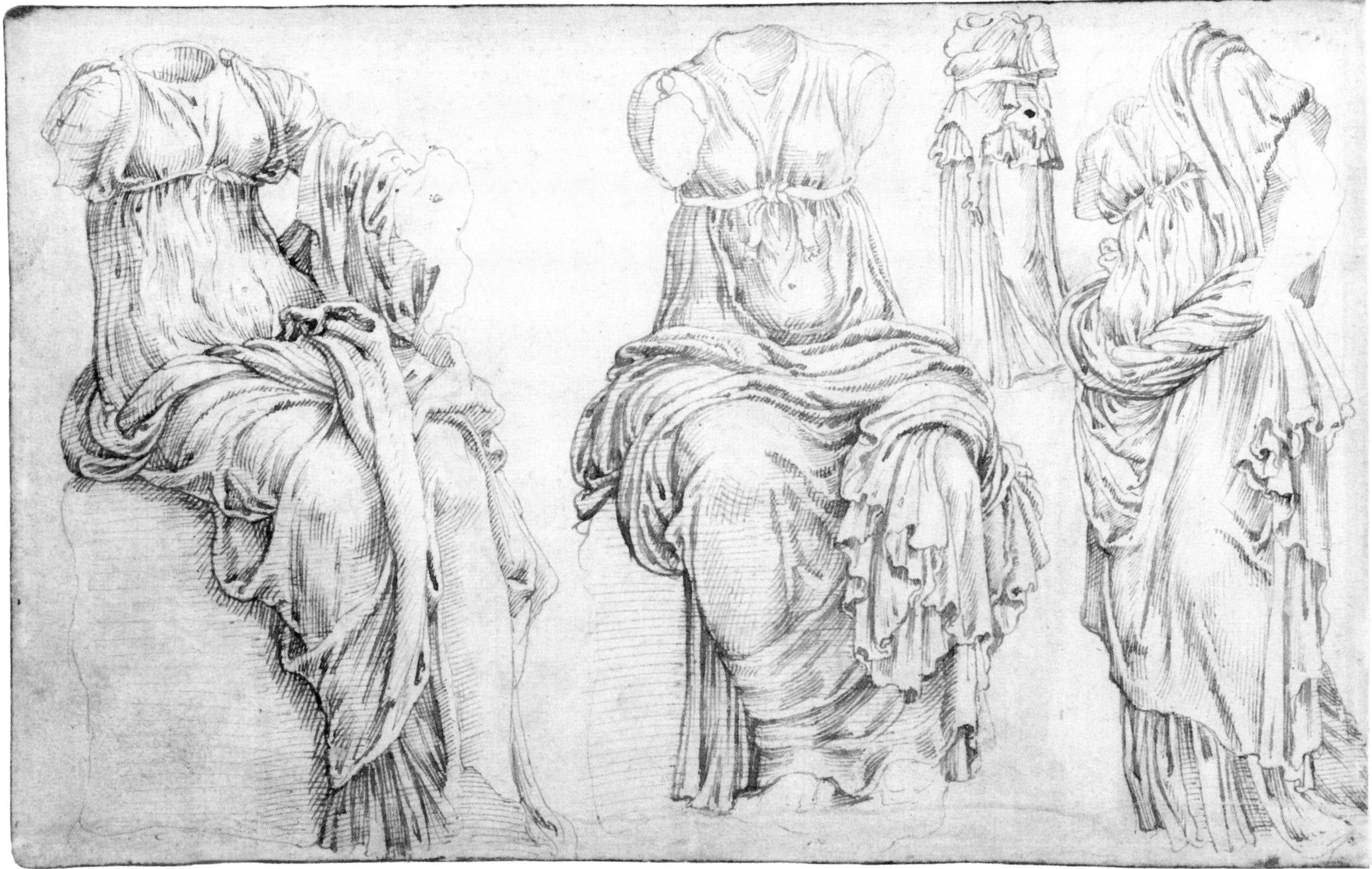

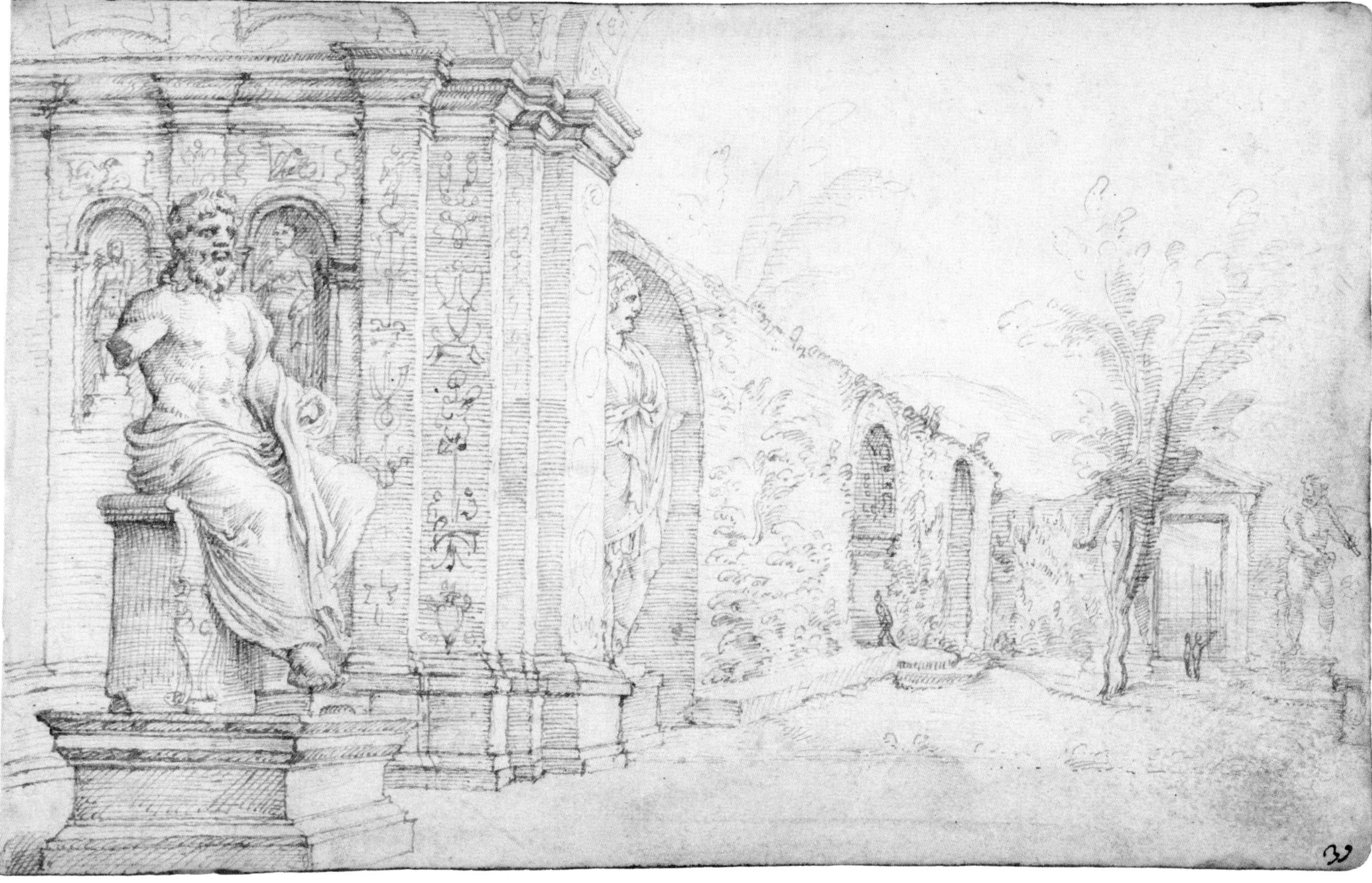

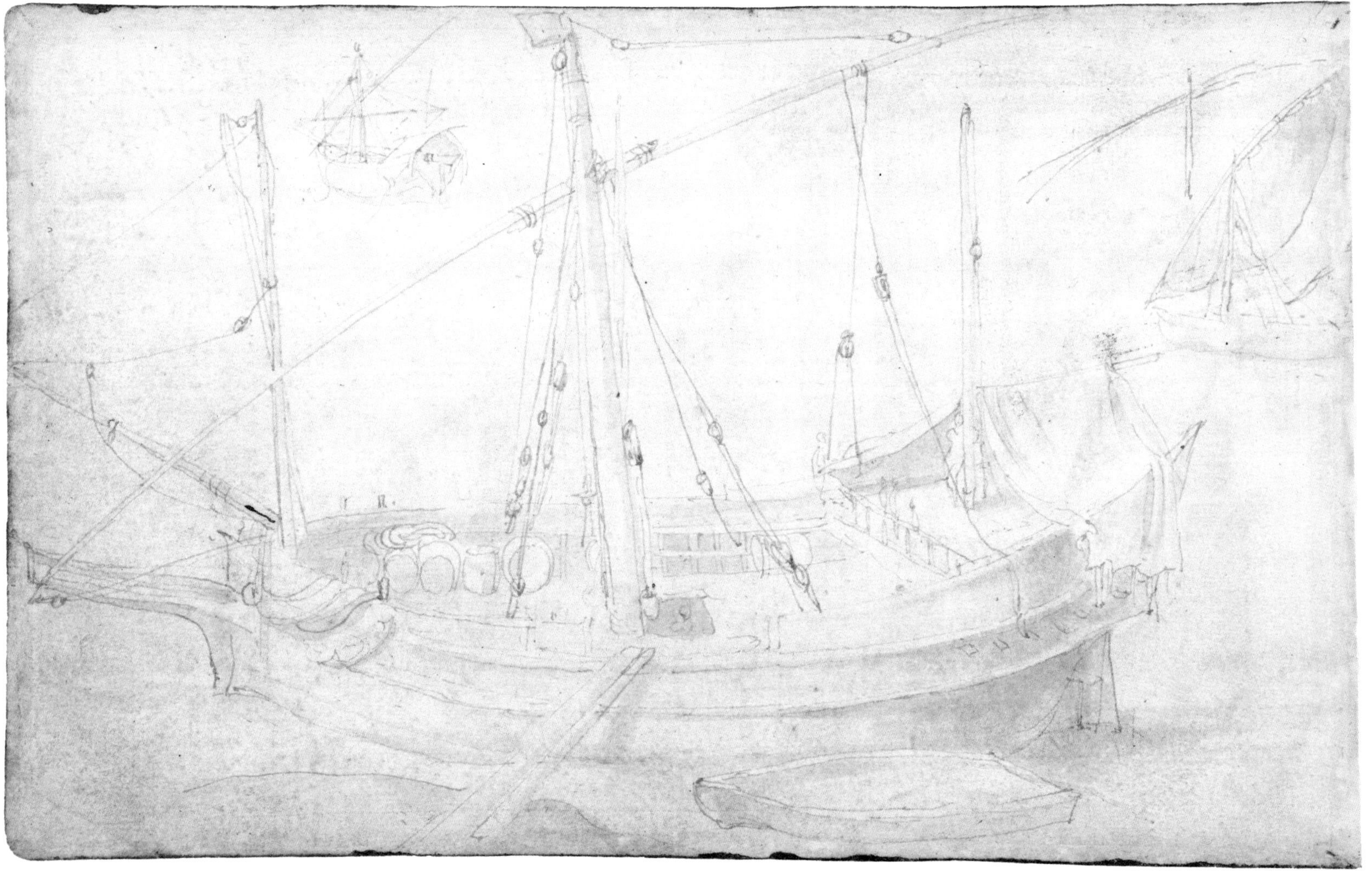

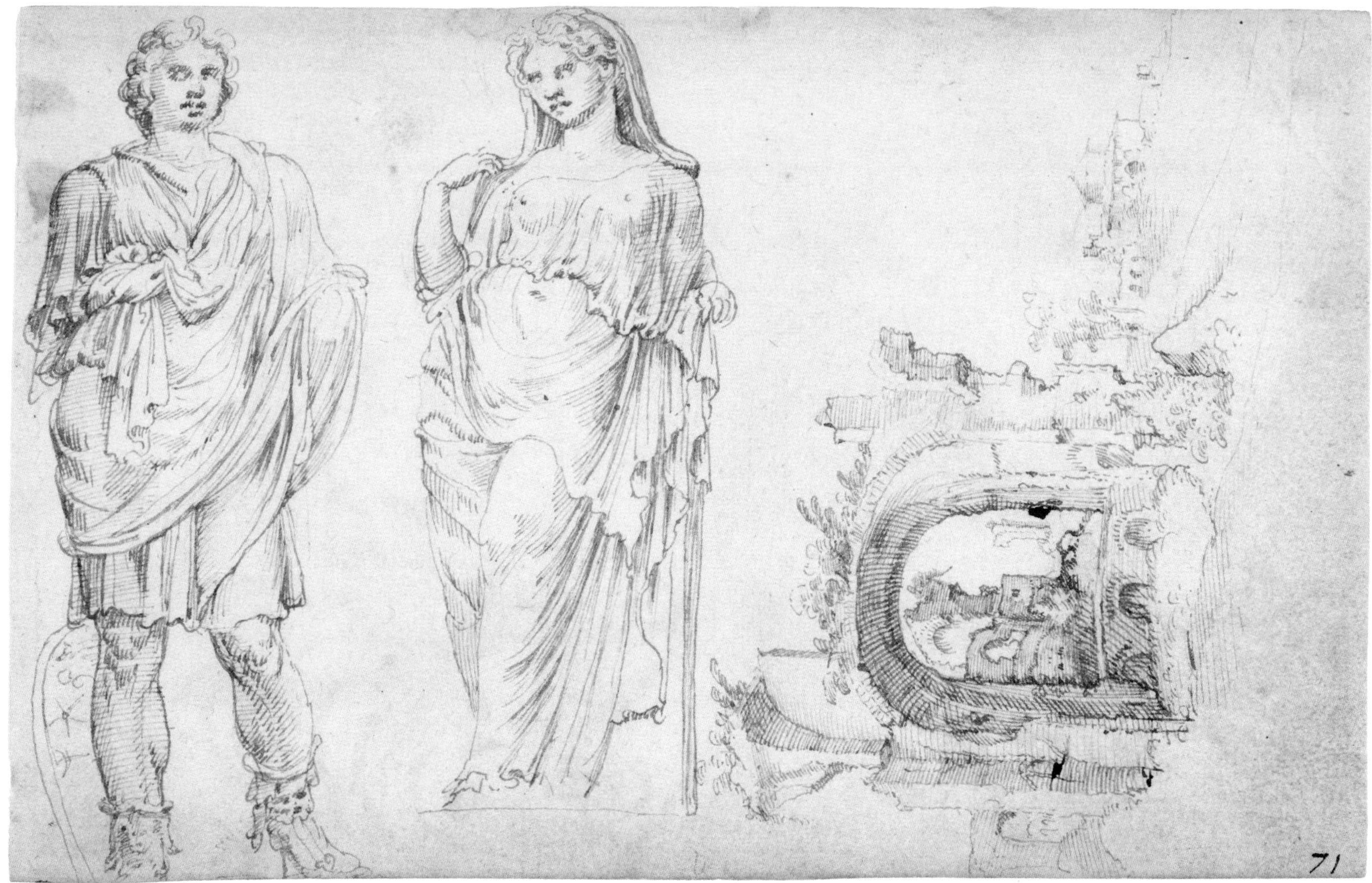

71

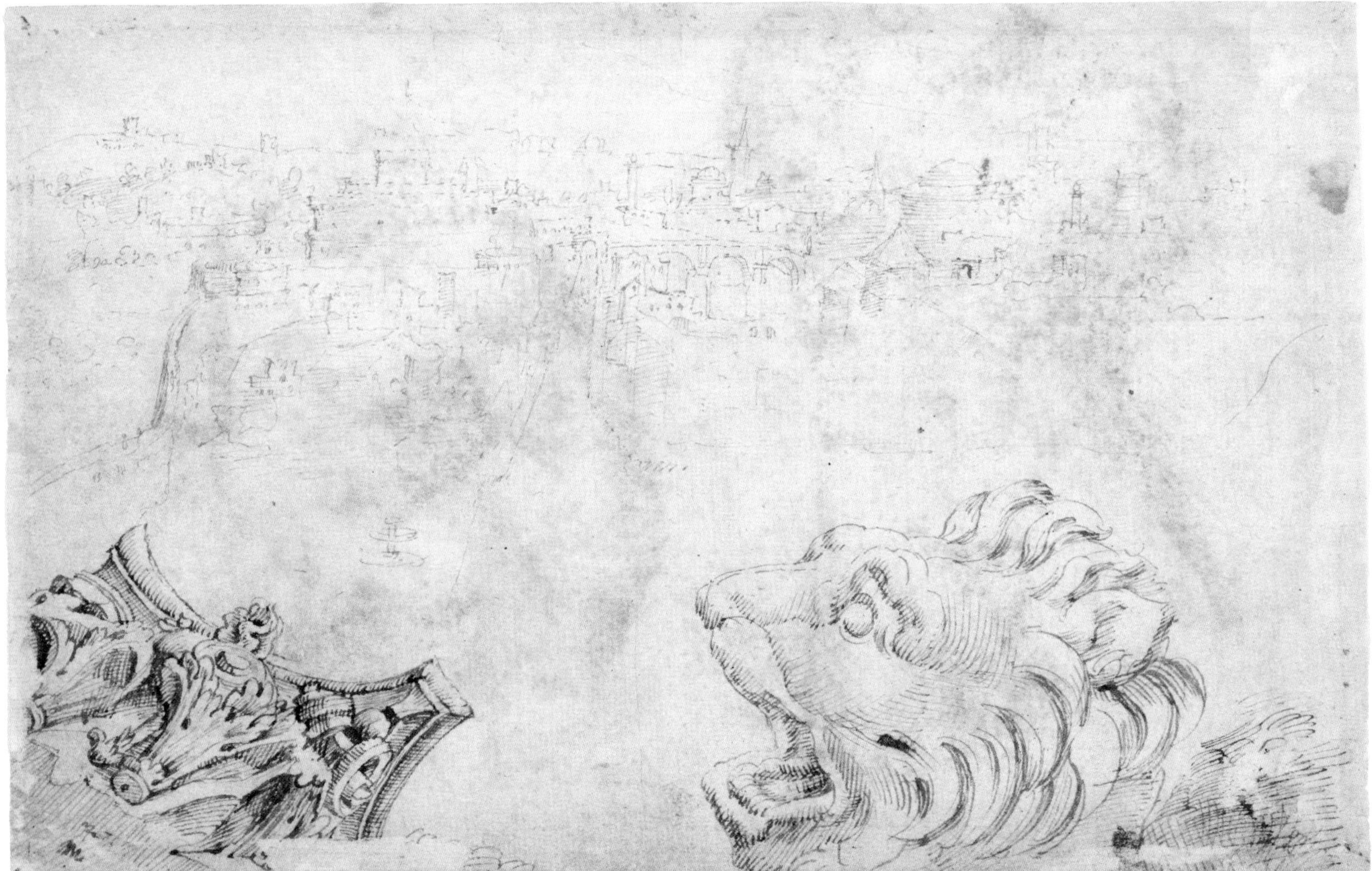

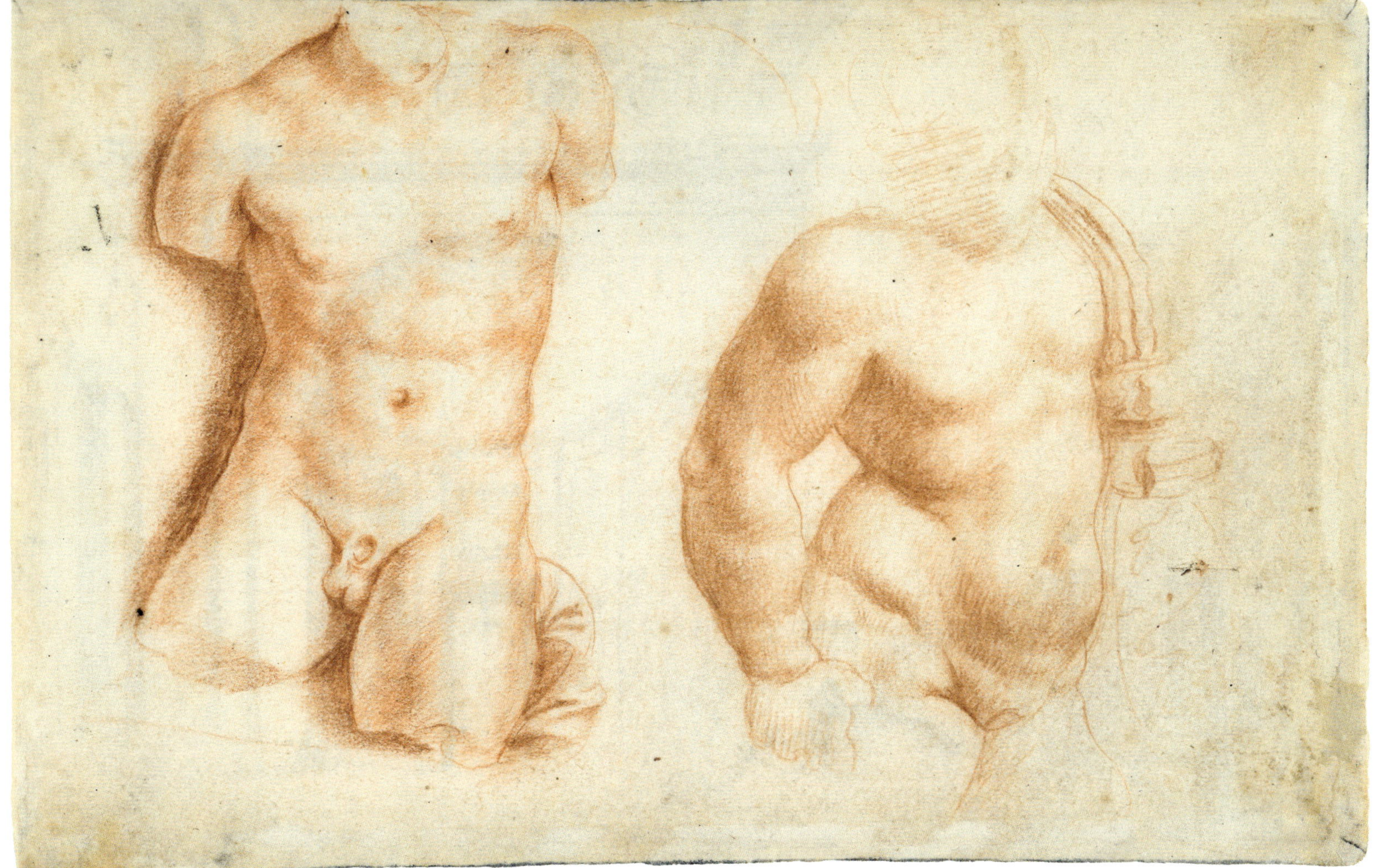

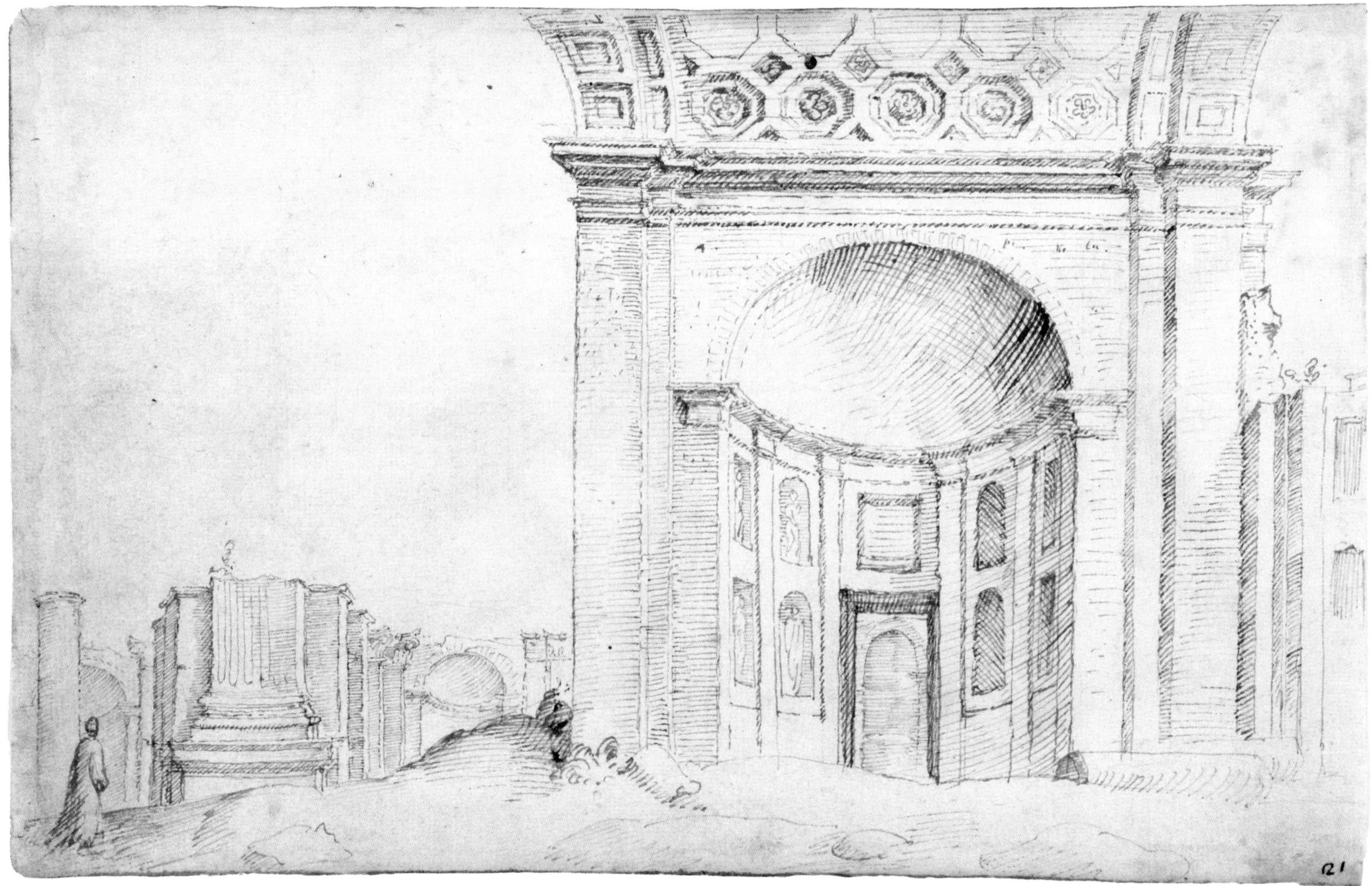
21

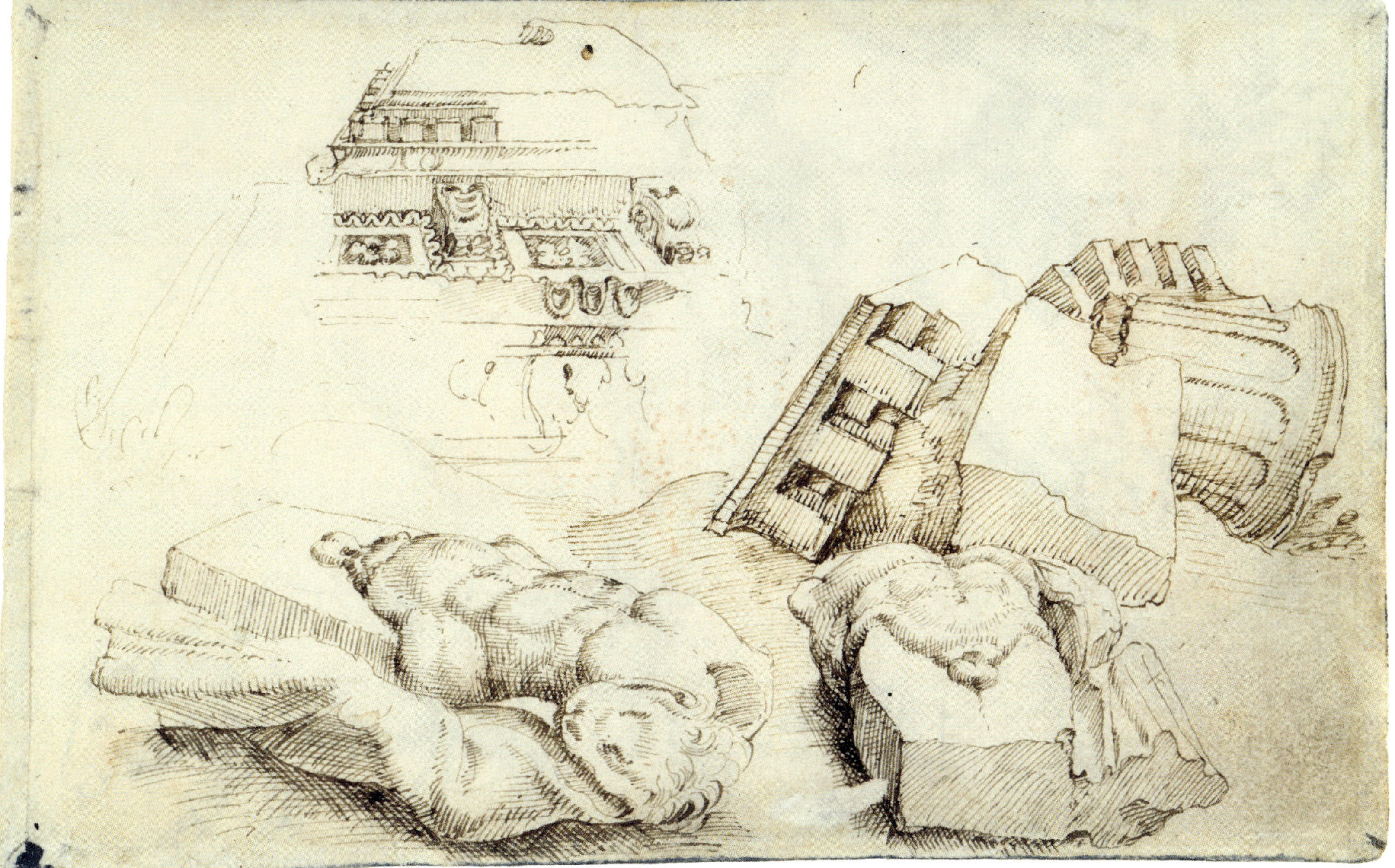

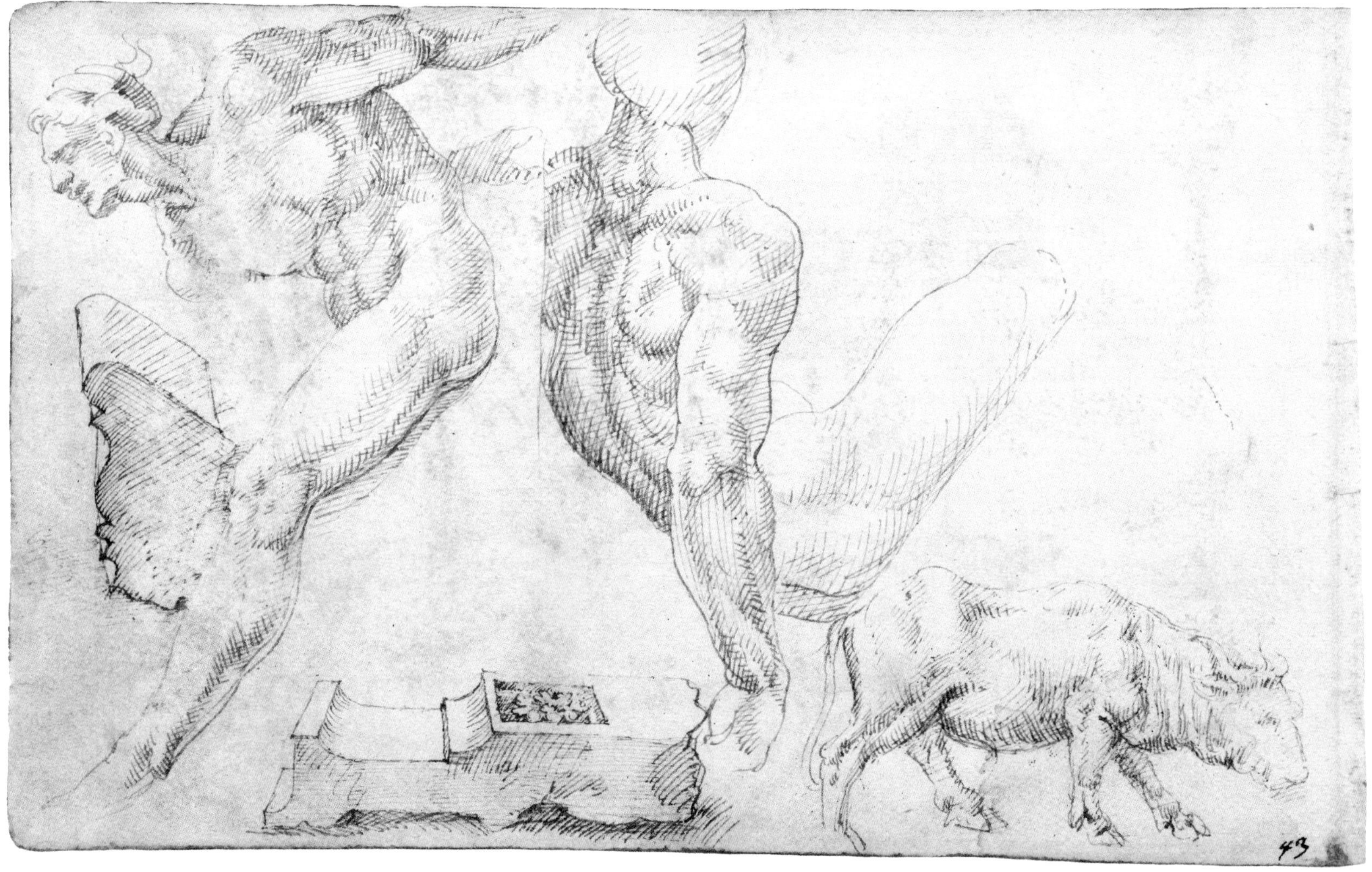

43

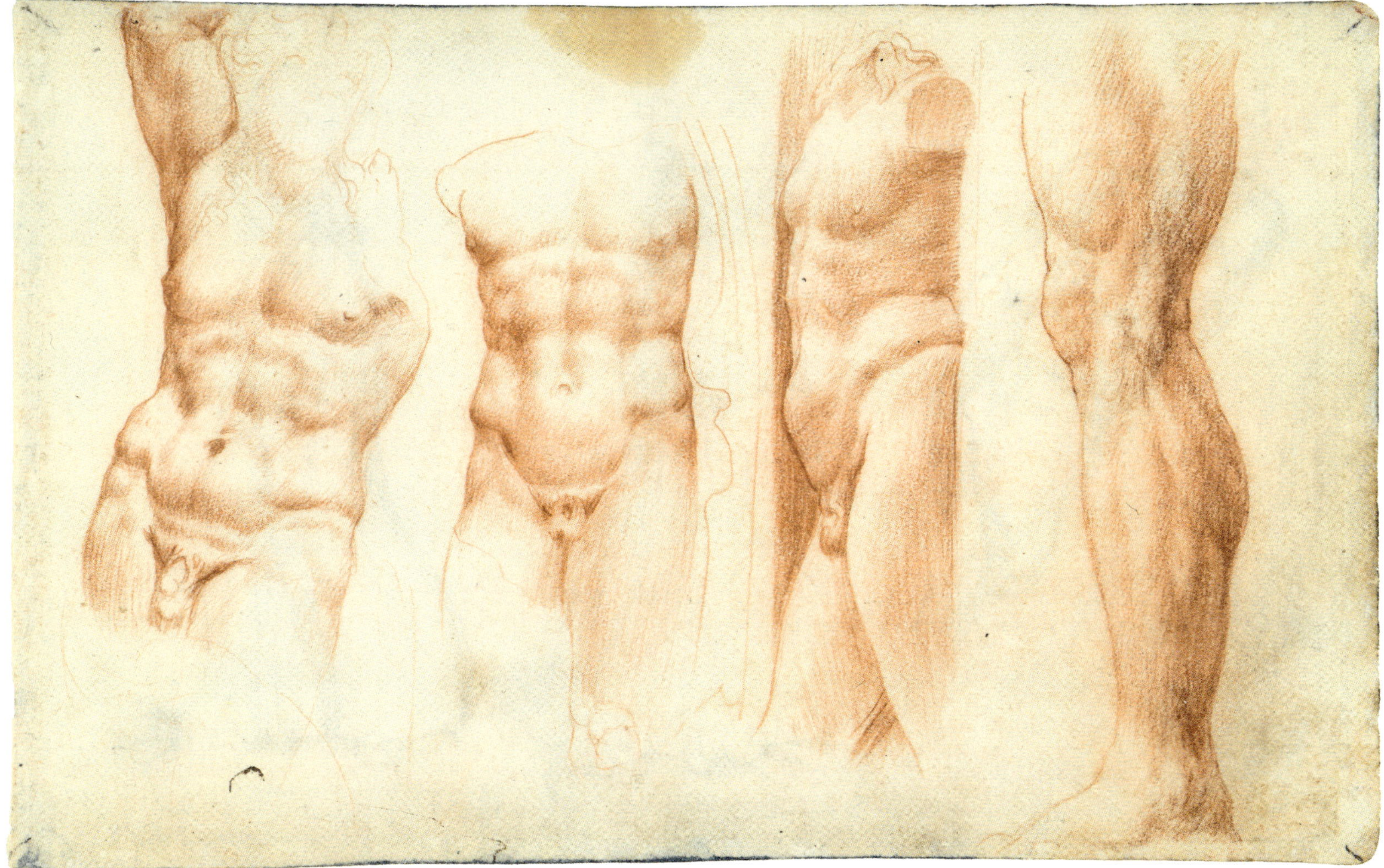

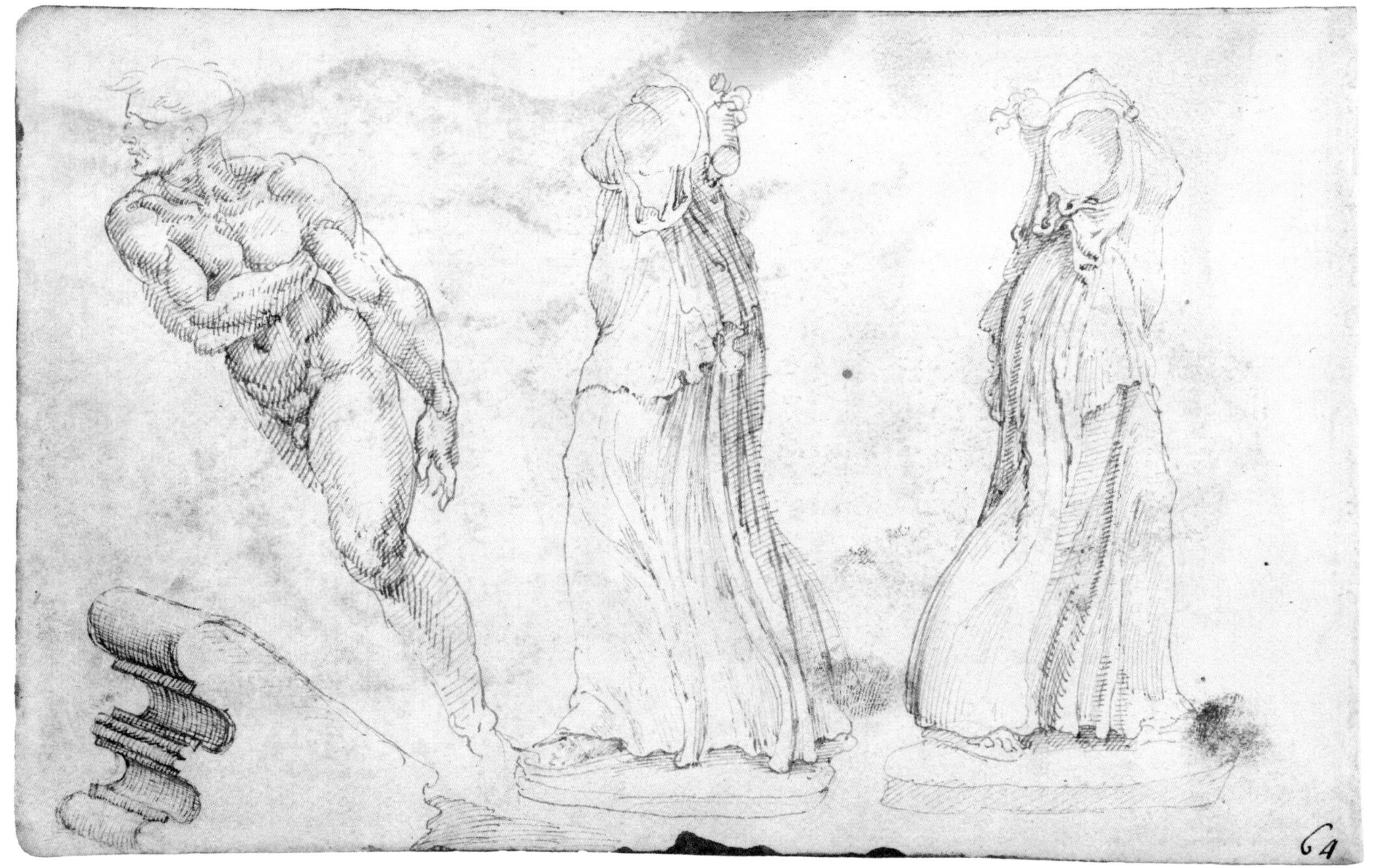

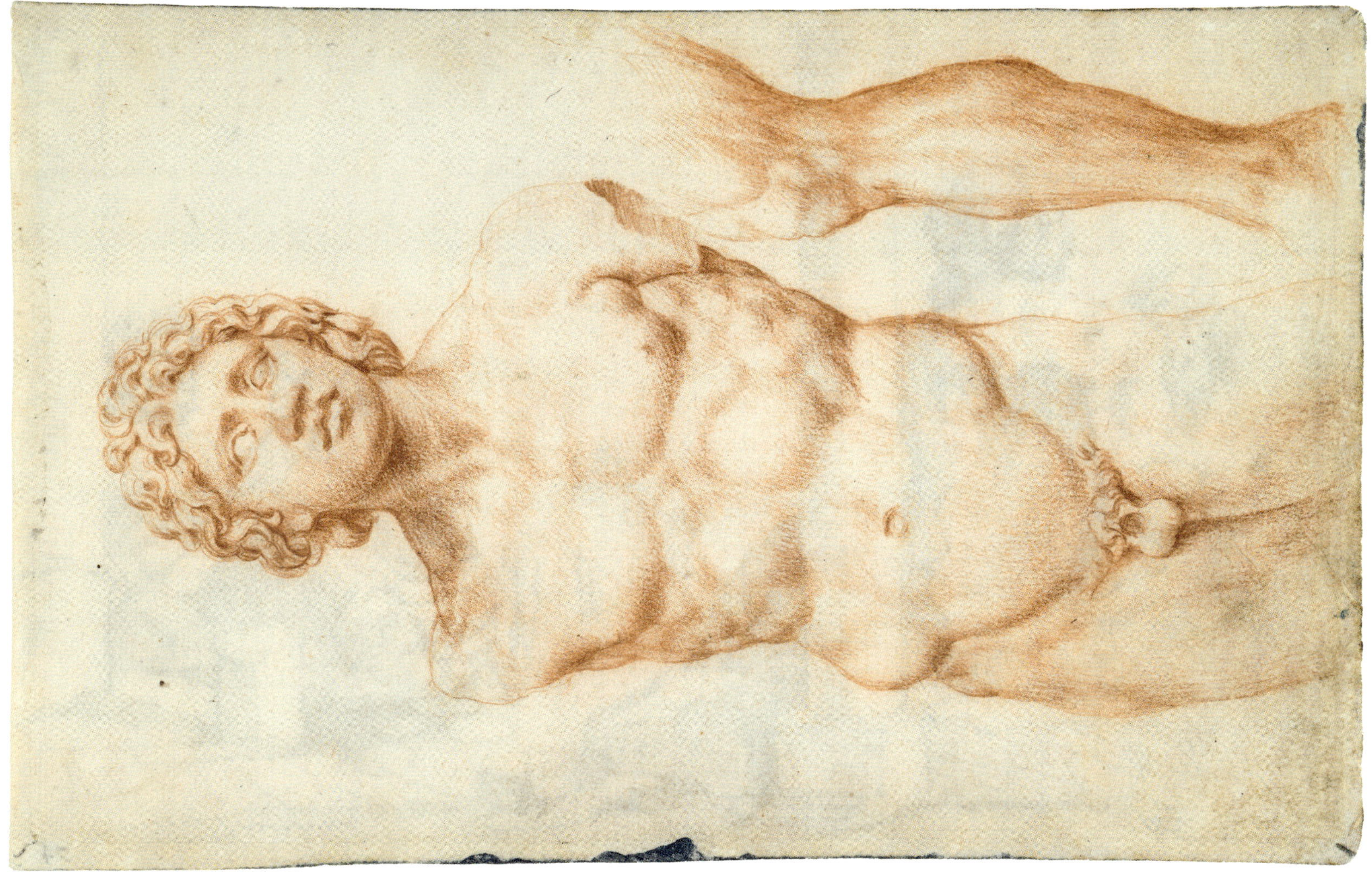

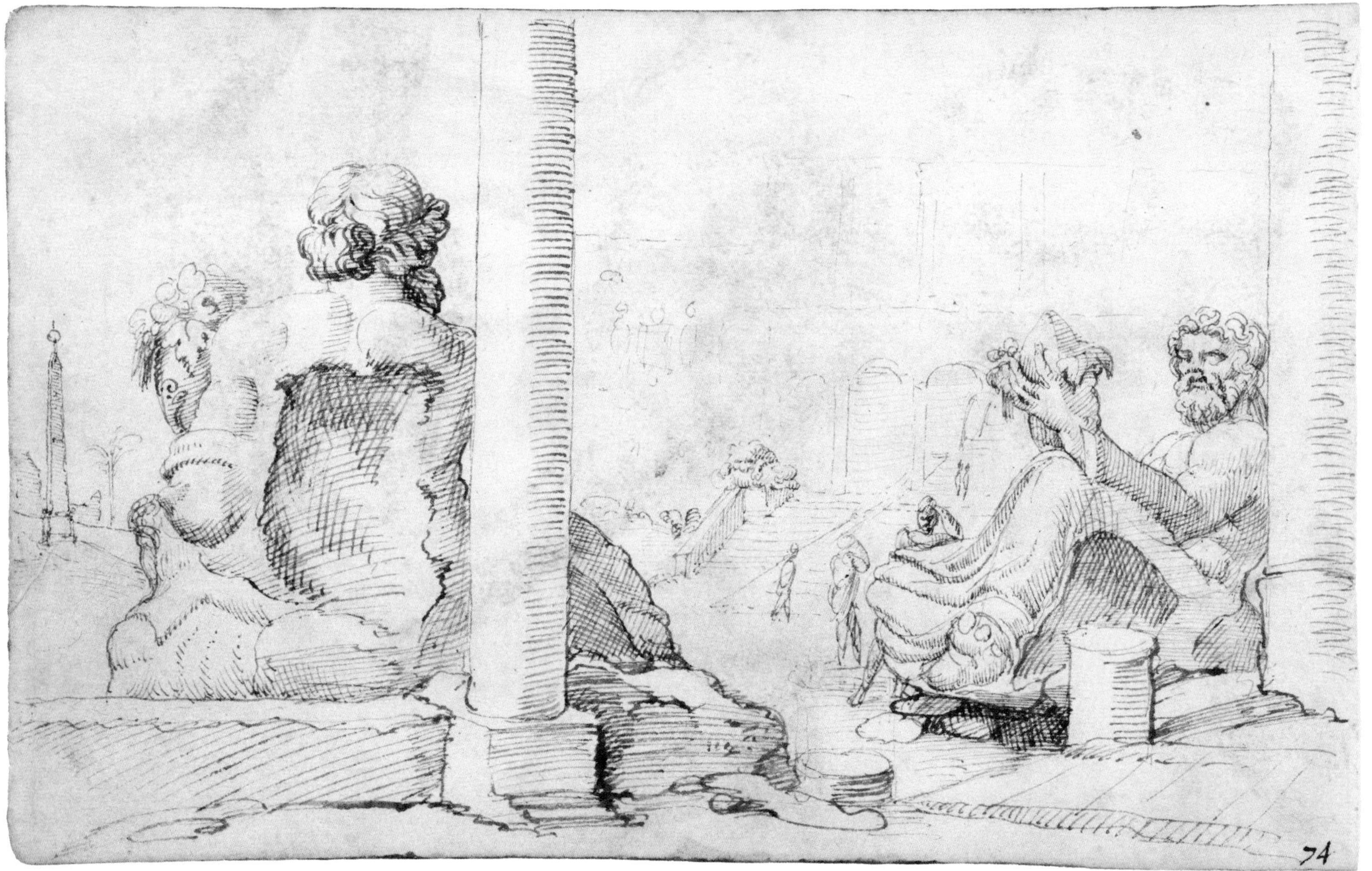

74

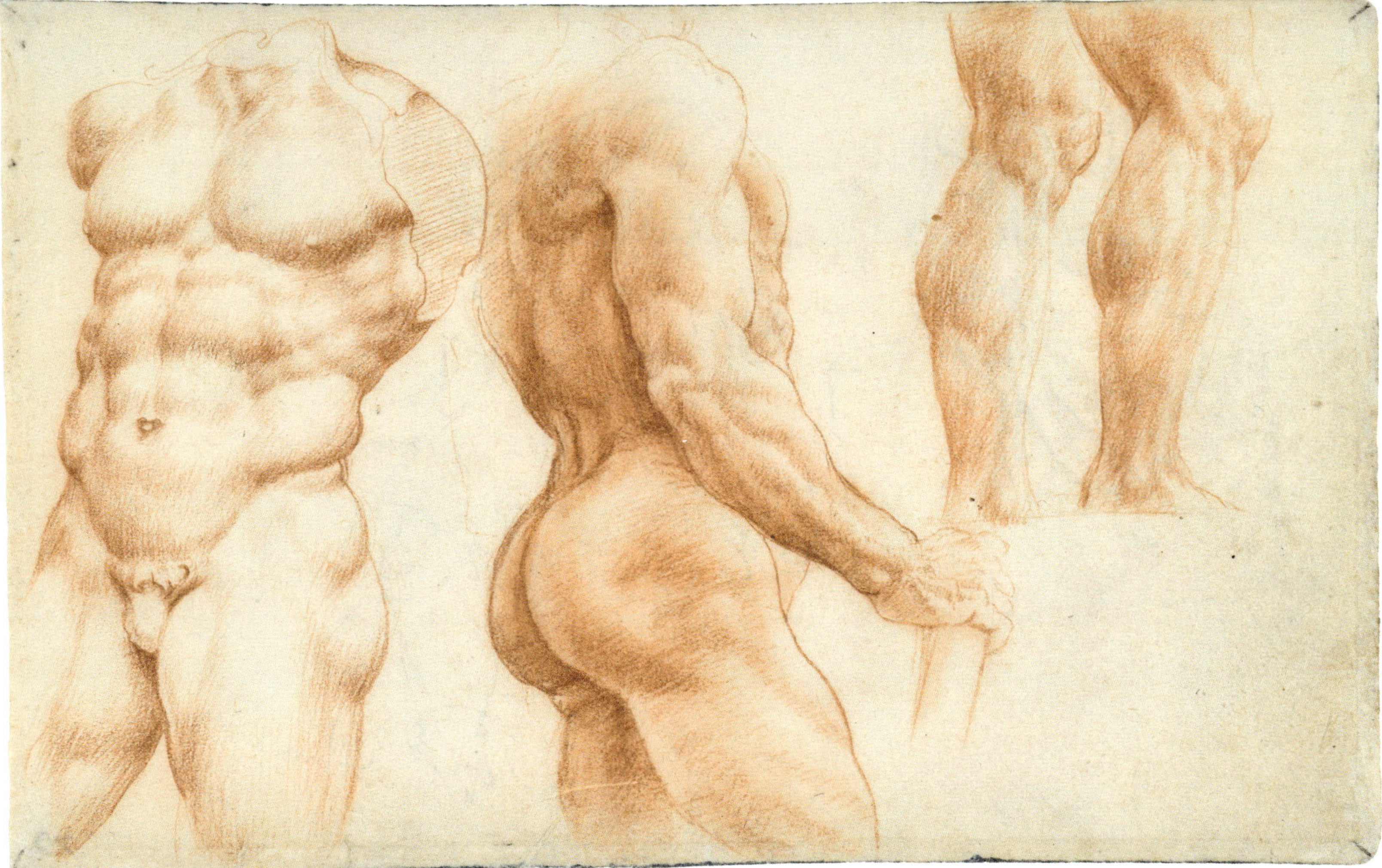

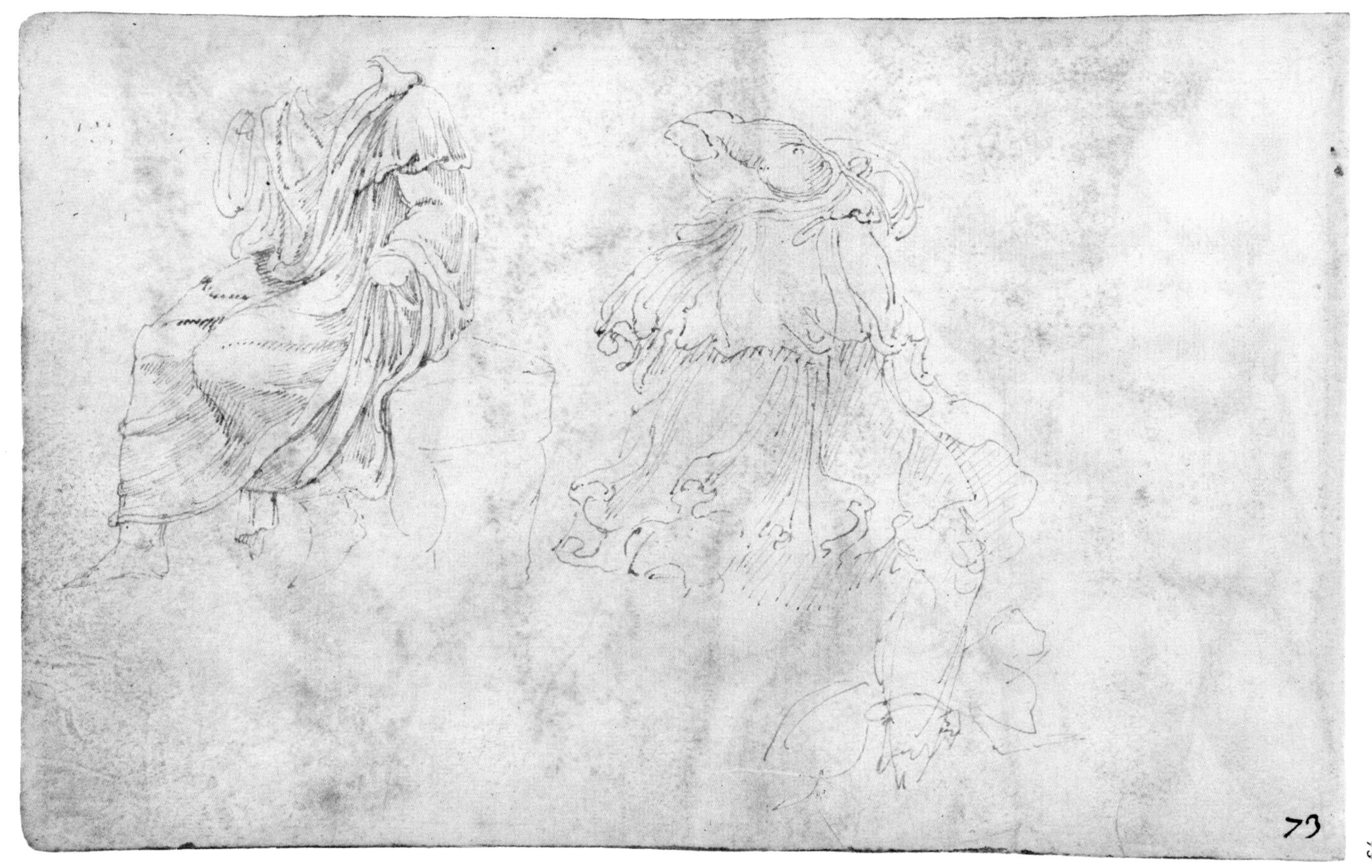

73

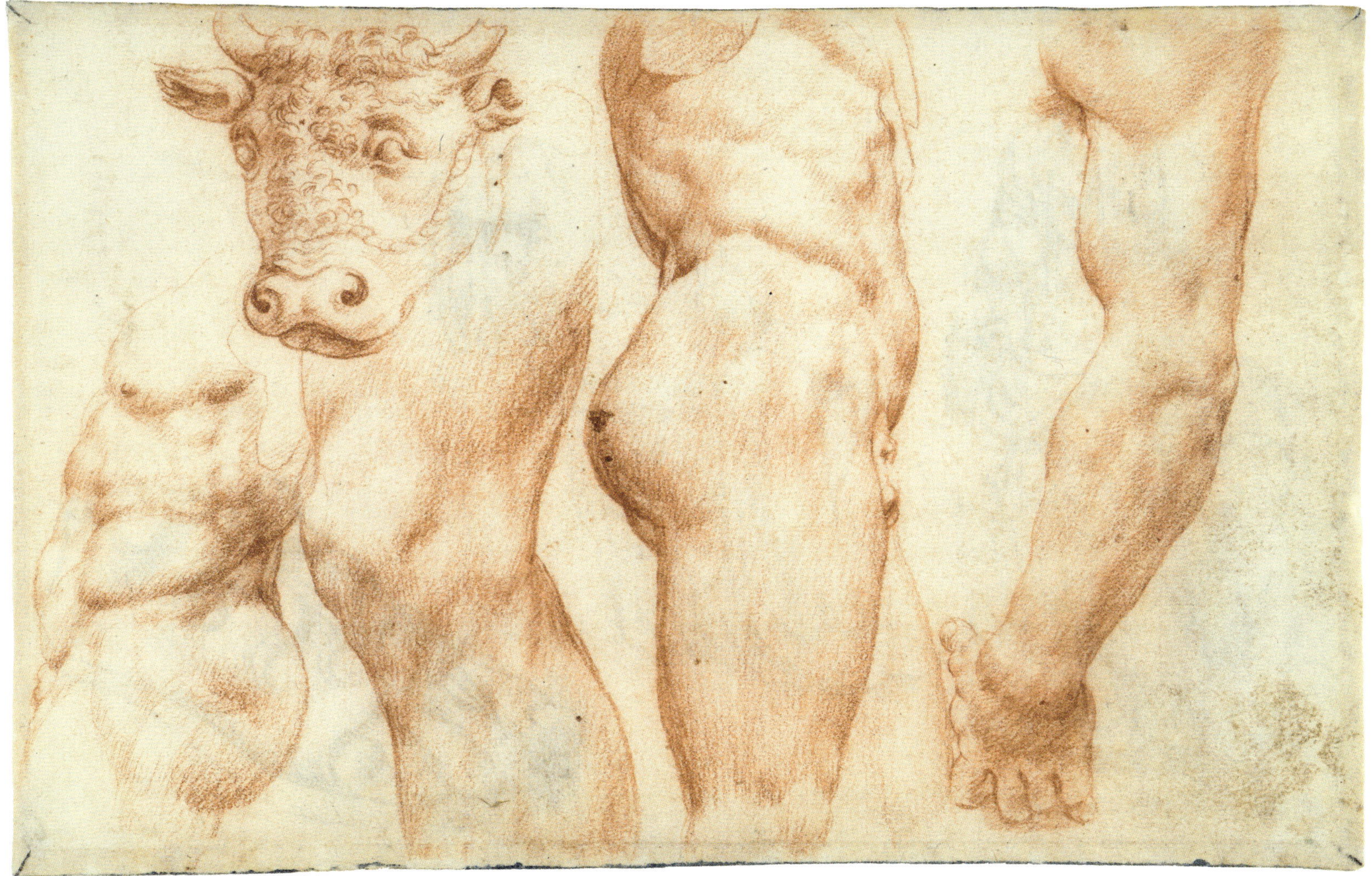

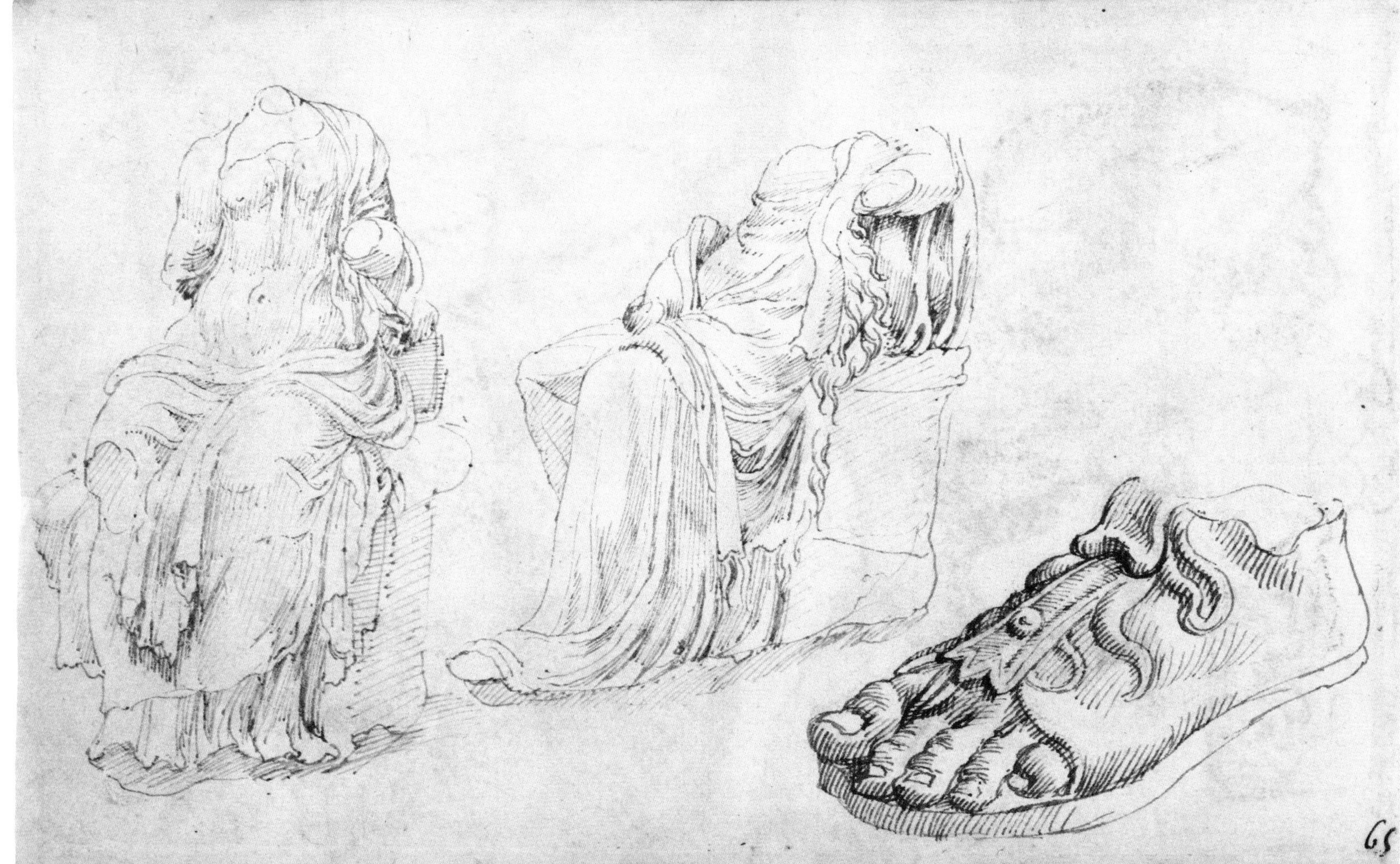

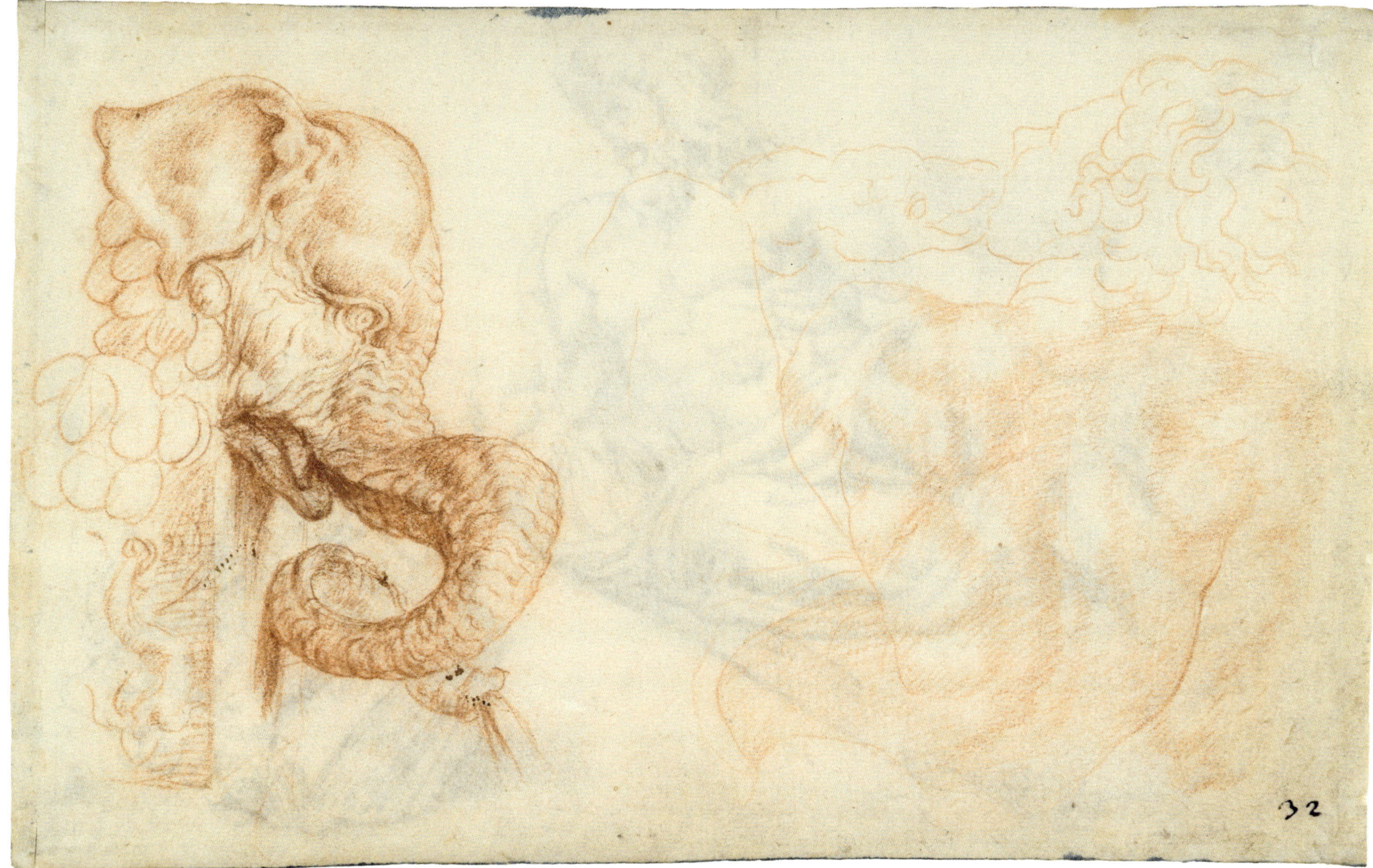

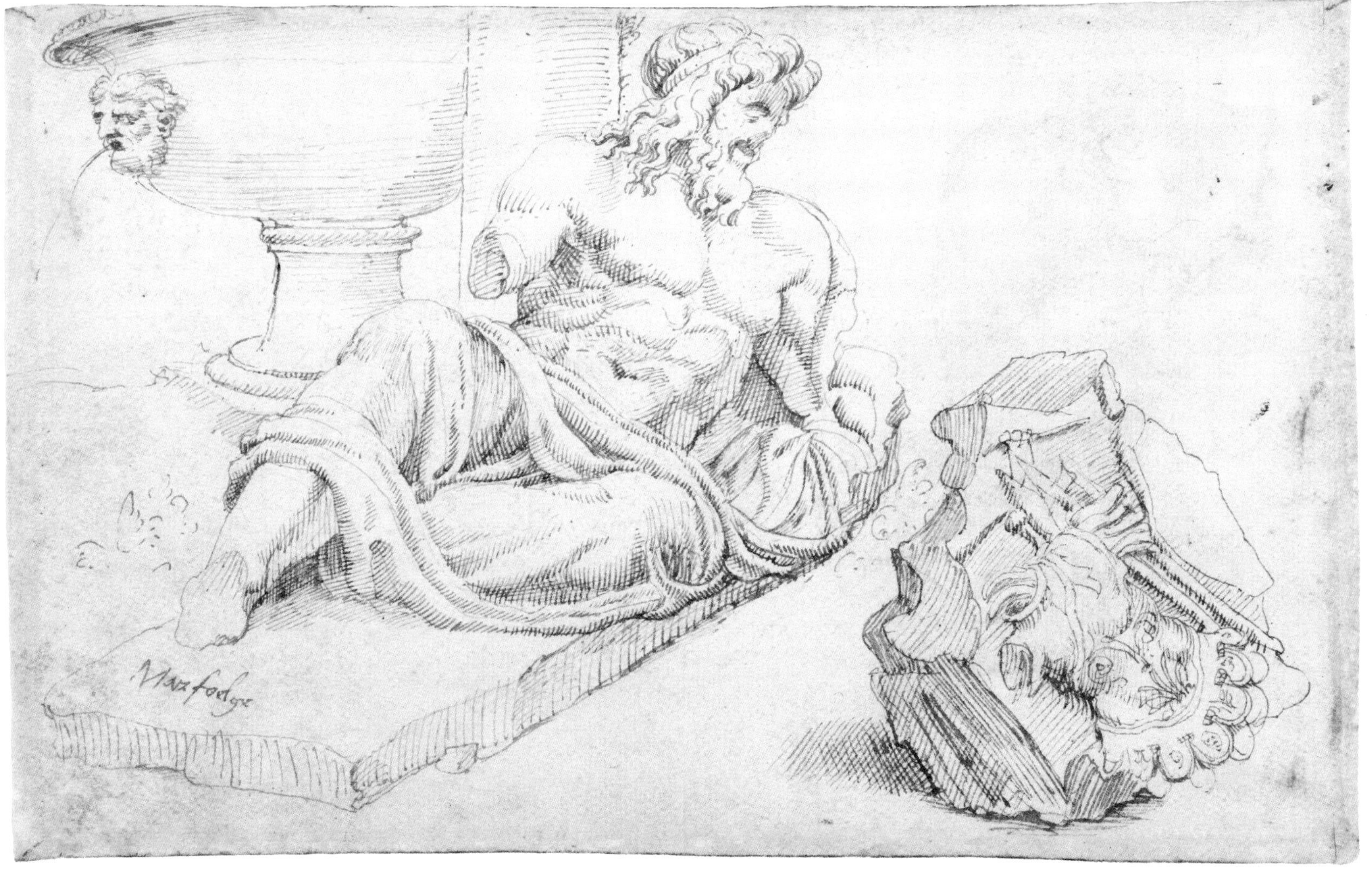

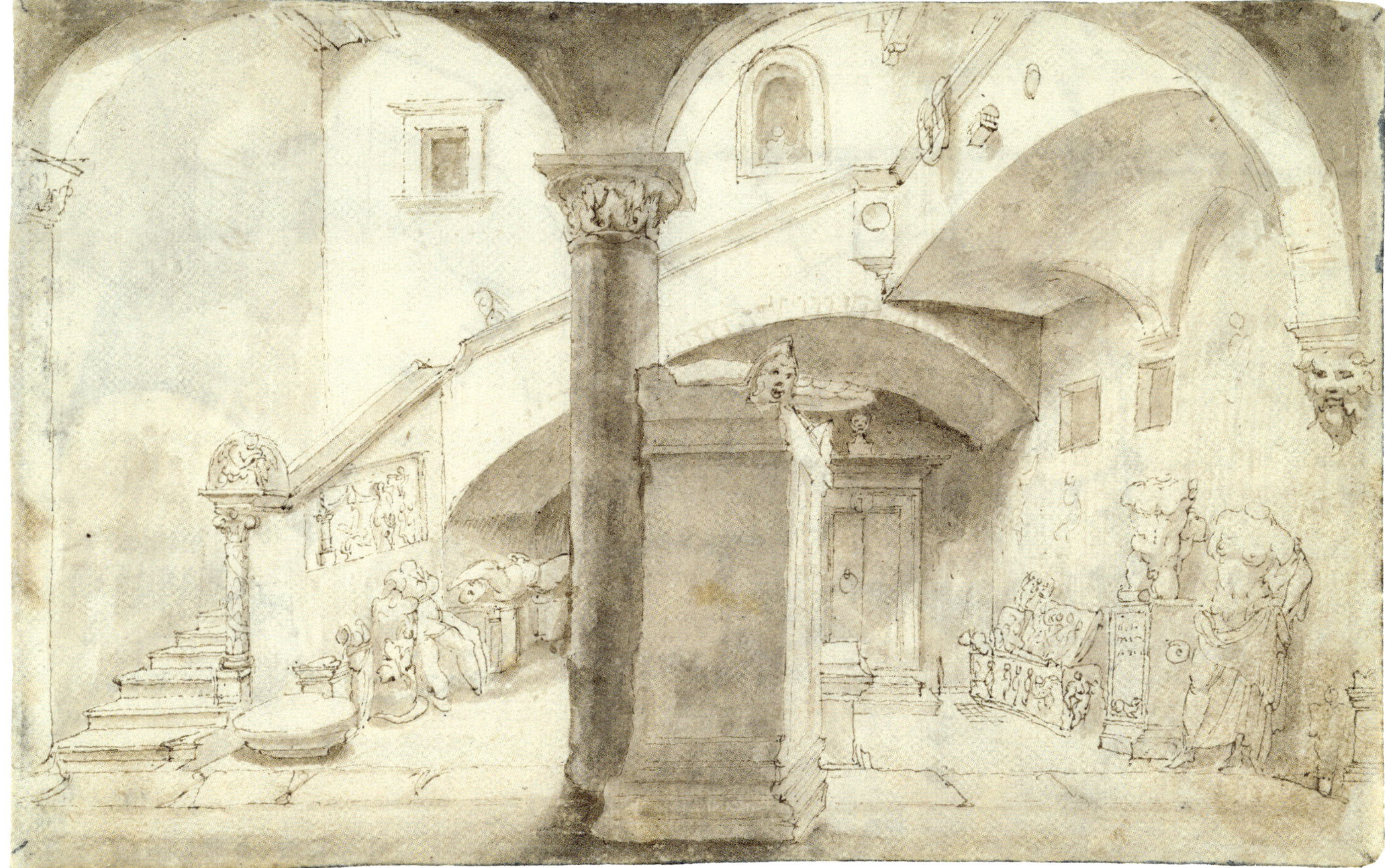

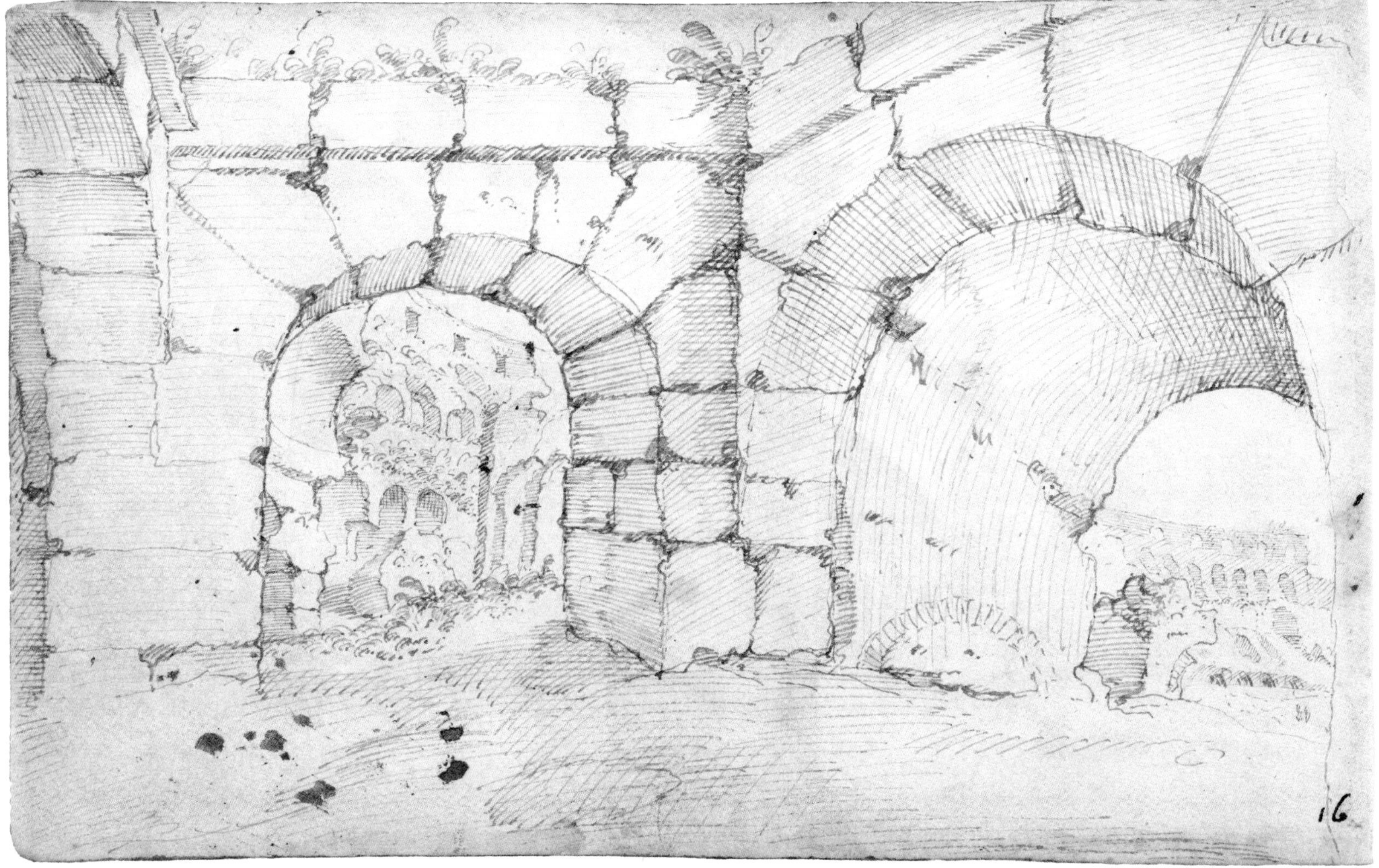
16

[ONE MISSING PAGE]

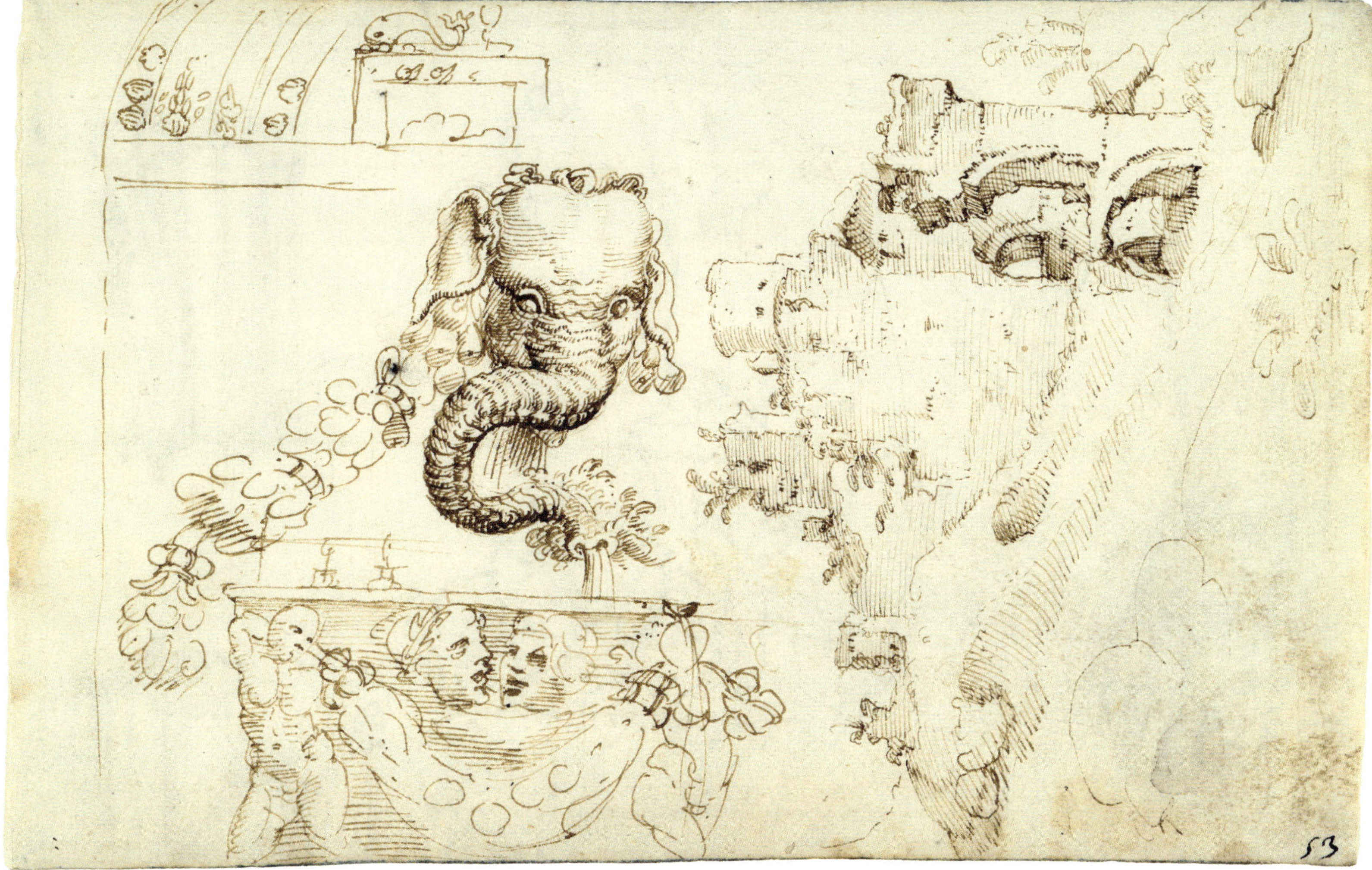

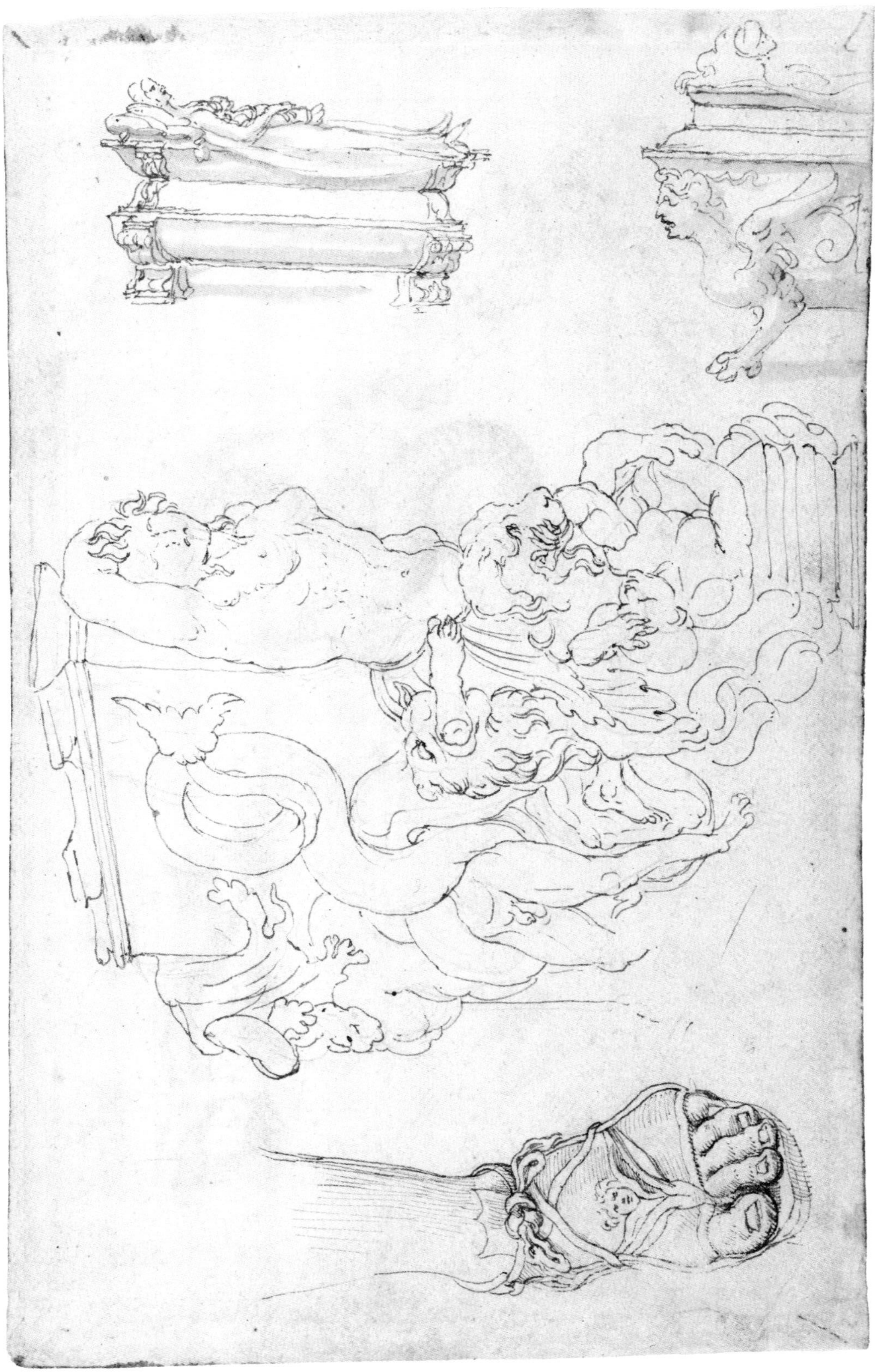

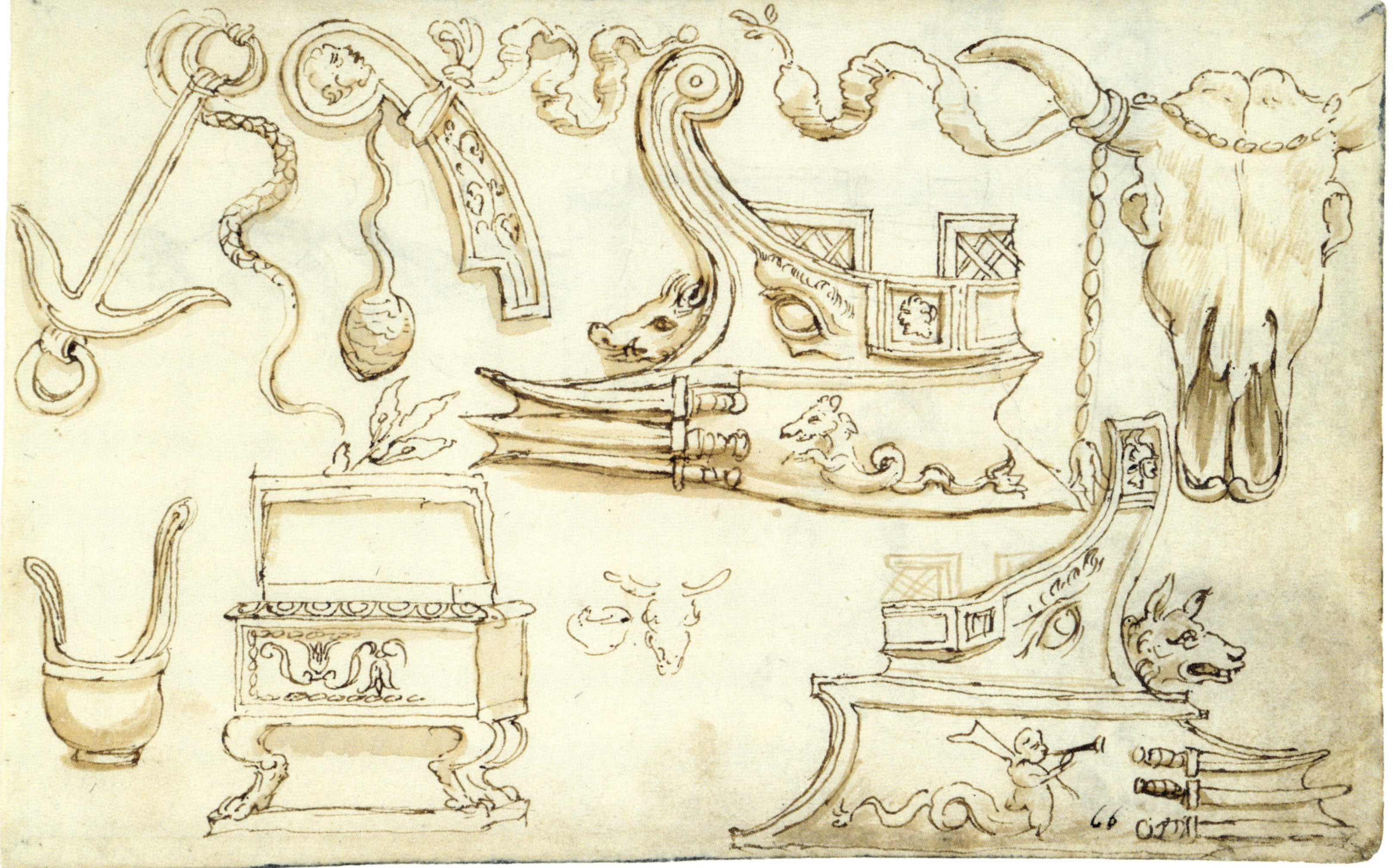

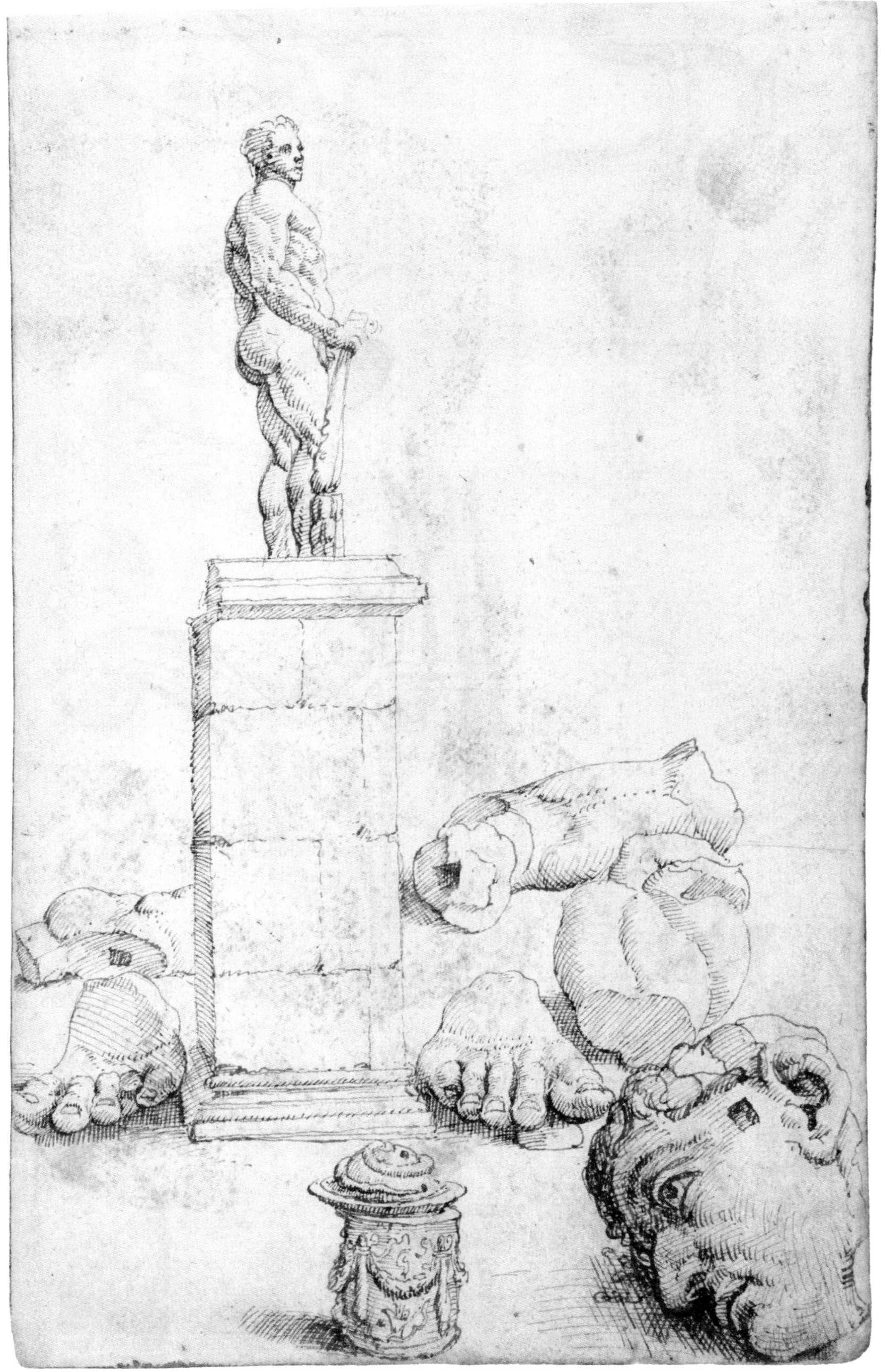

[ONE MISSING PAGE]

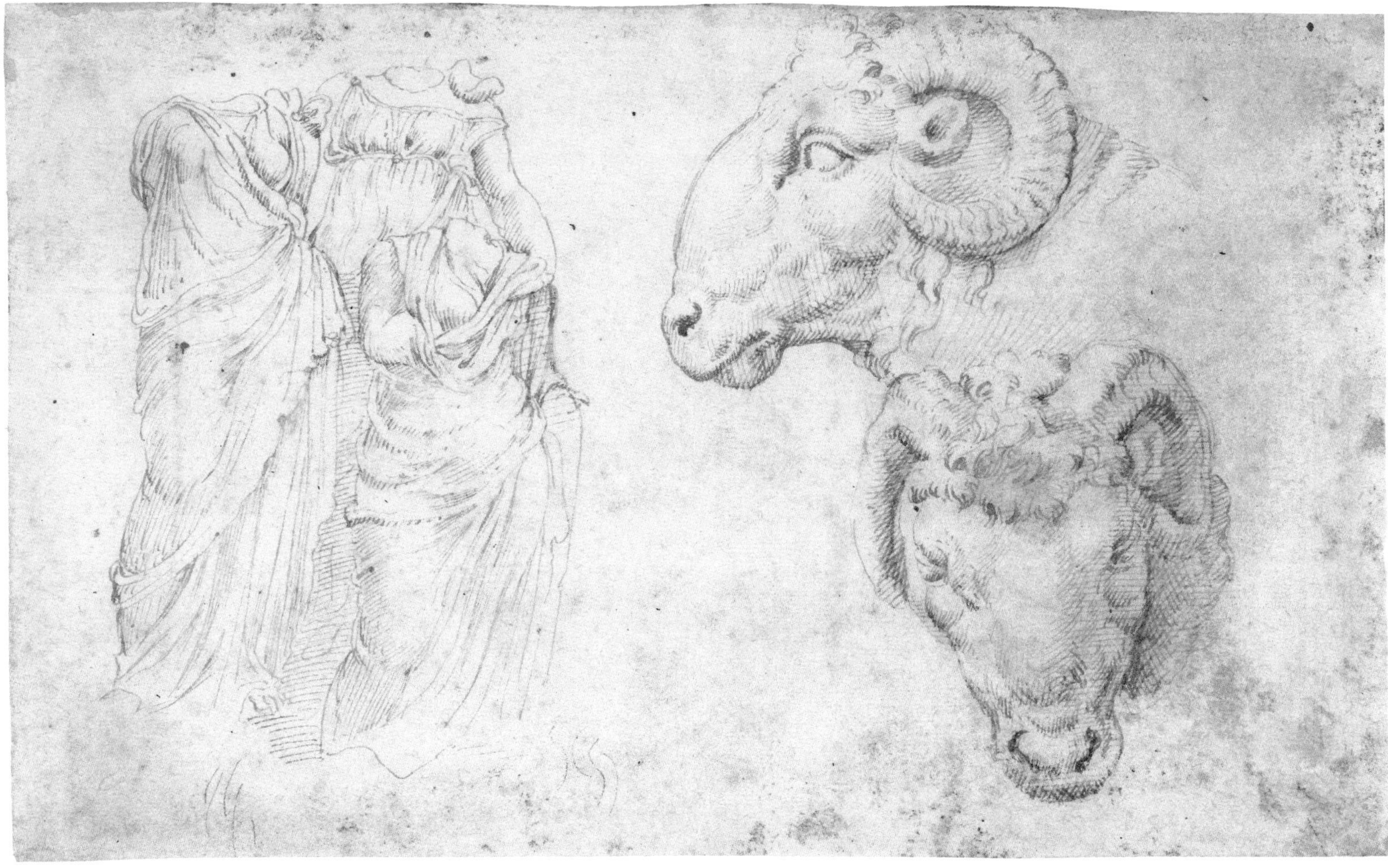

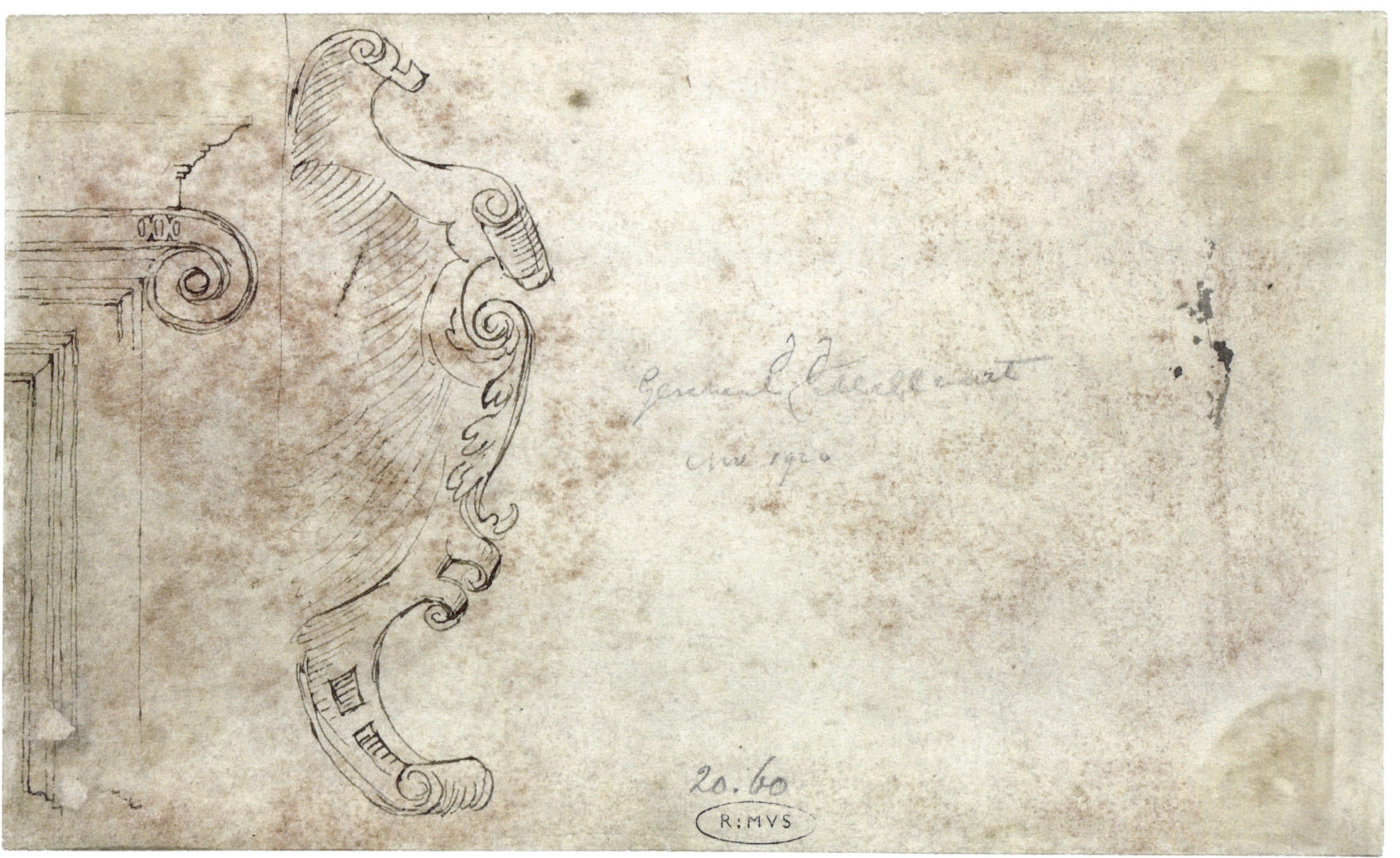
20.60
R:MVS

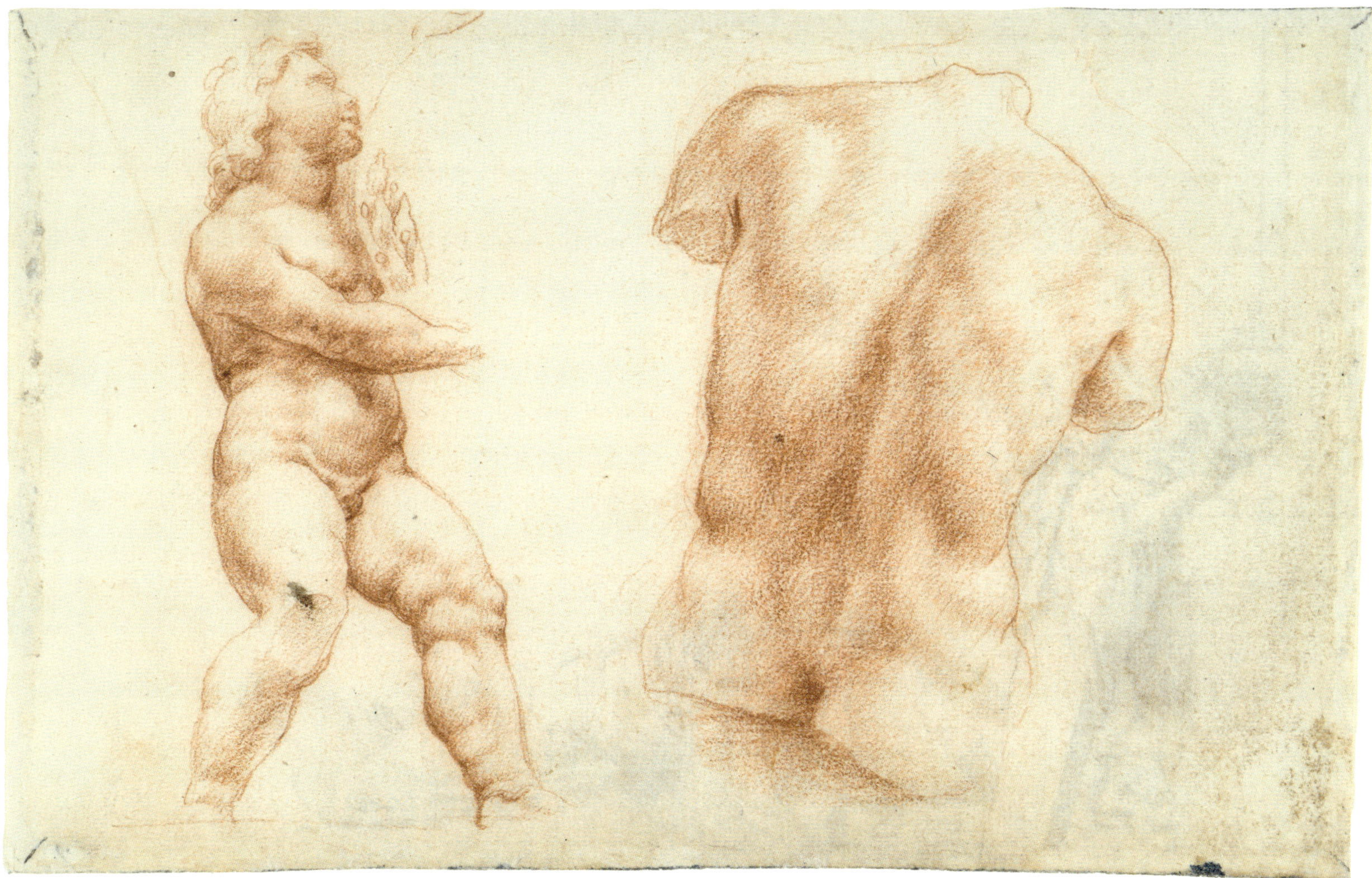

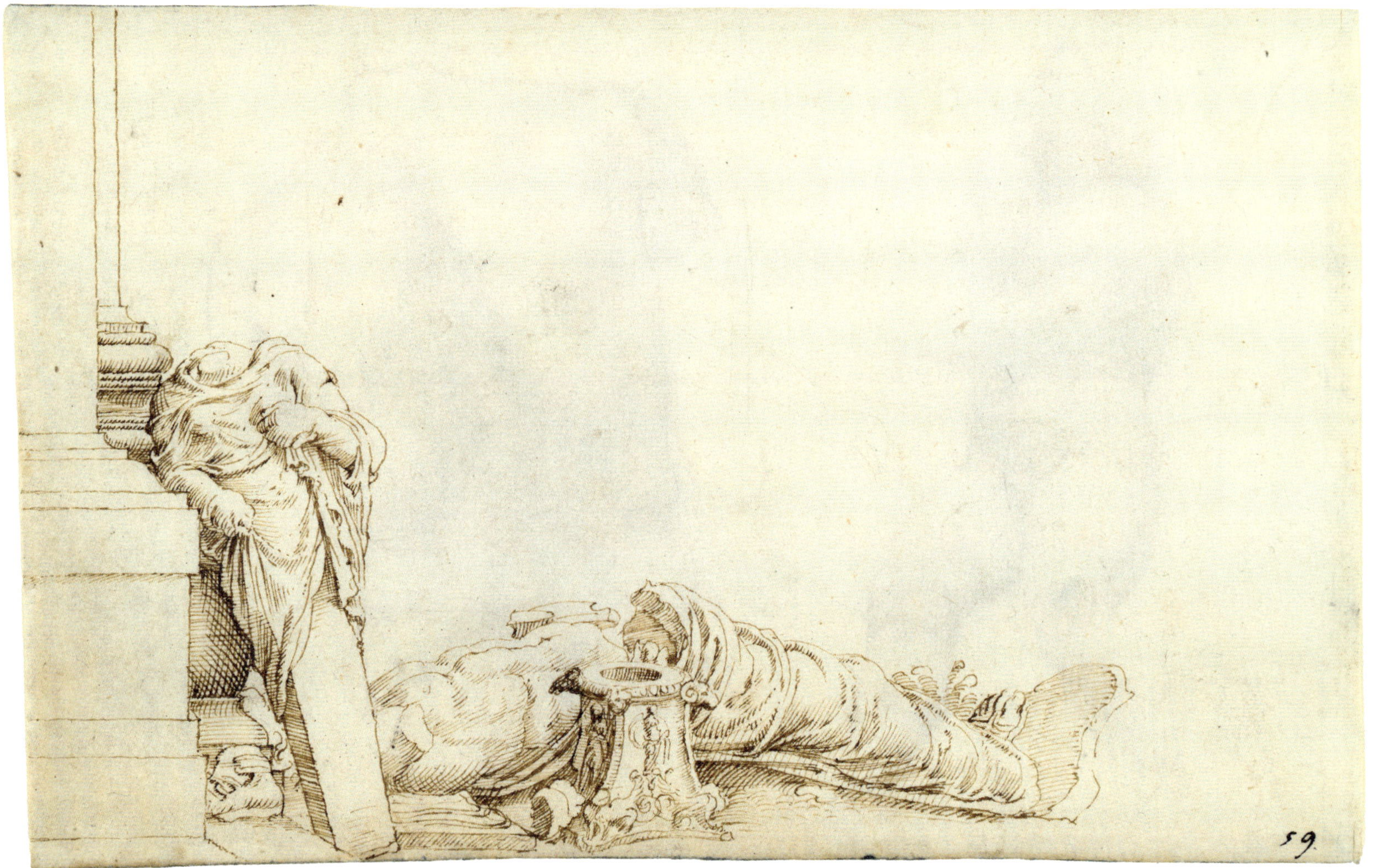

59.

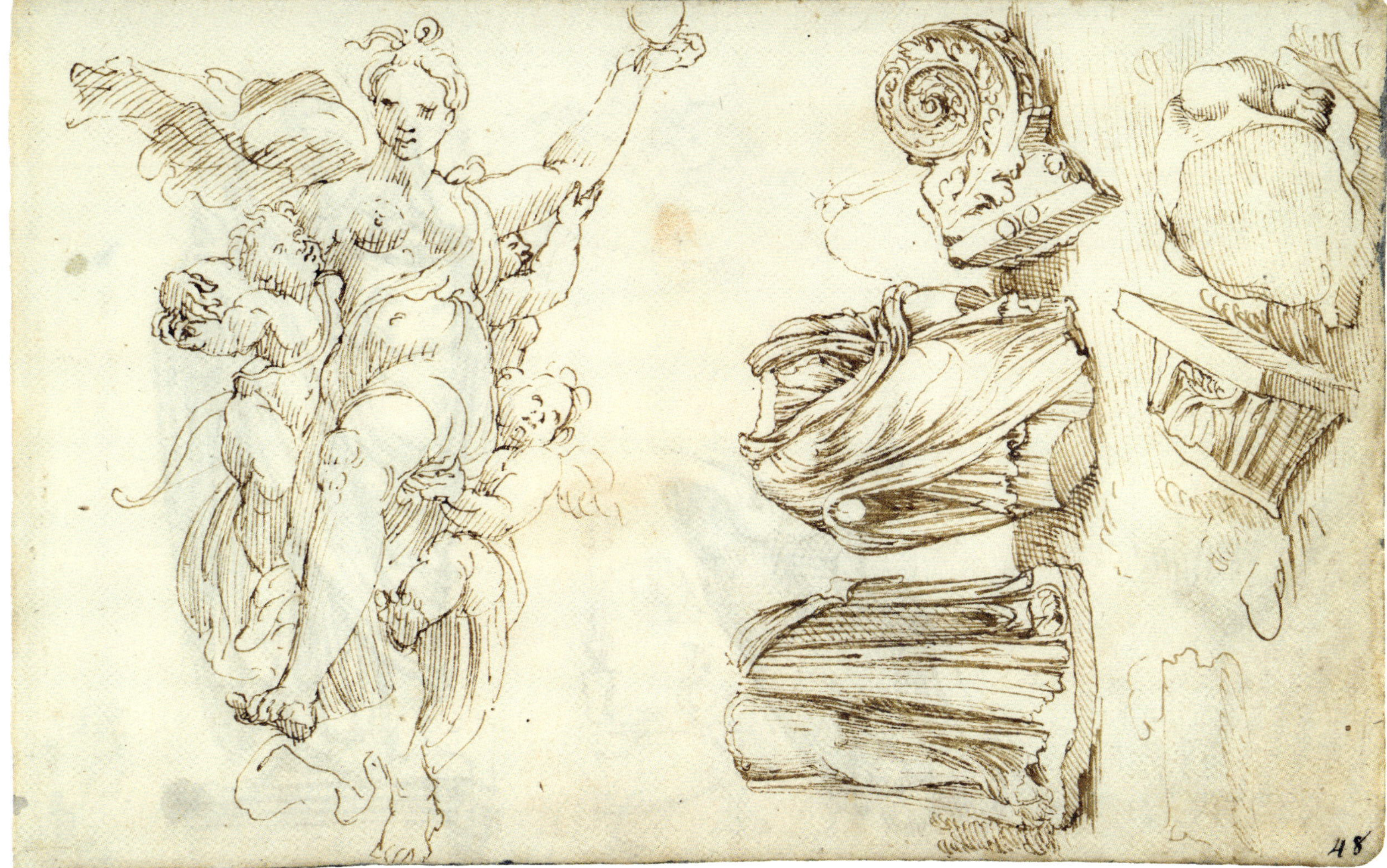

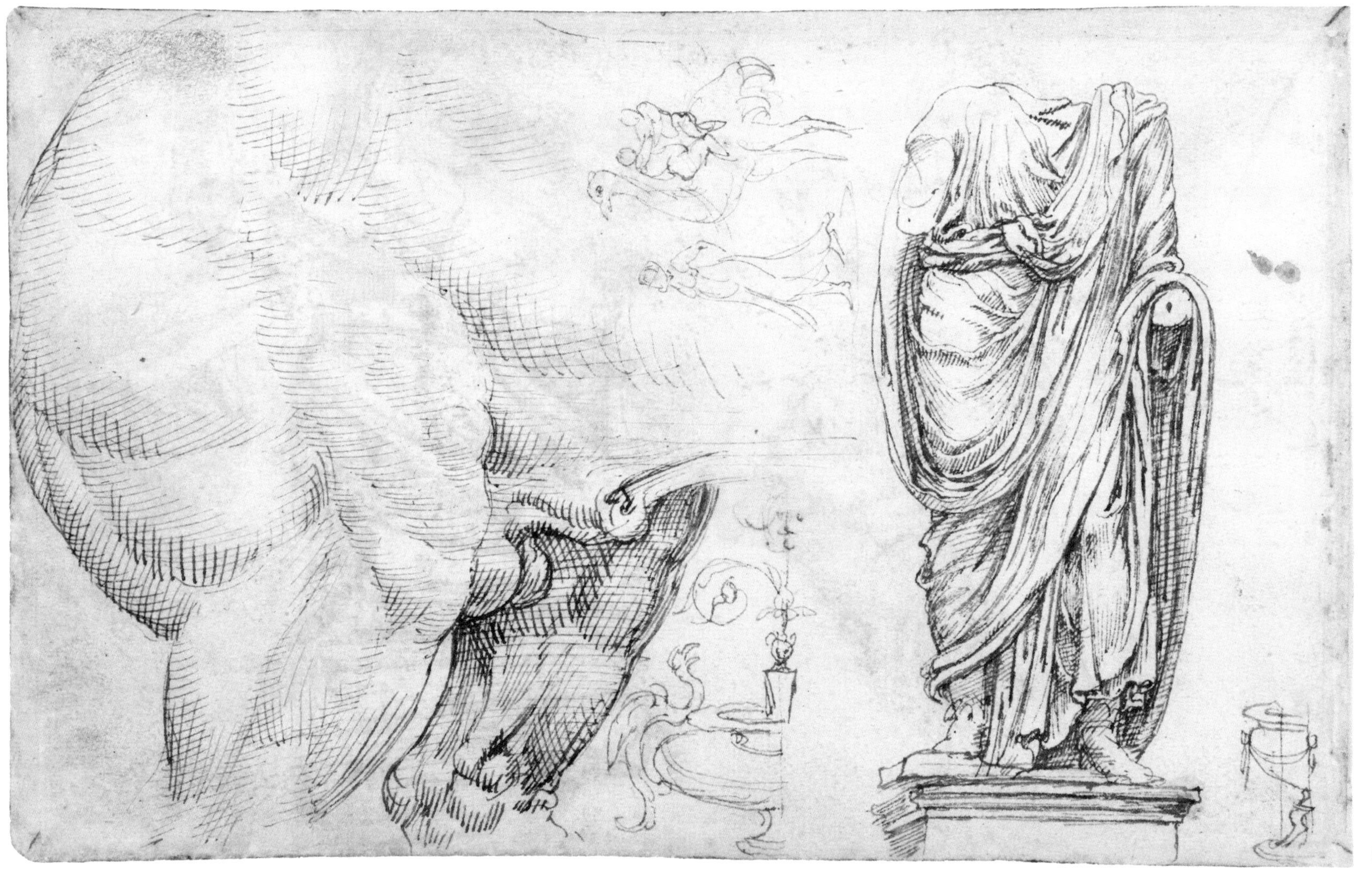

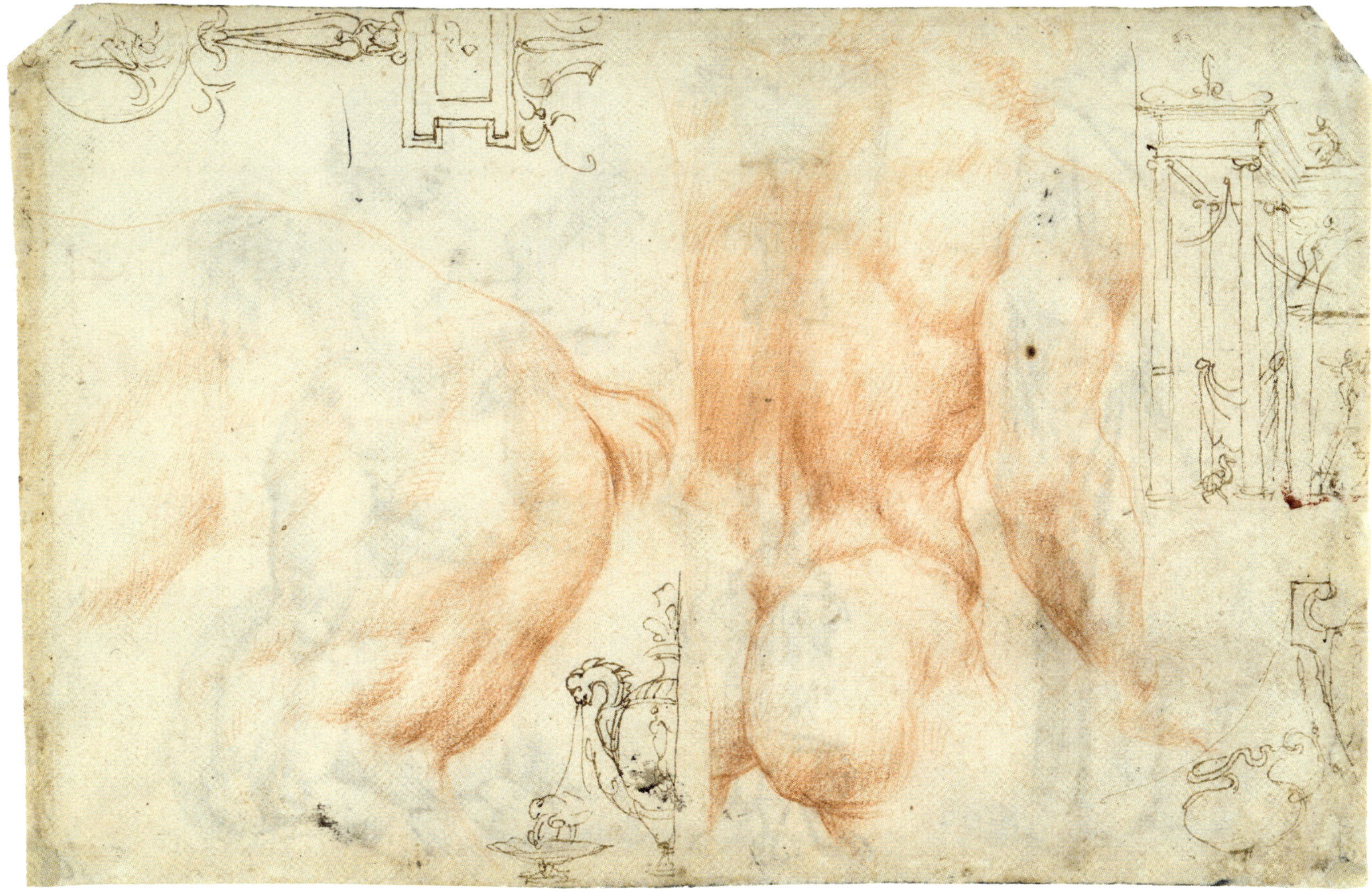

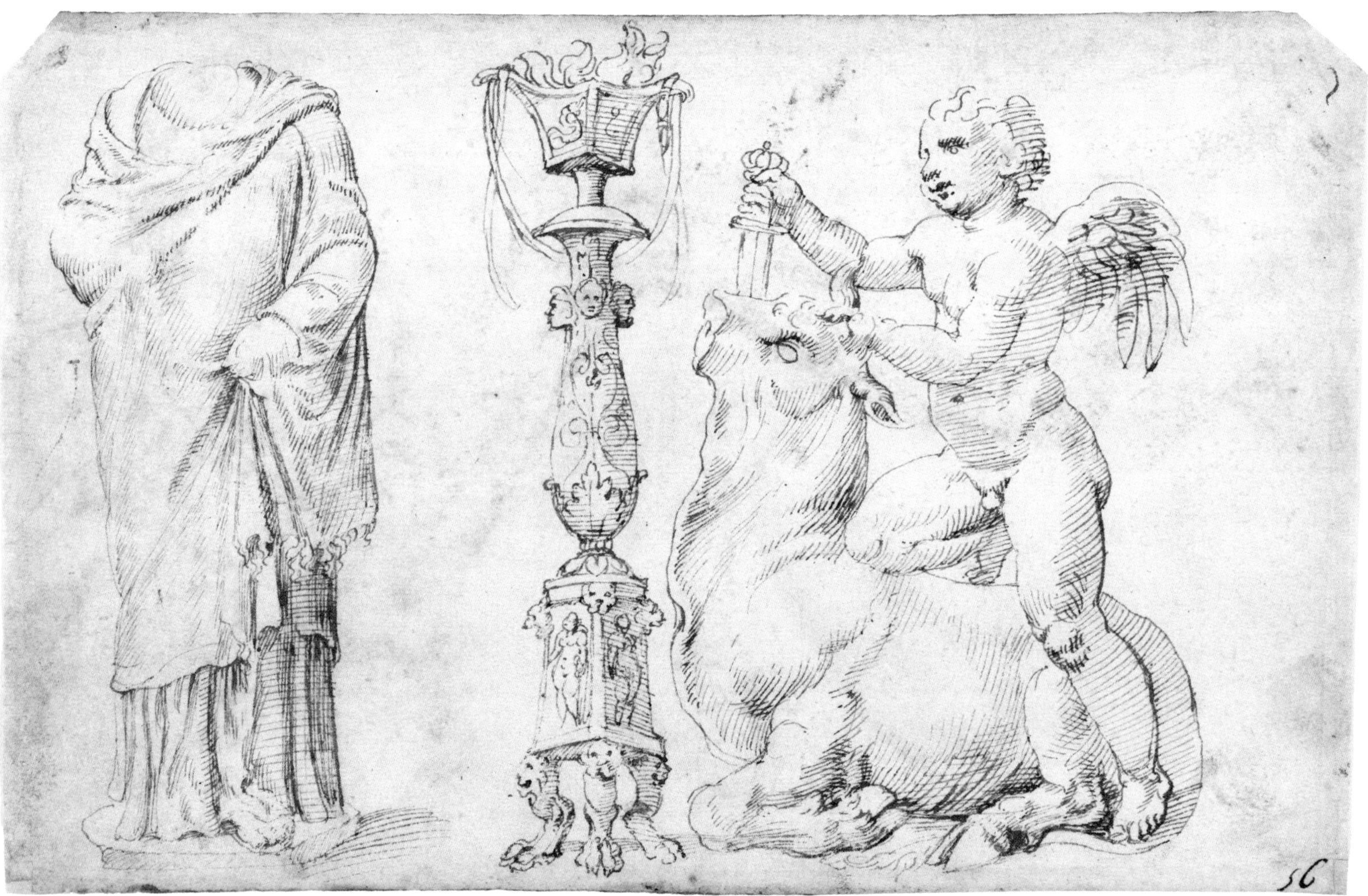

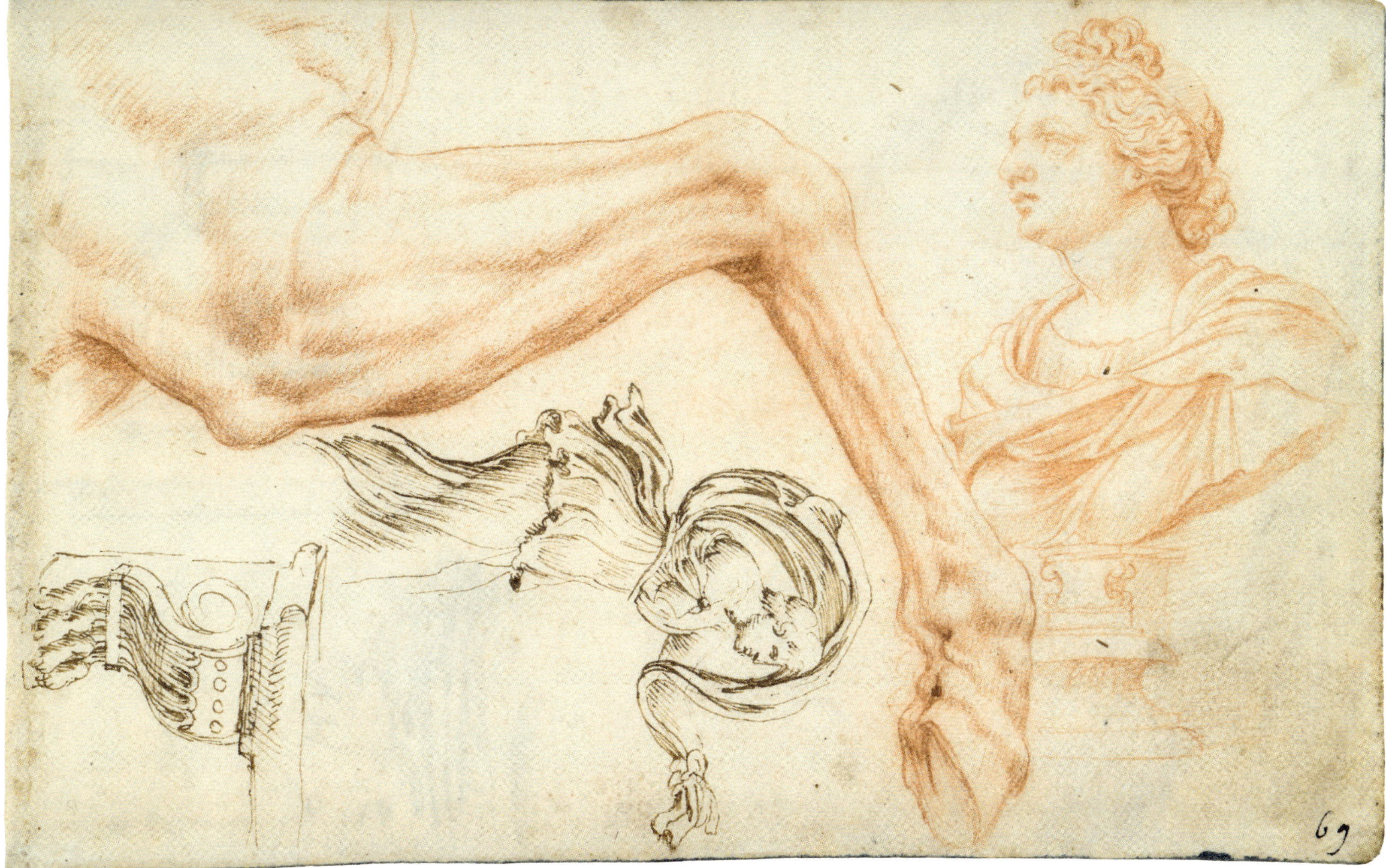

69

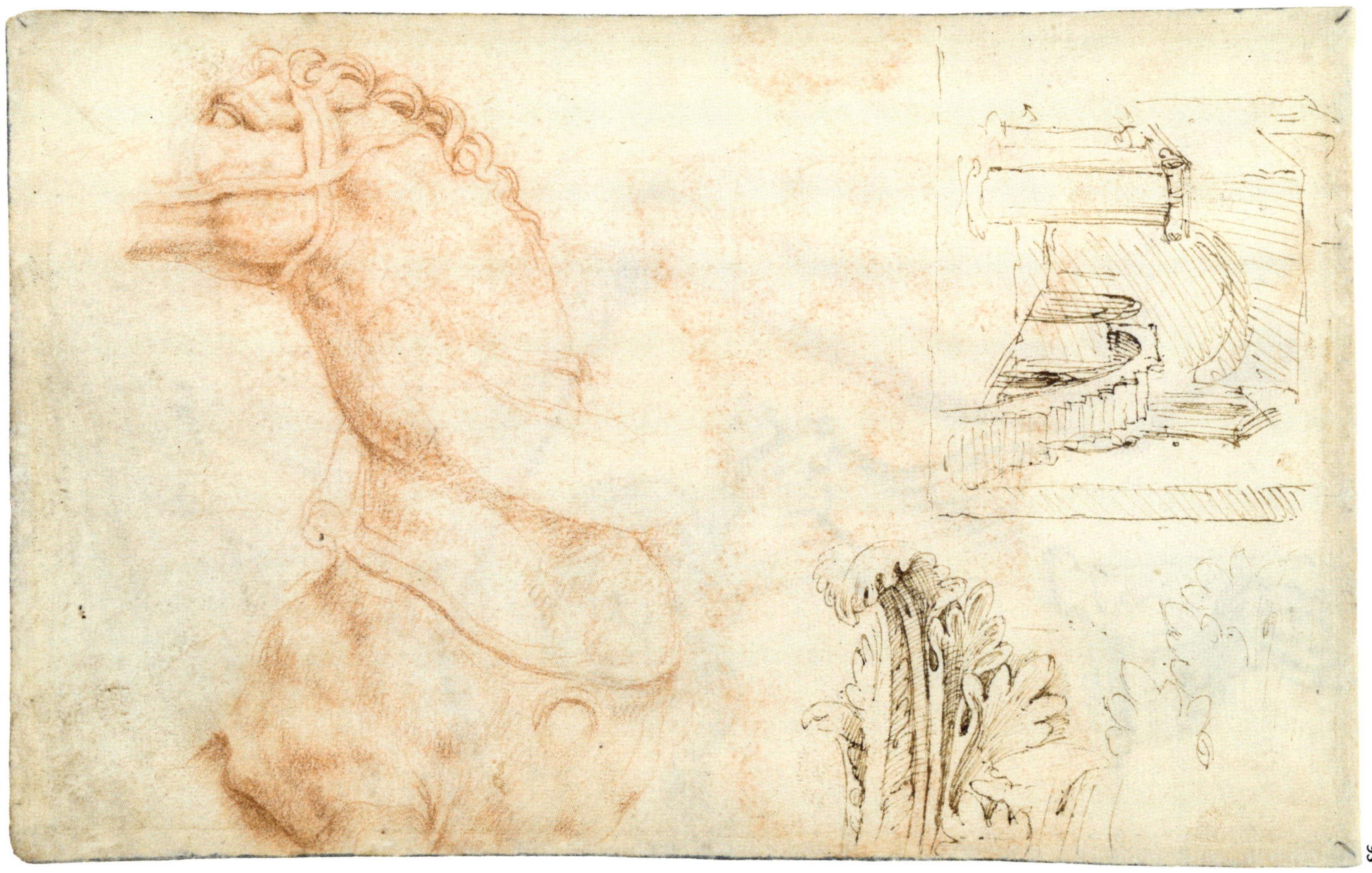

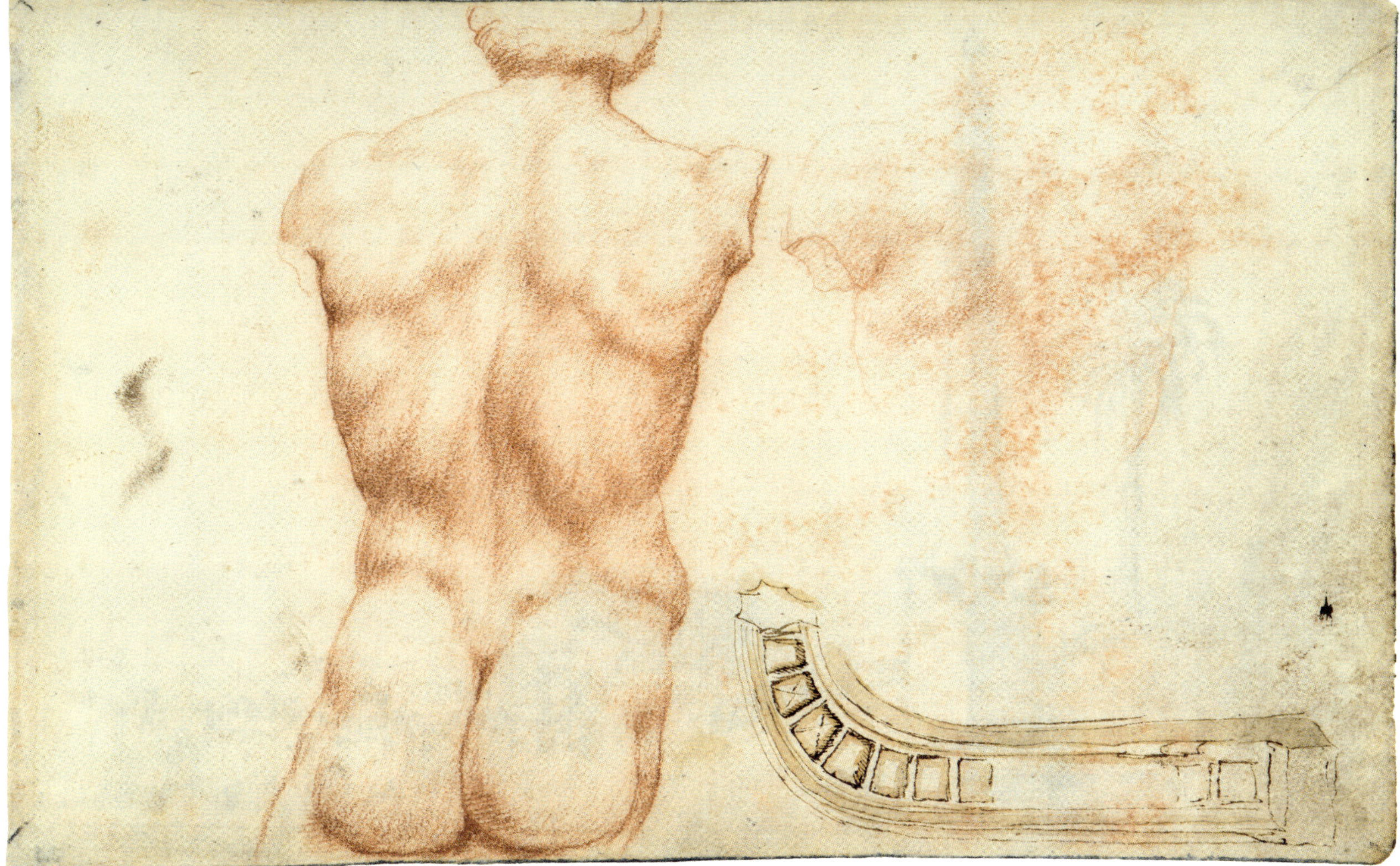

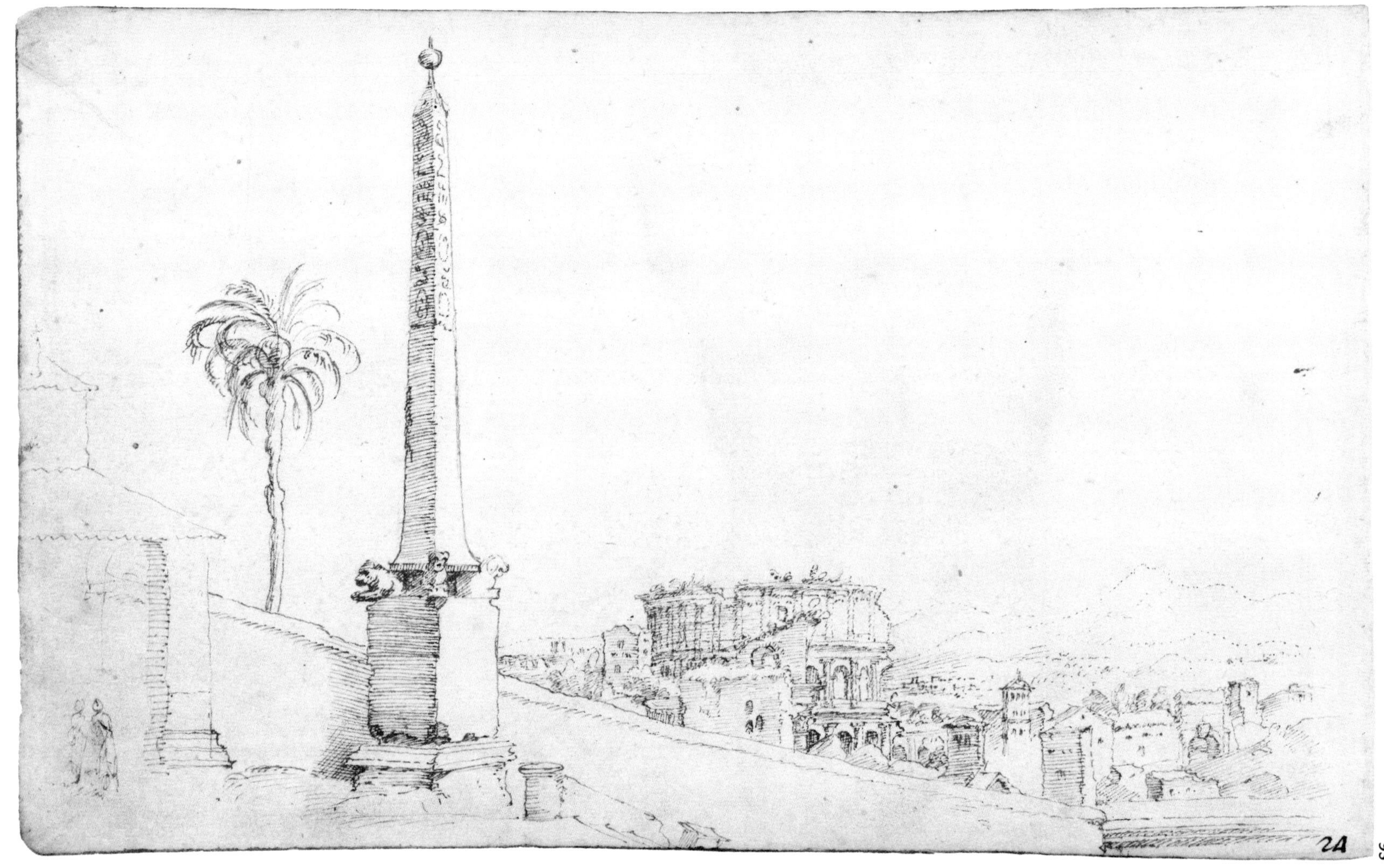

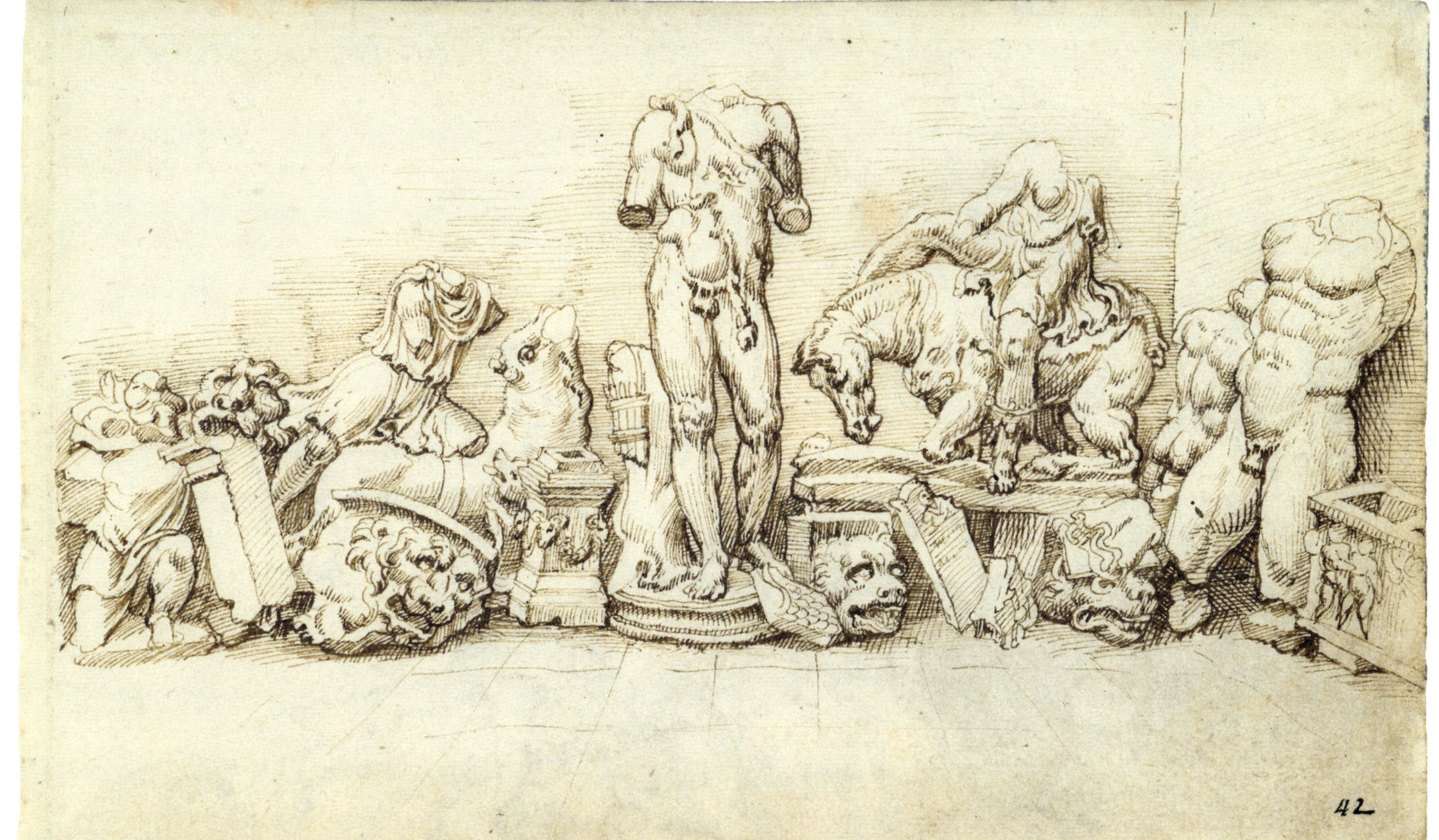

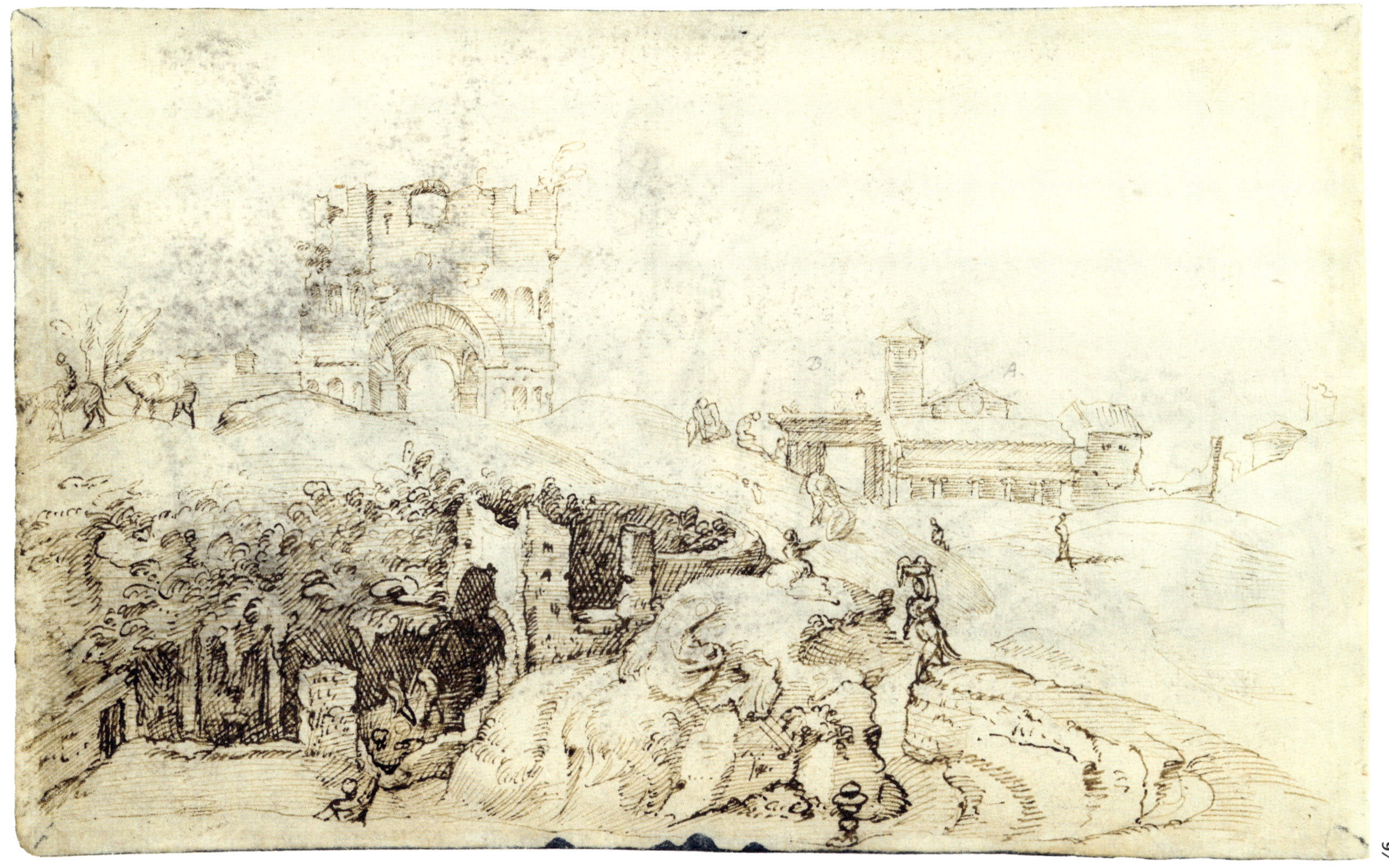

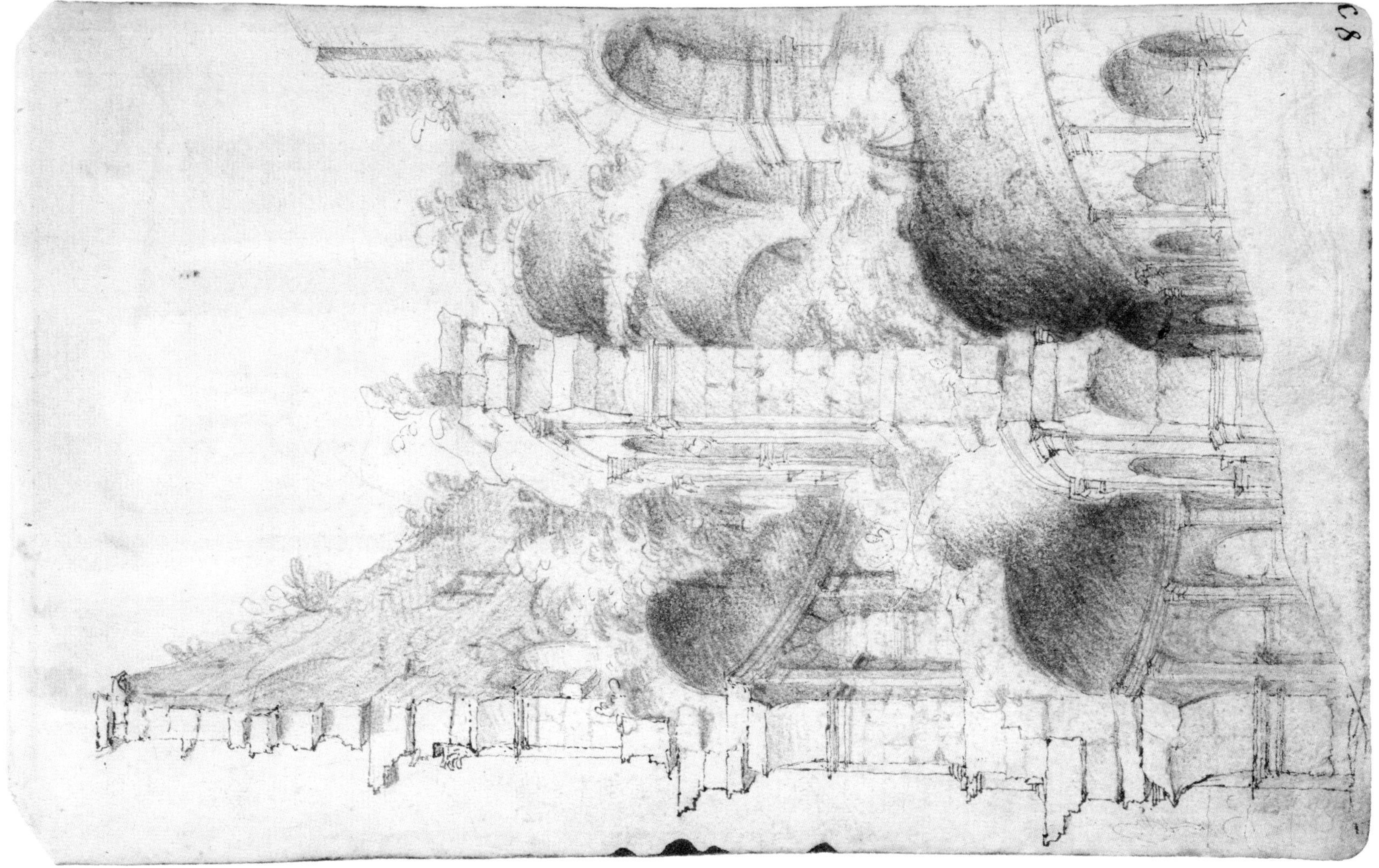

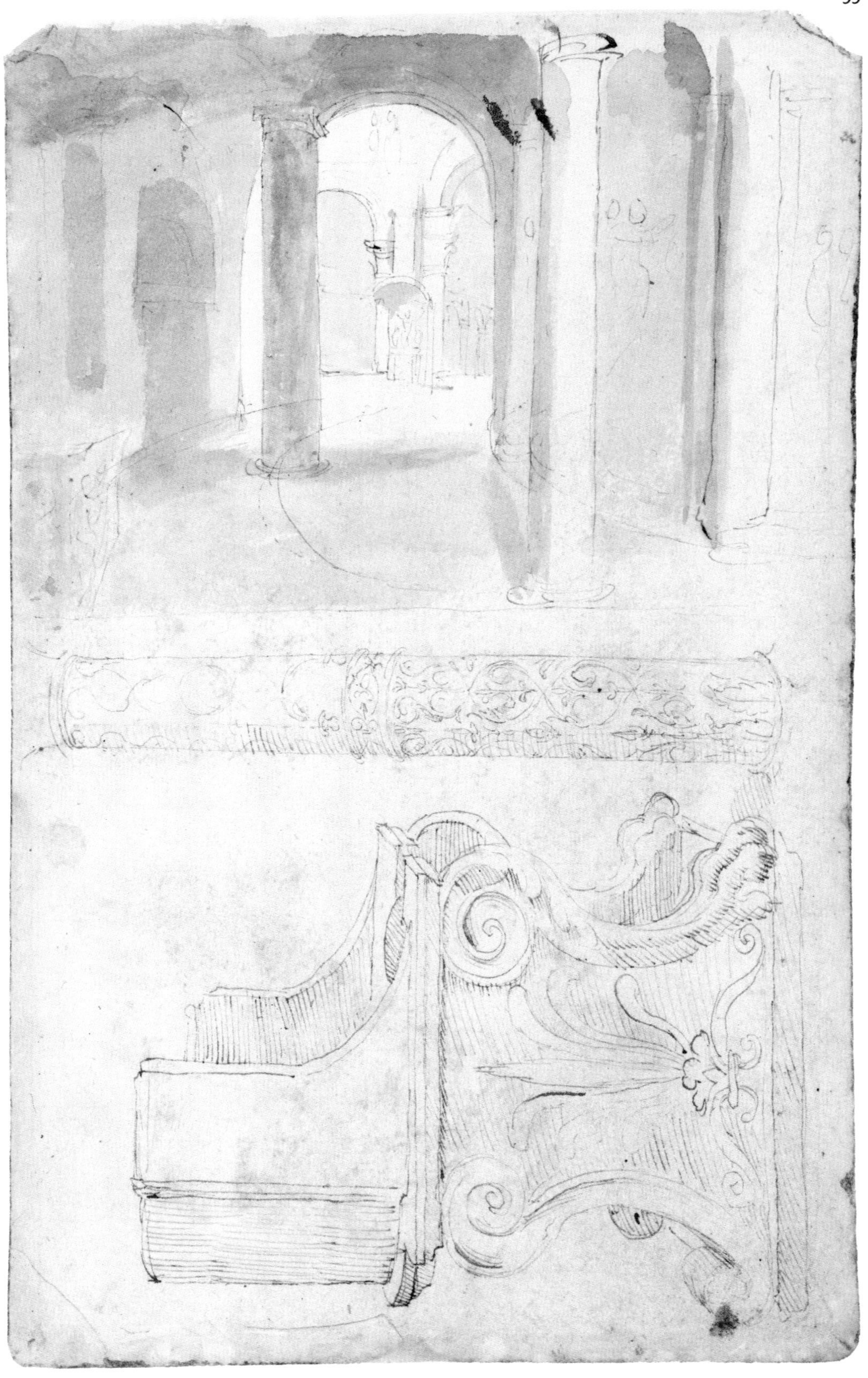

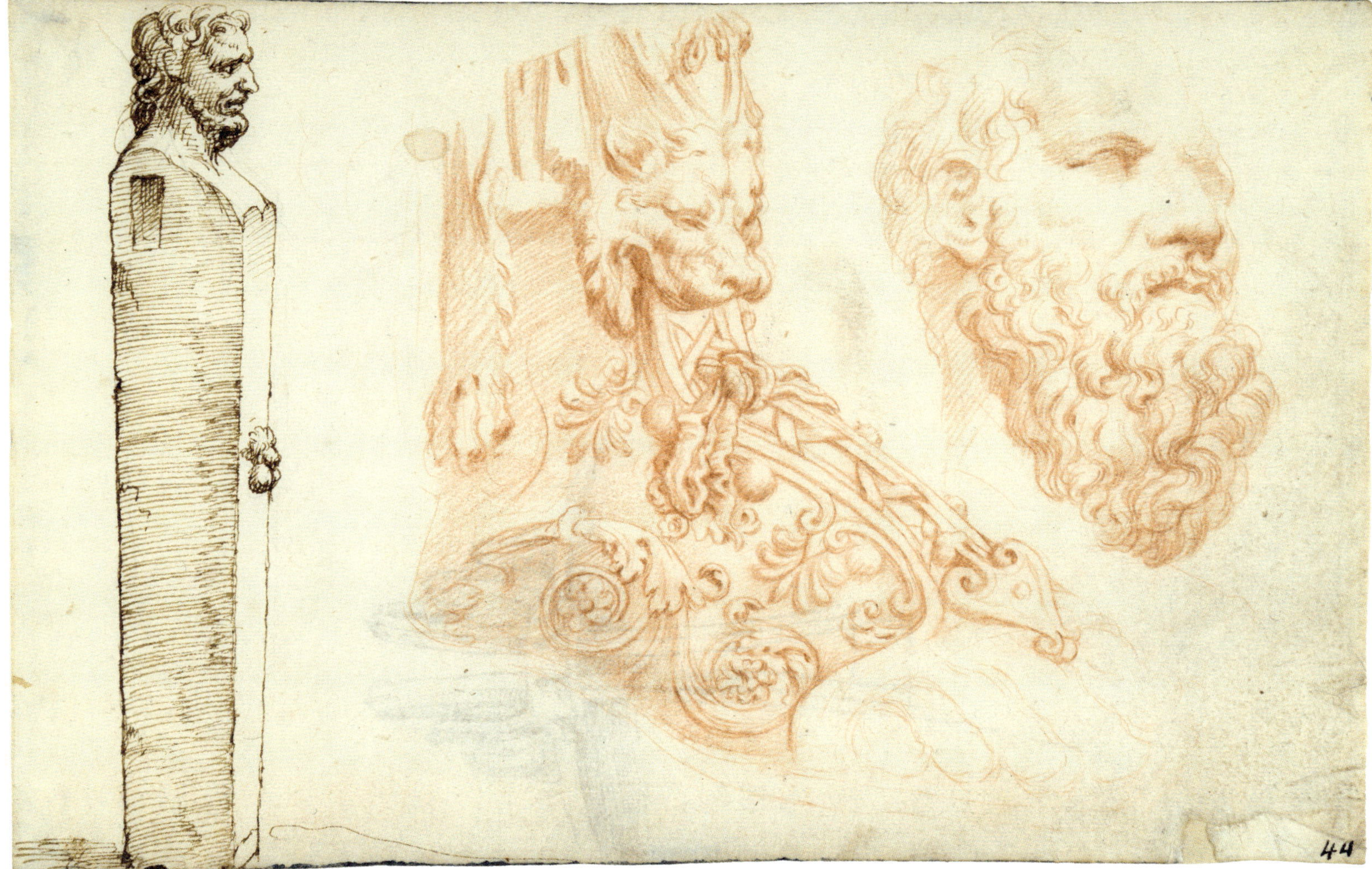

44

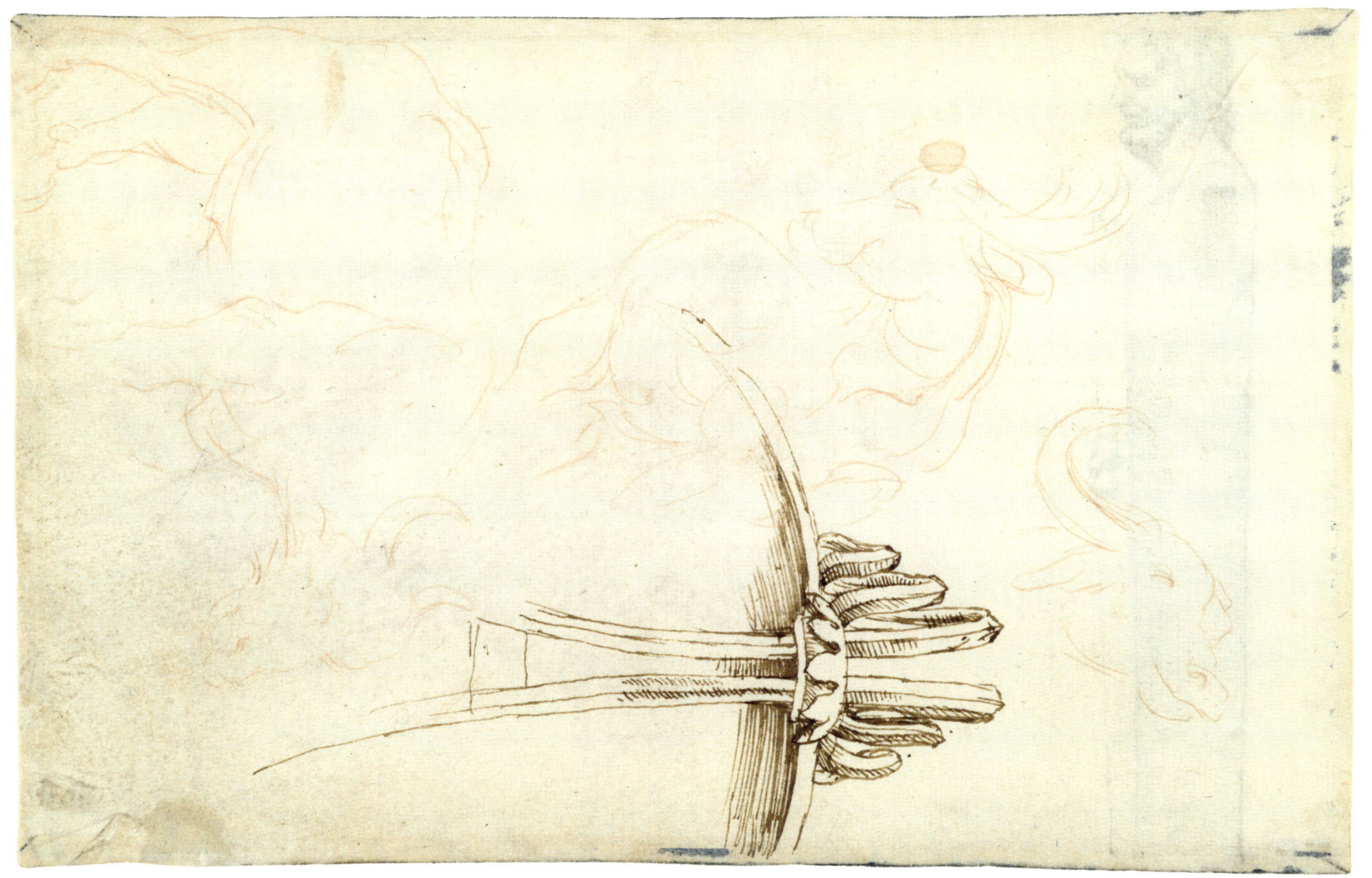

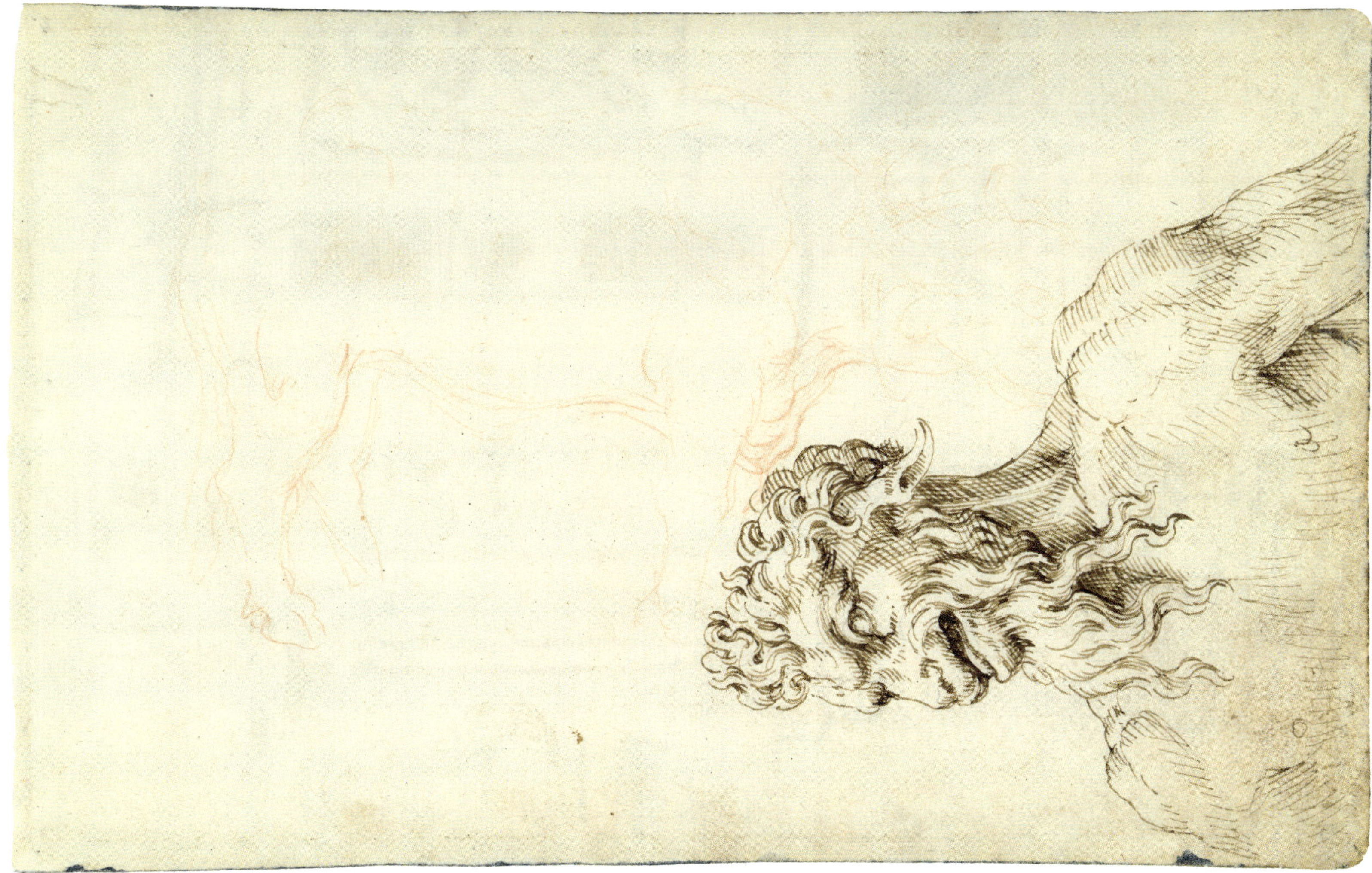

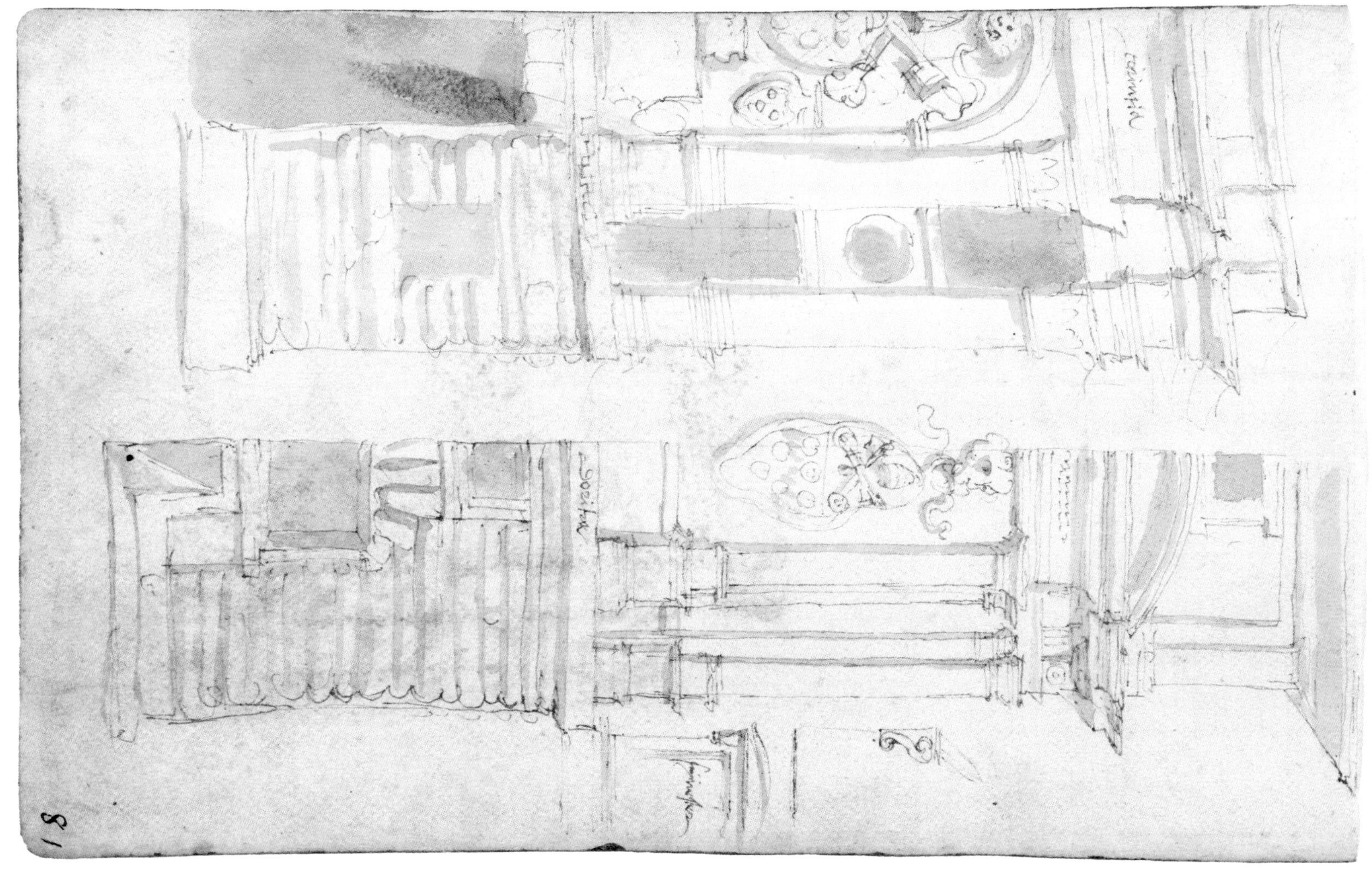

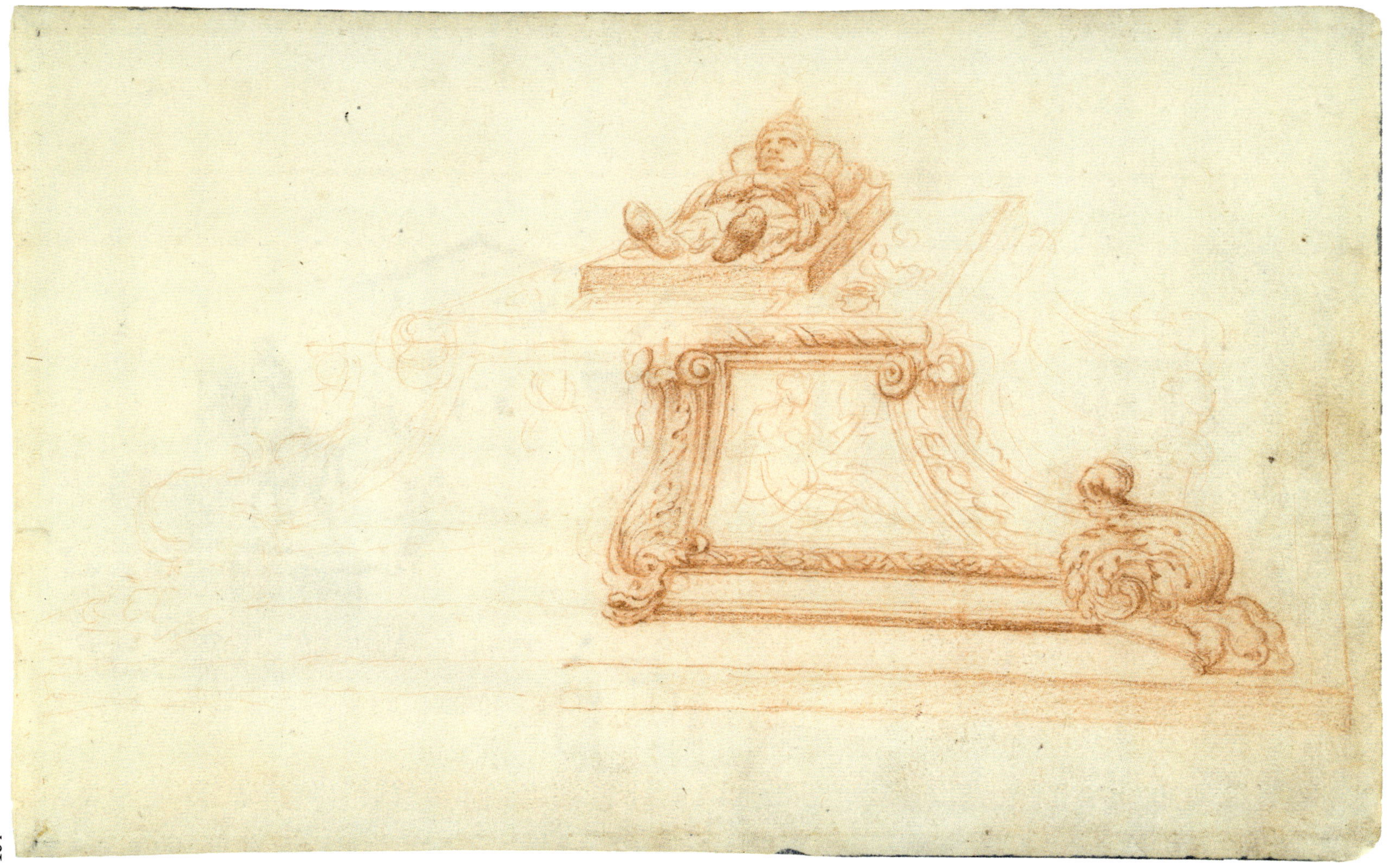

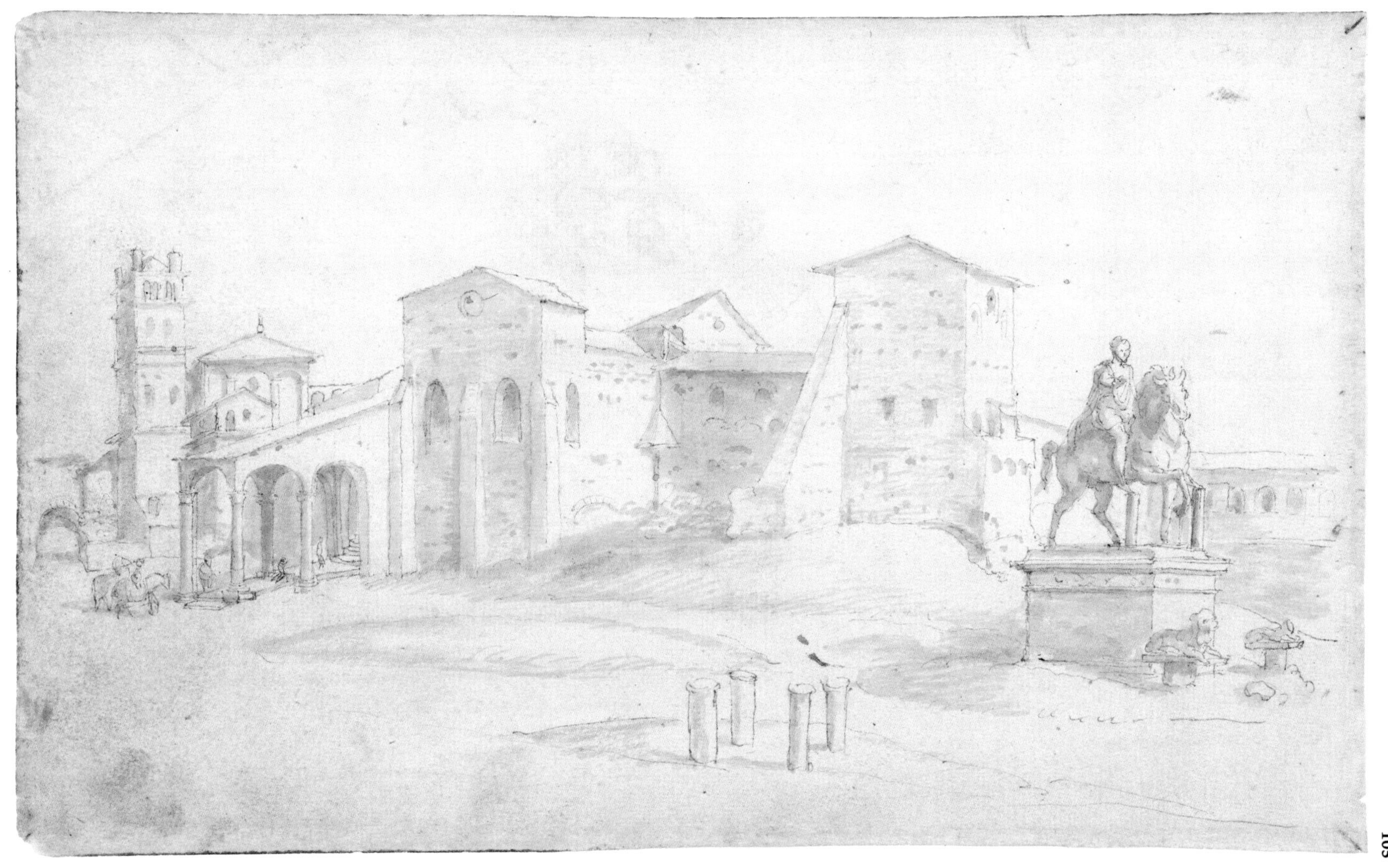

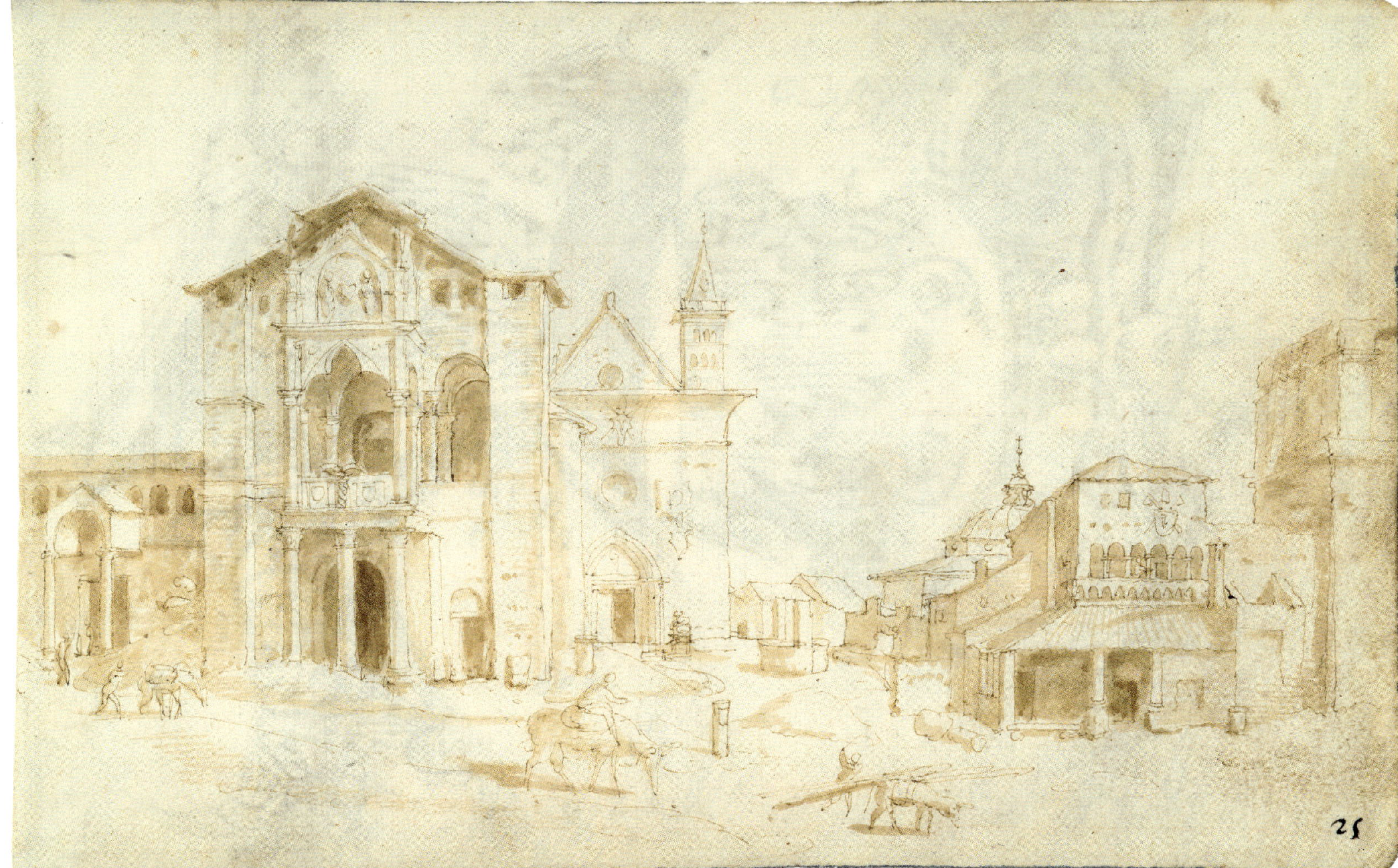

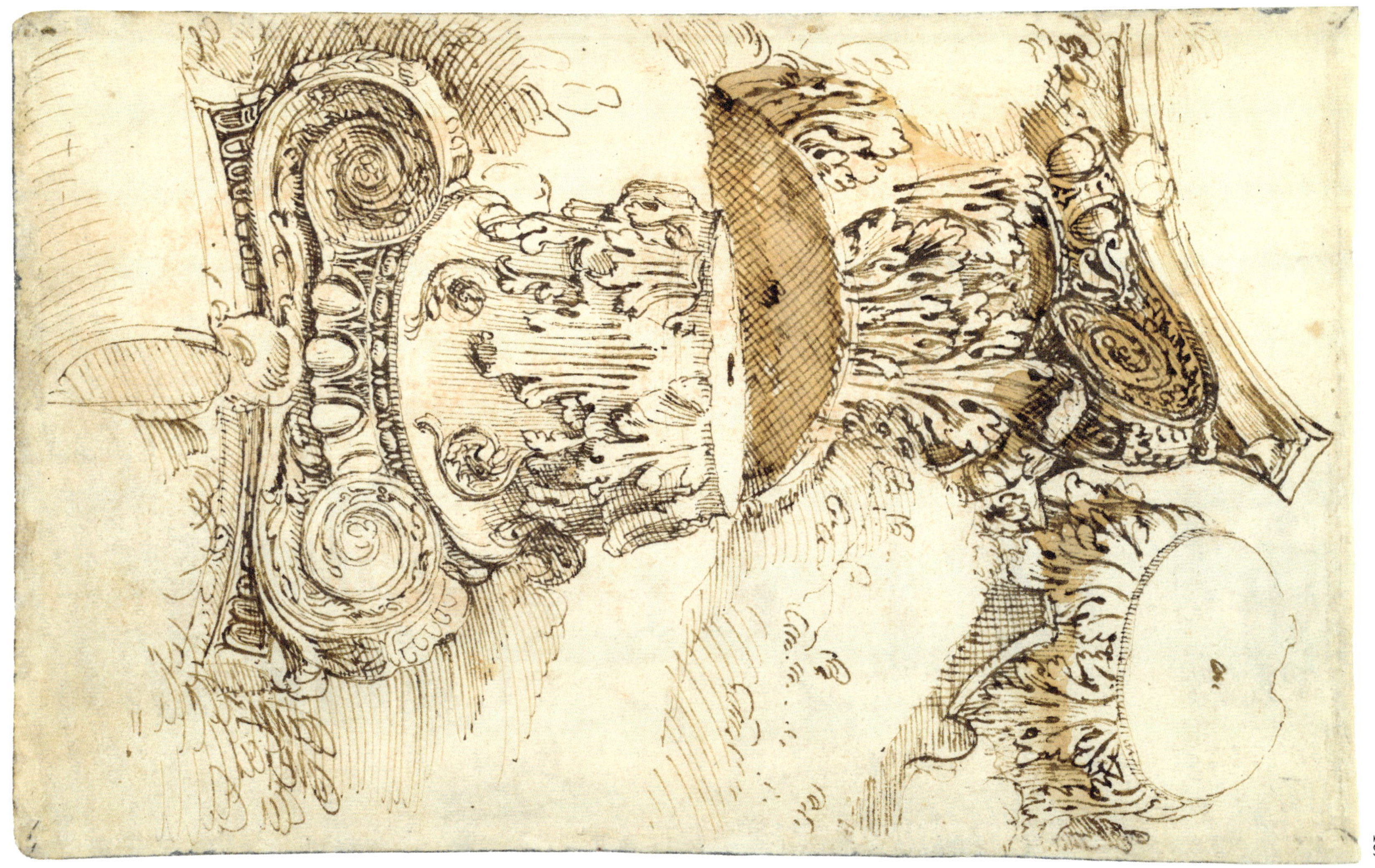

[ONE MISSING PAGE]

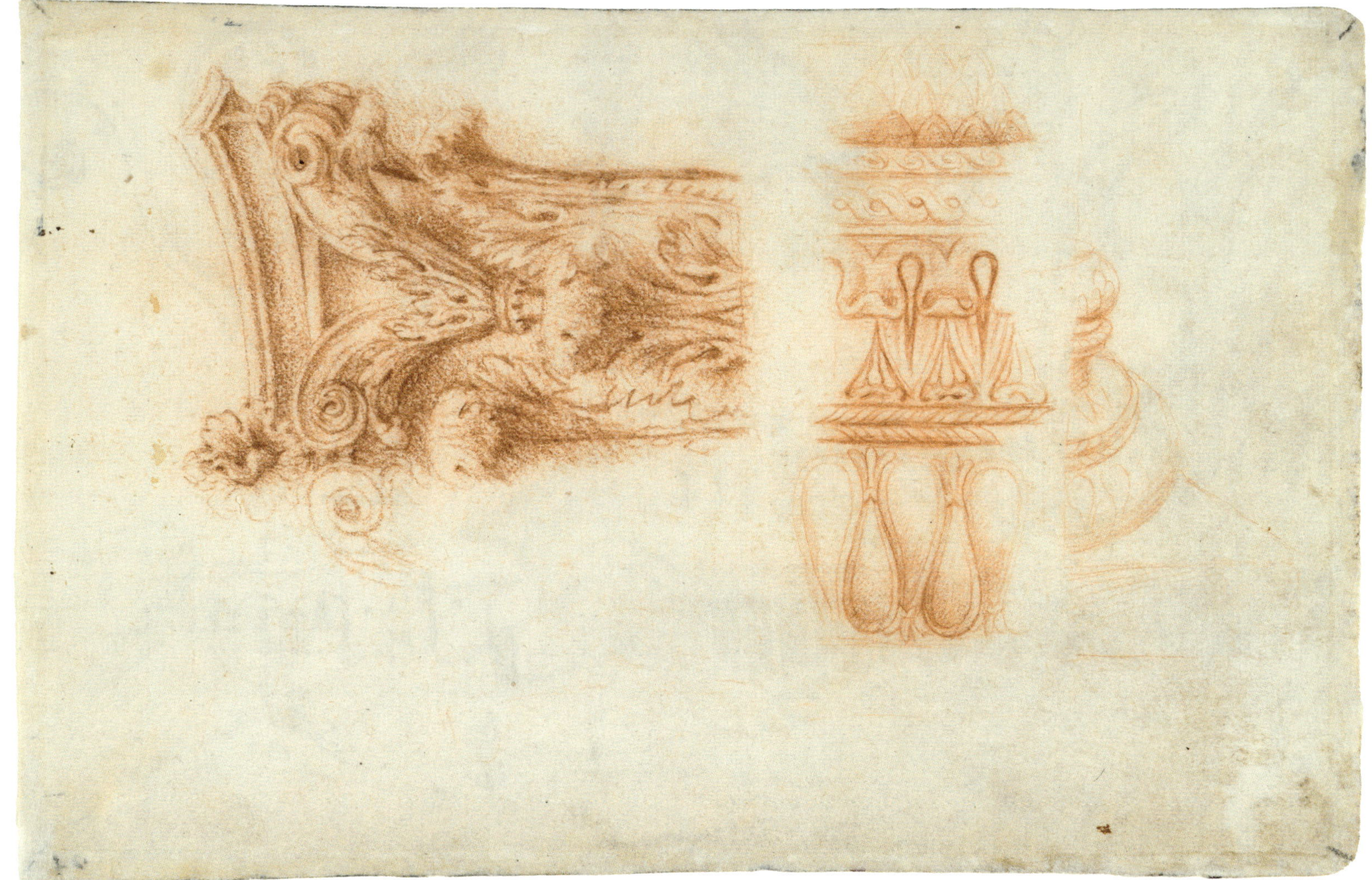

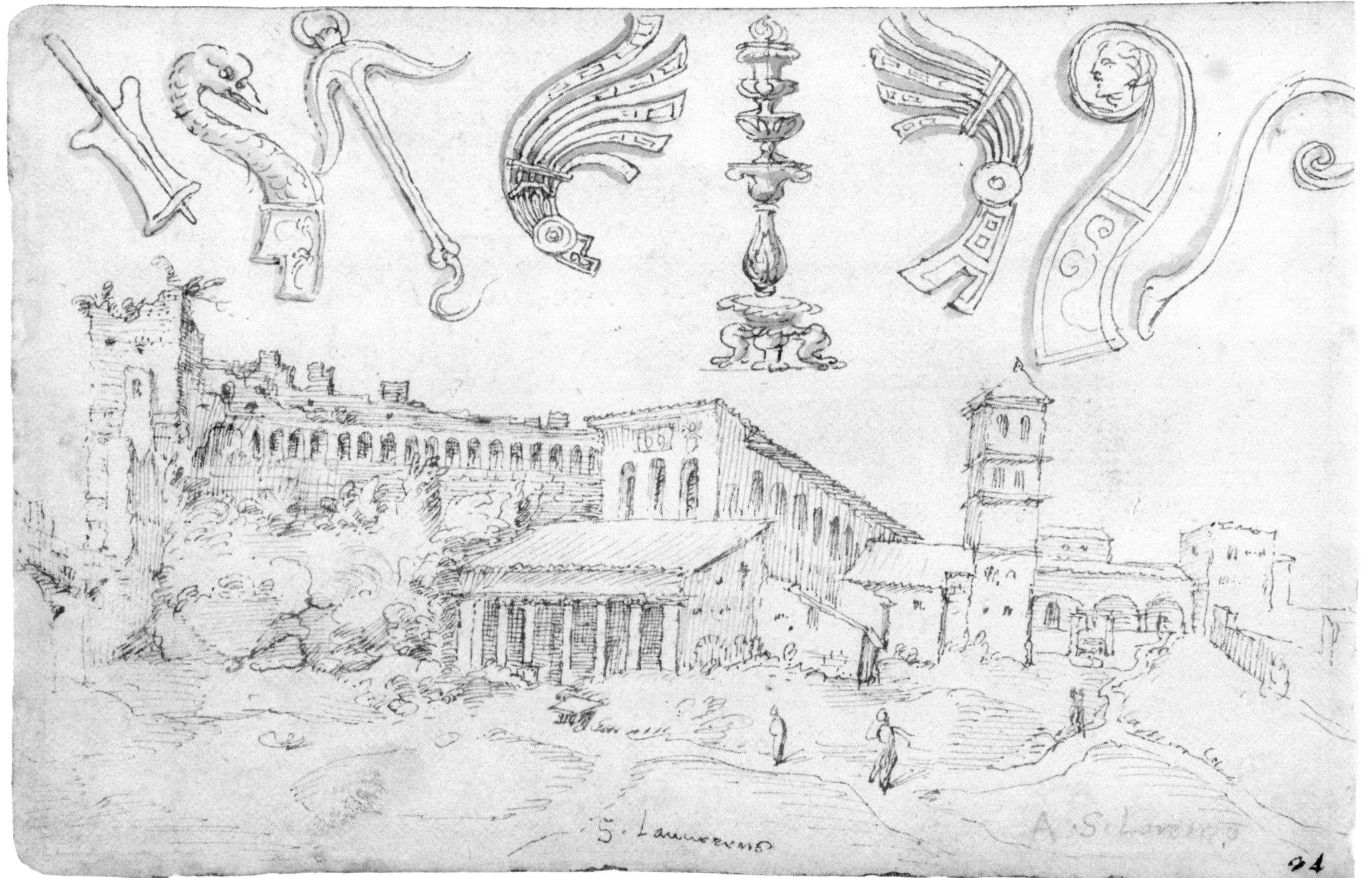
S. Laurentio
A S Lorenzo

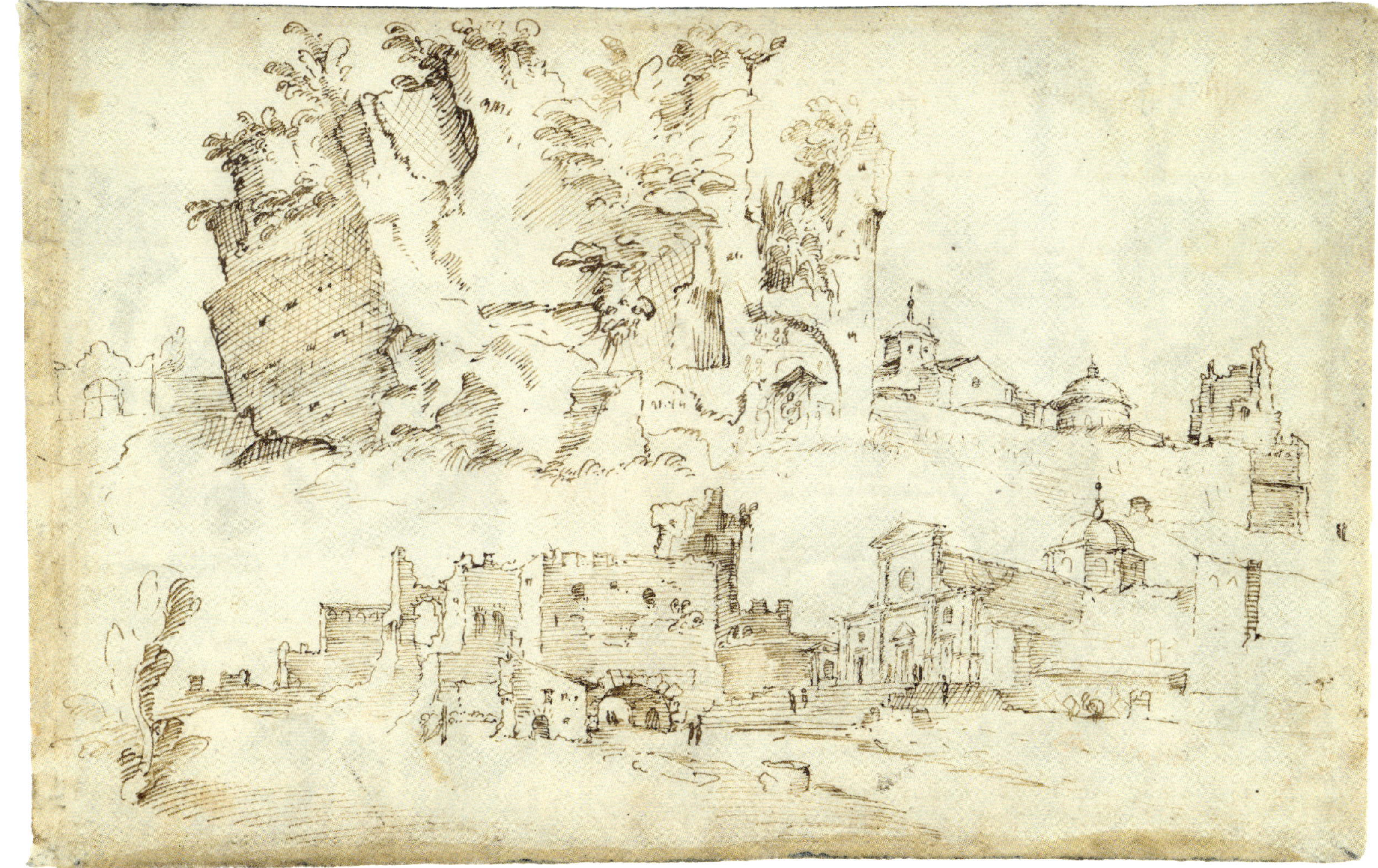

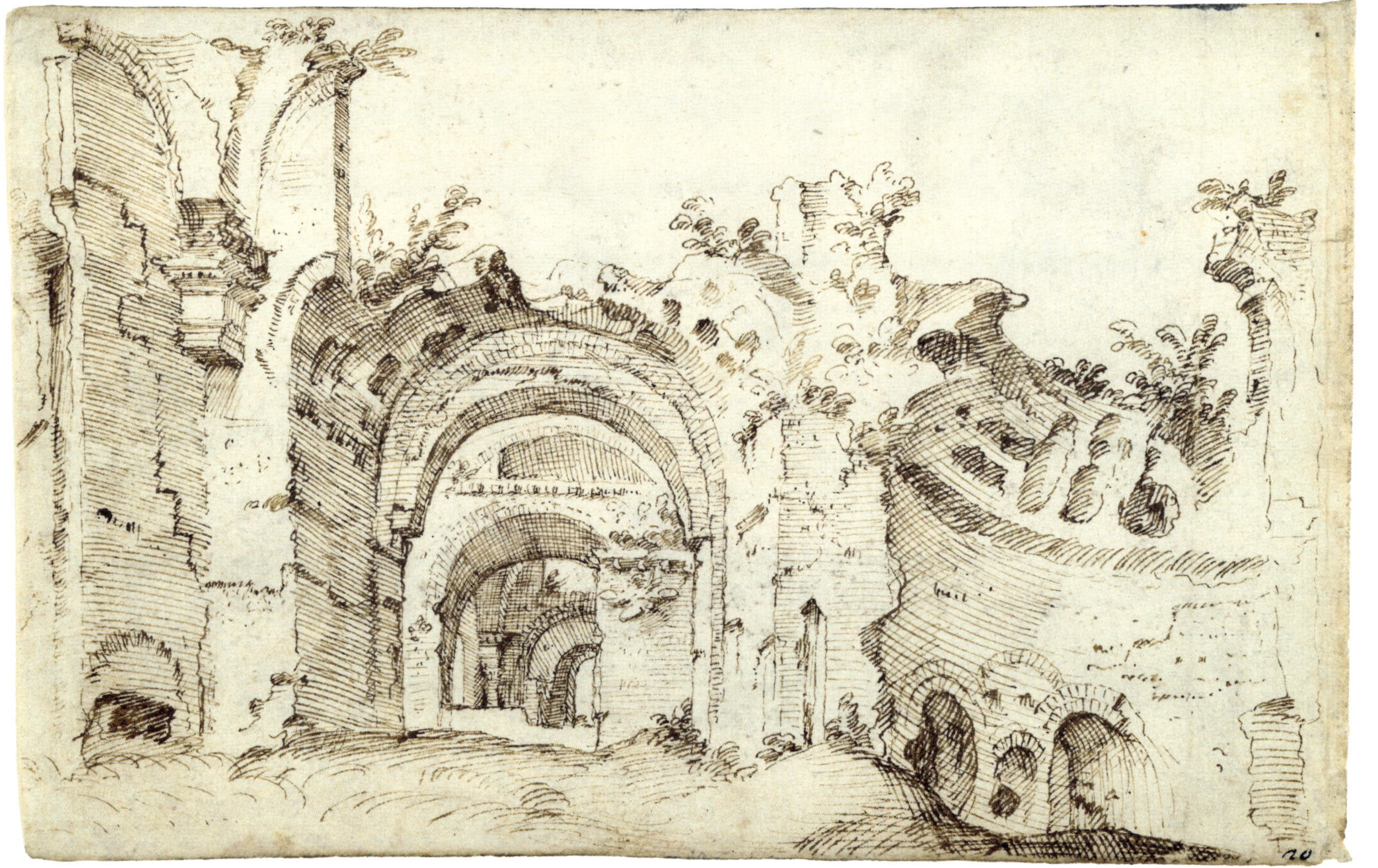

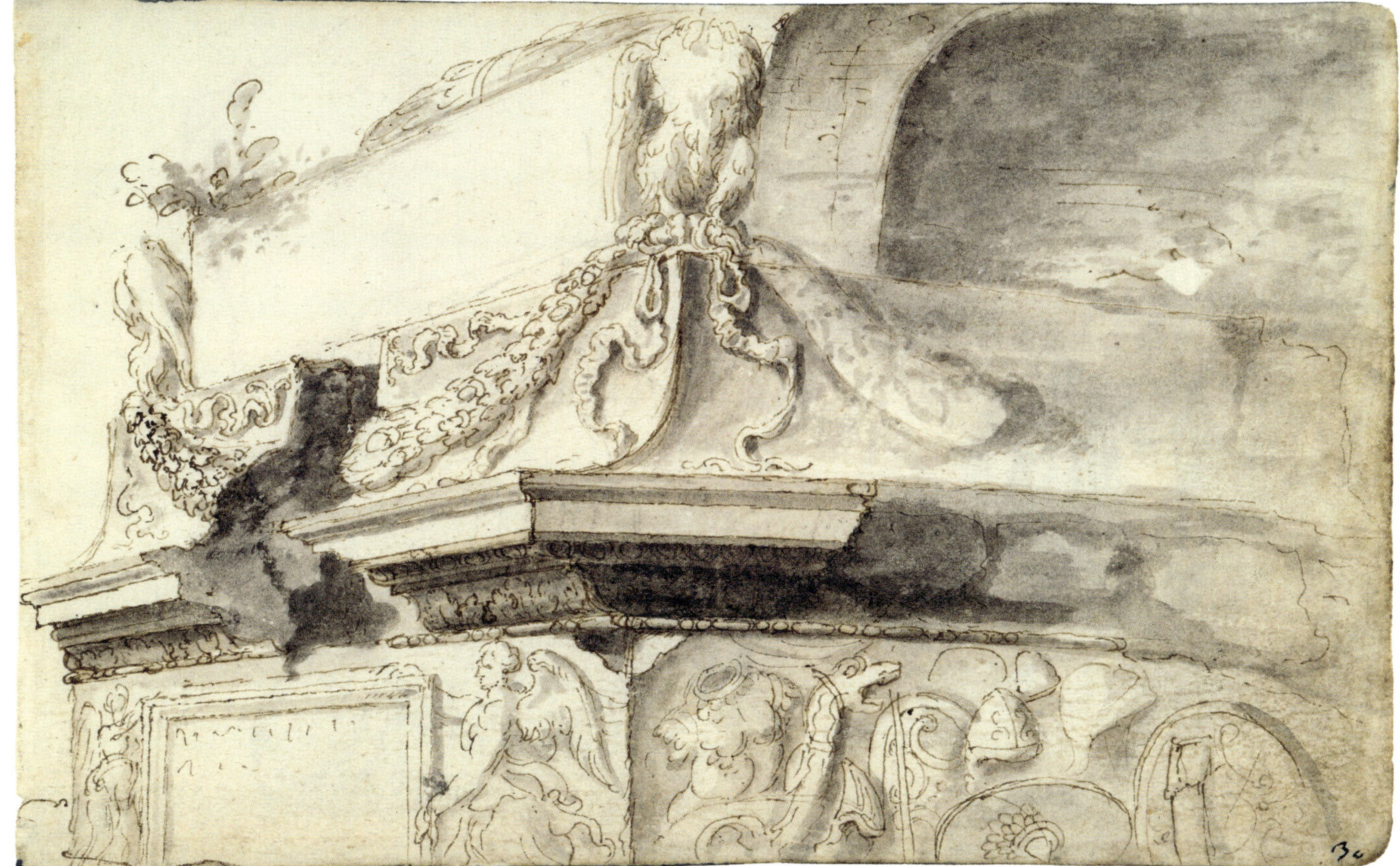

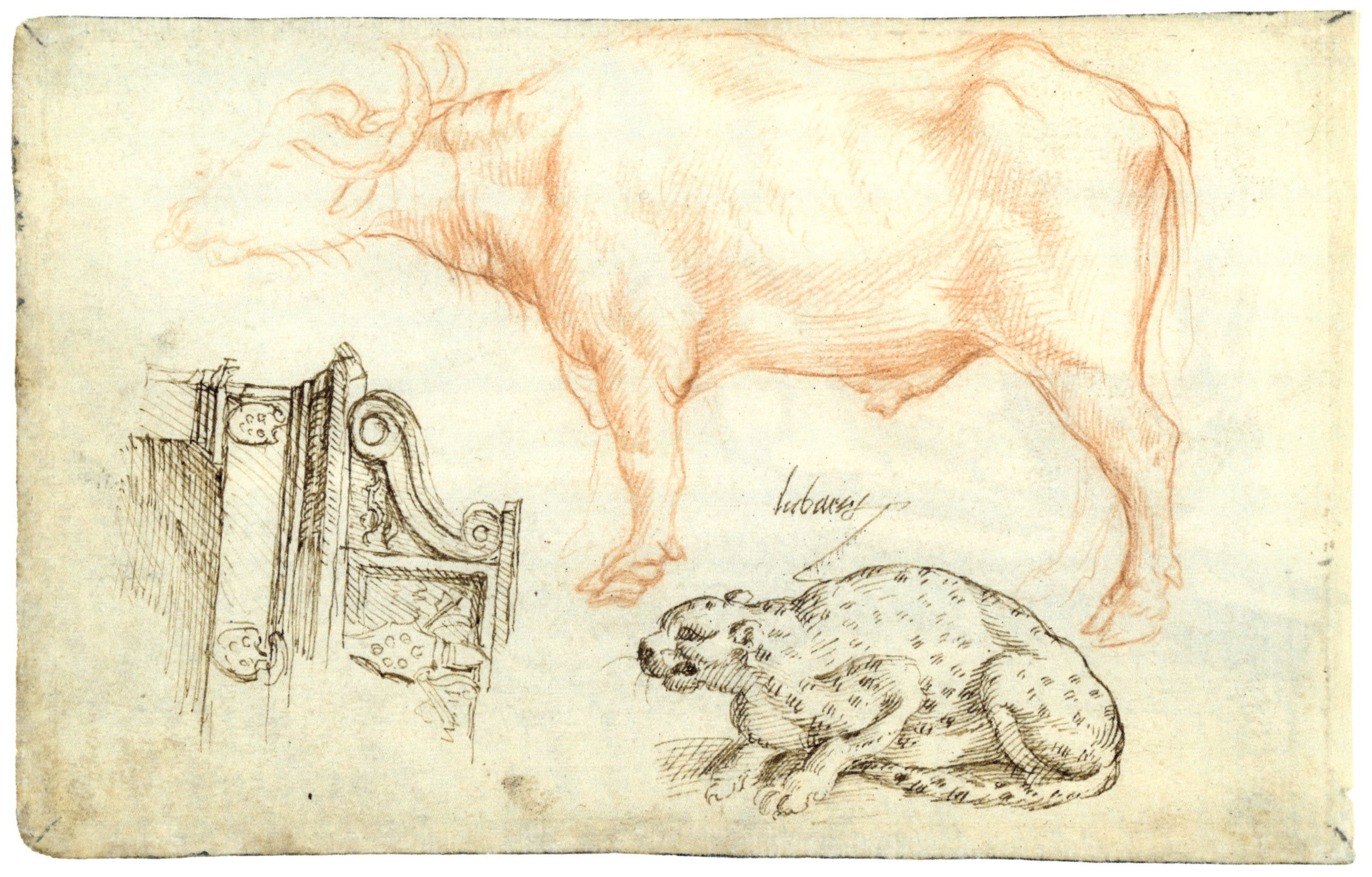
lubaus

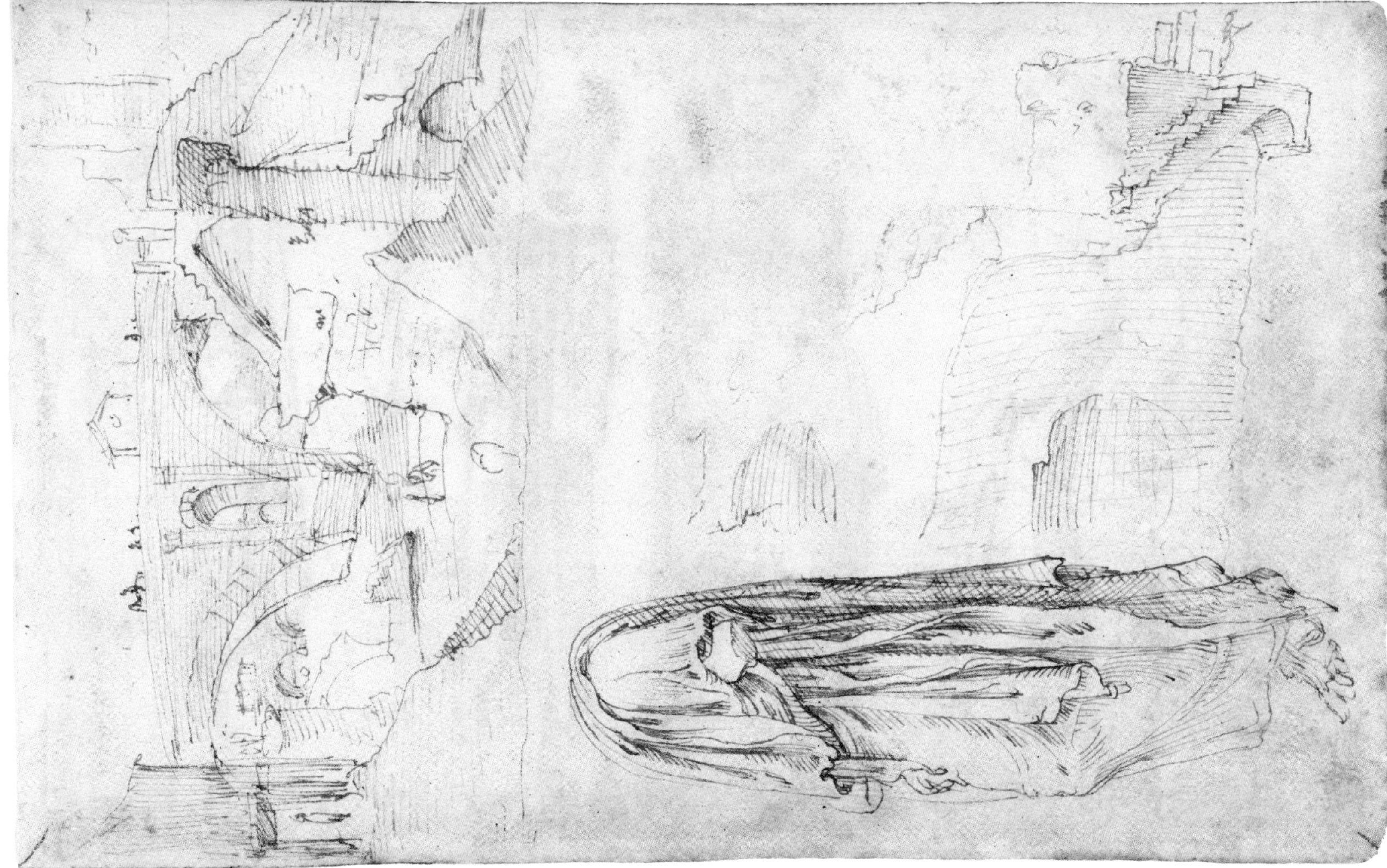

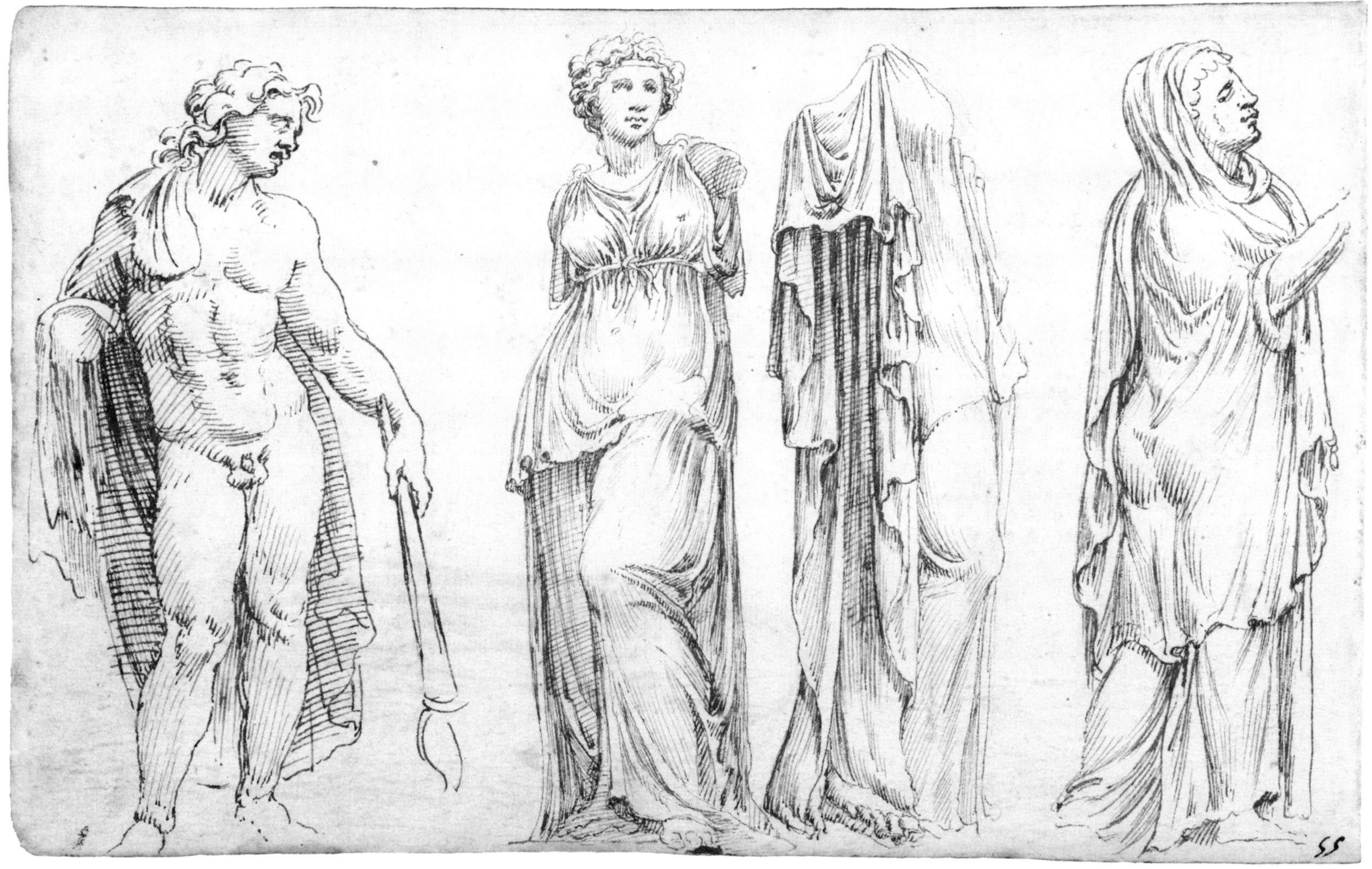

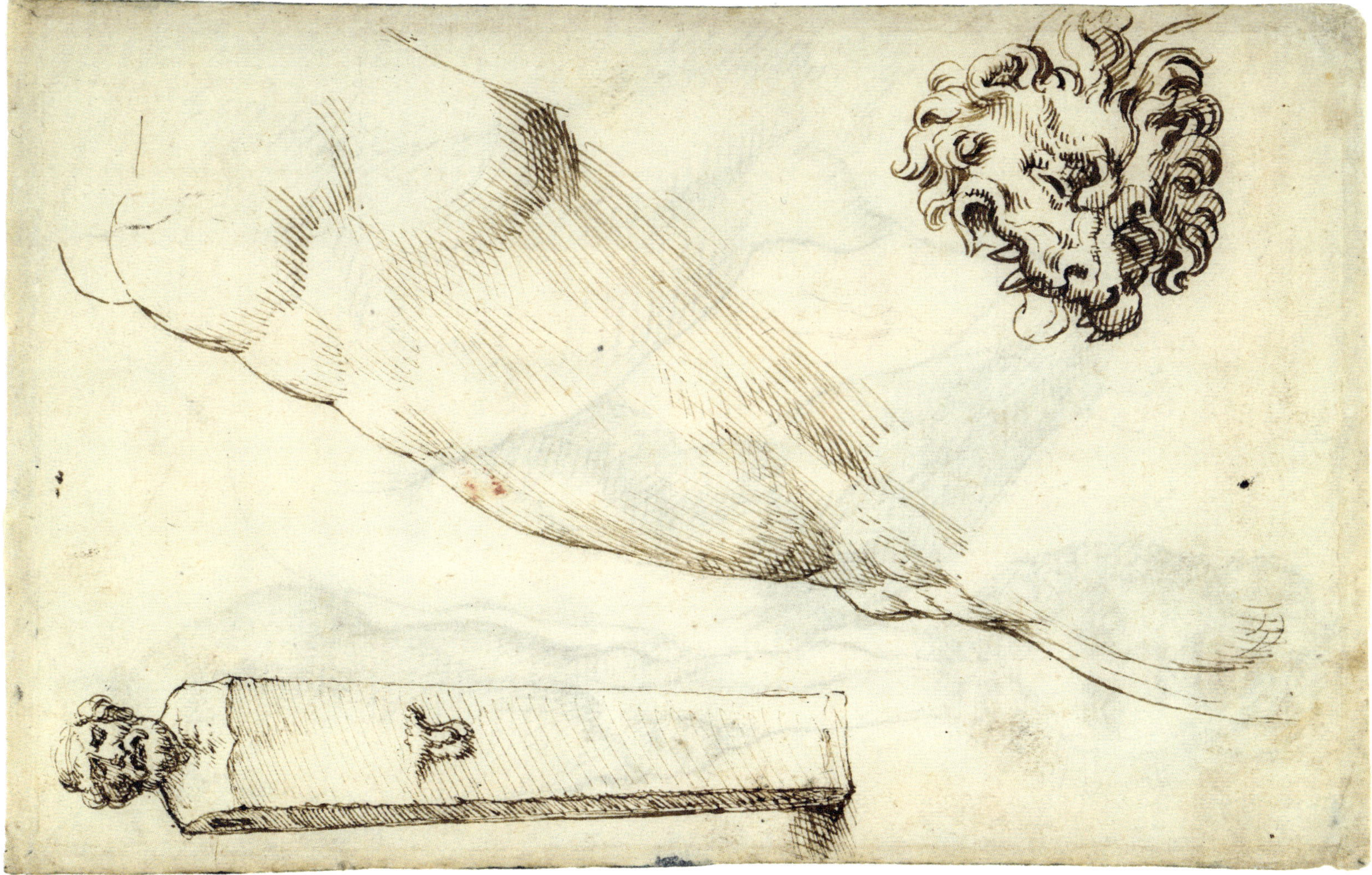

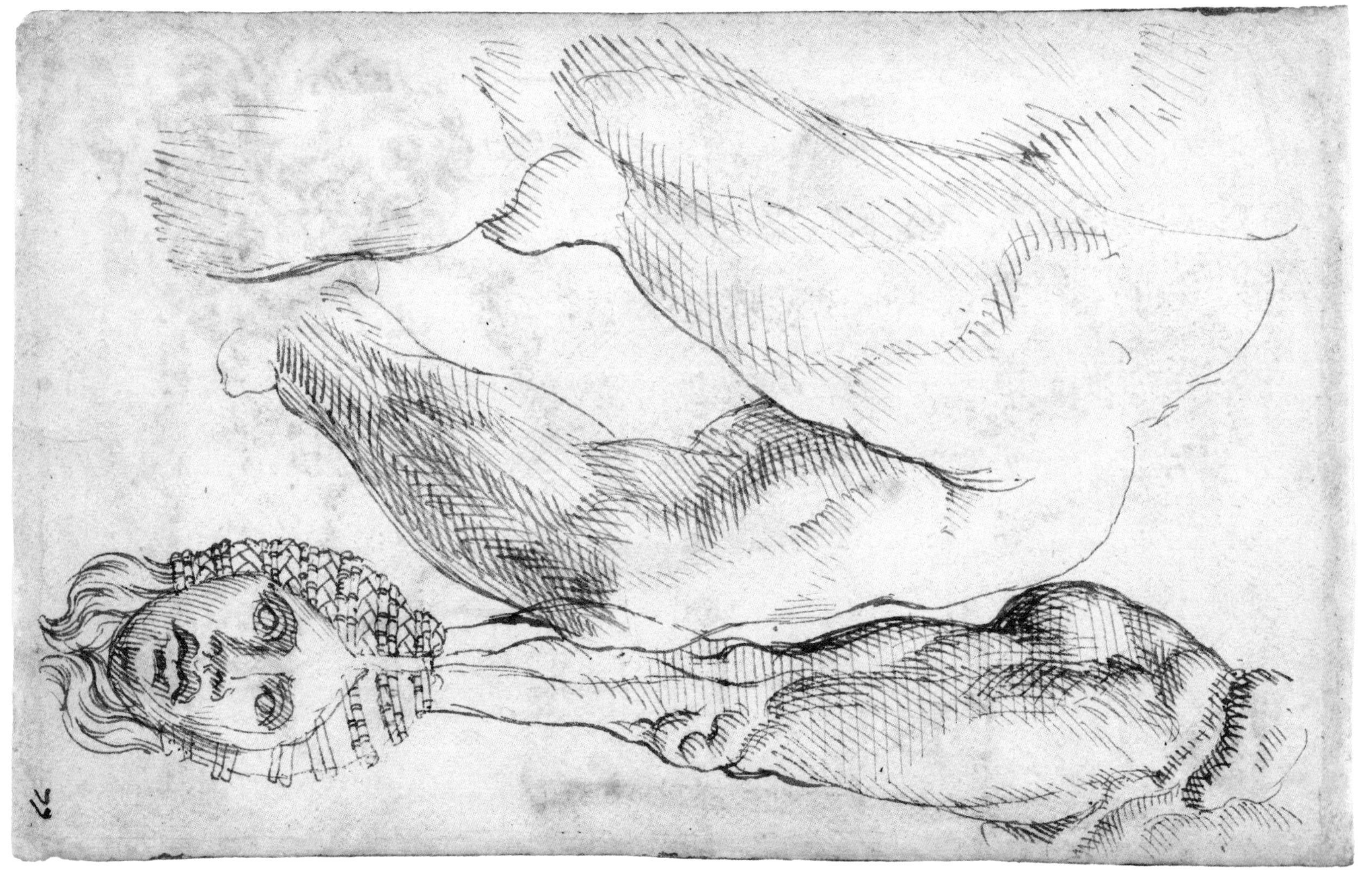

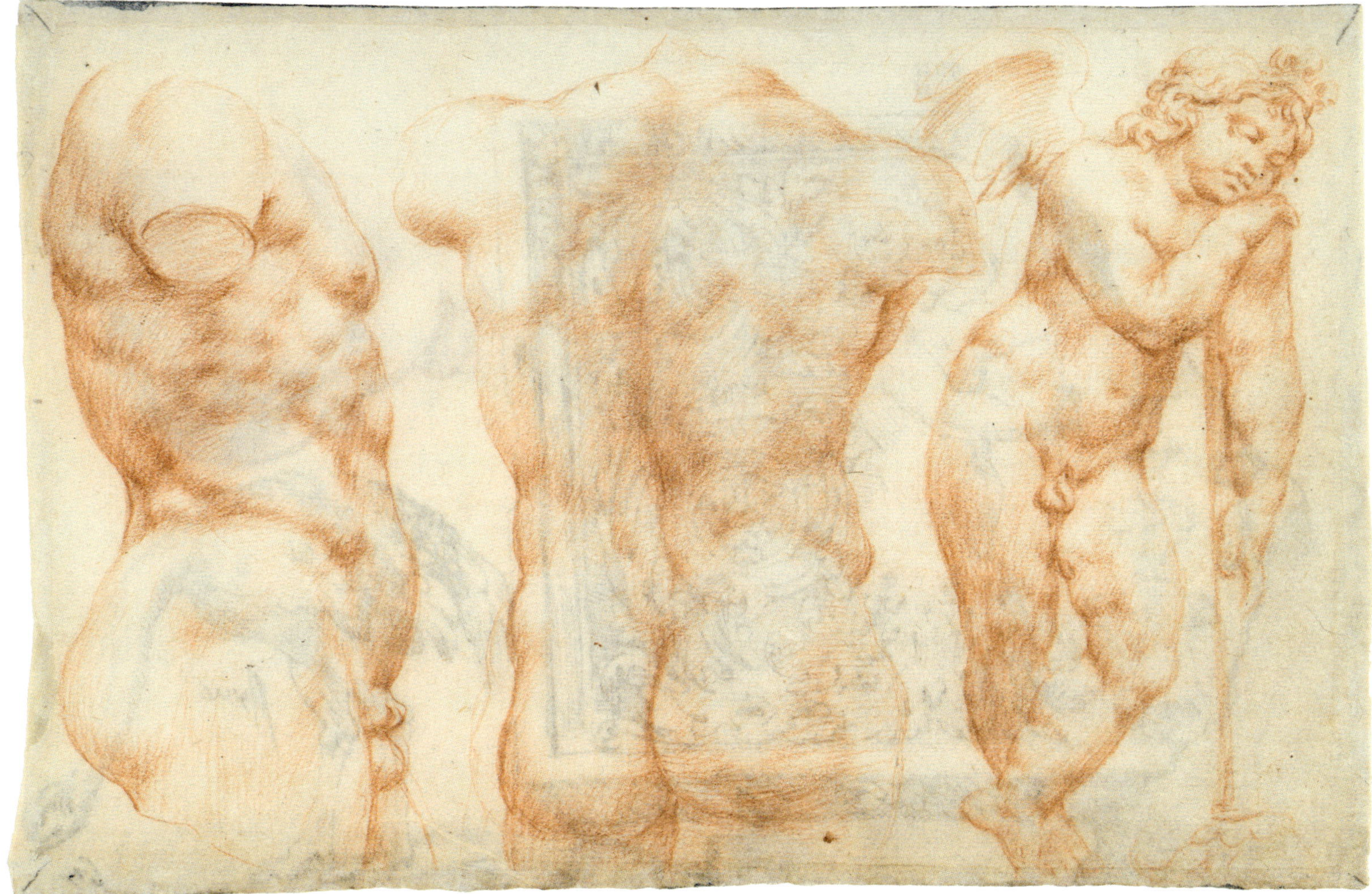

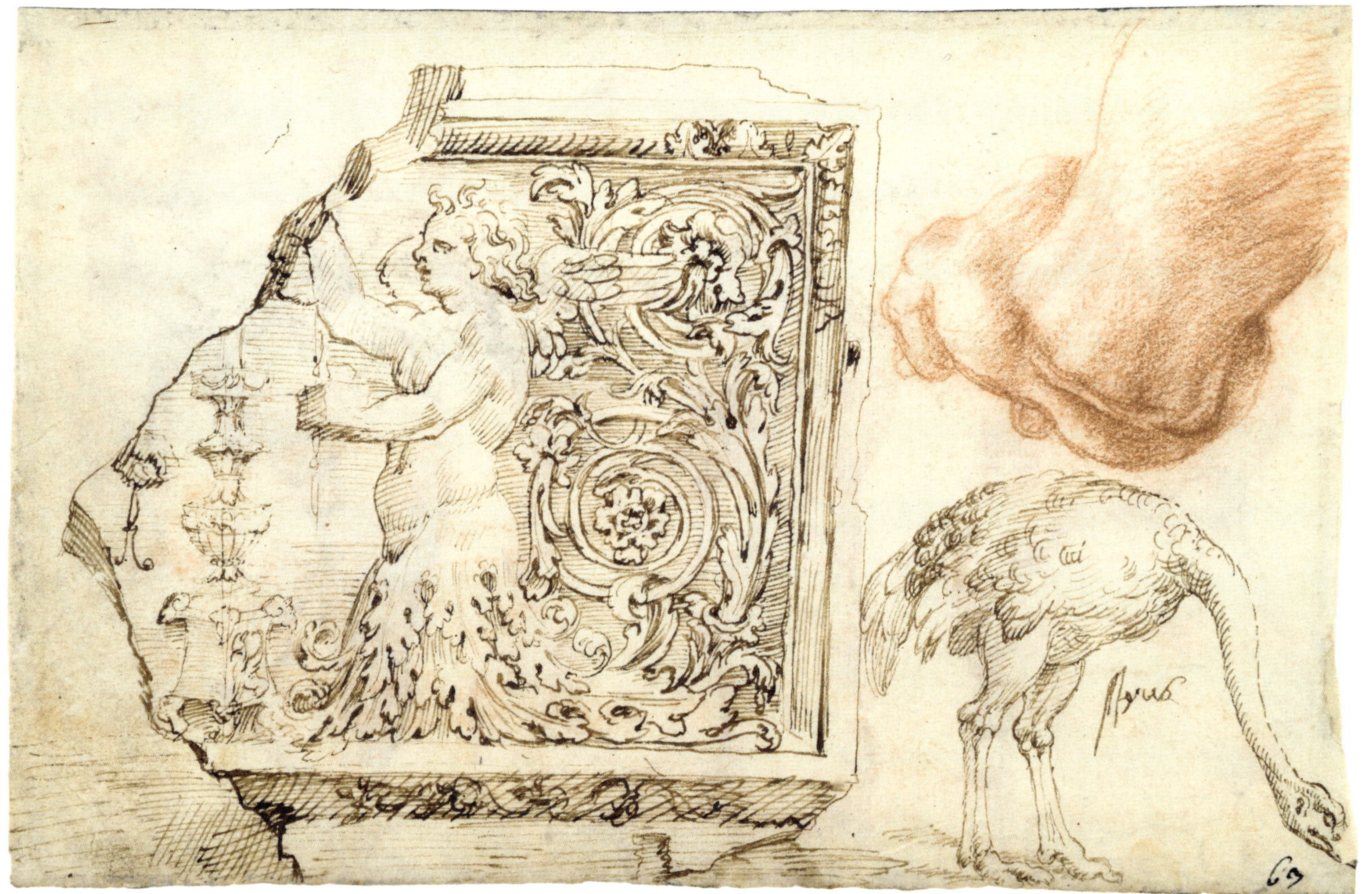

[TWO MISSING PAGES]

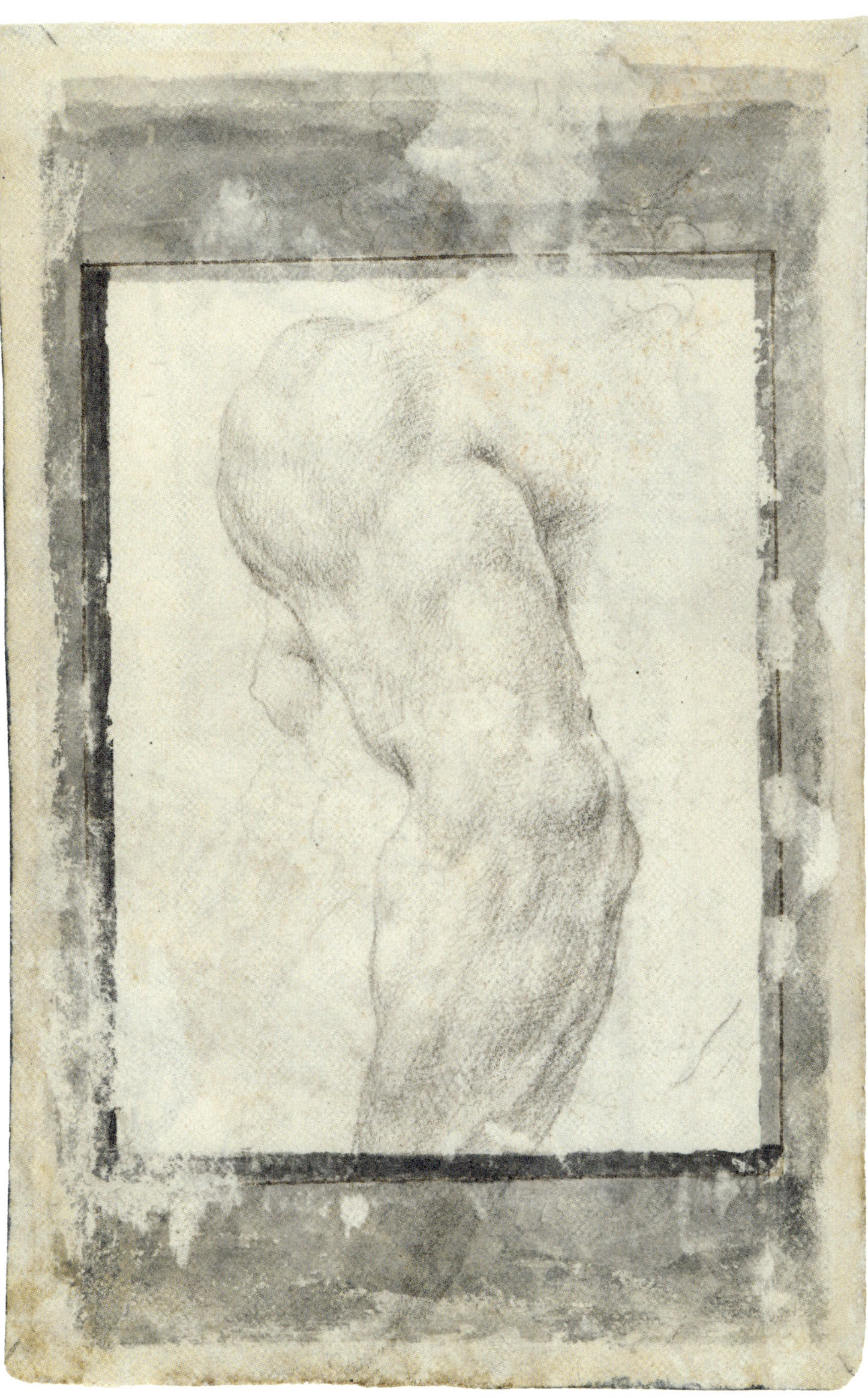

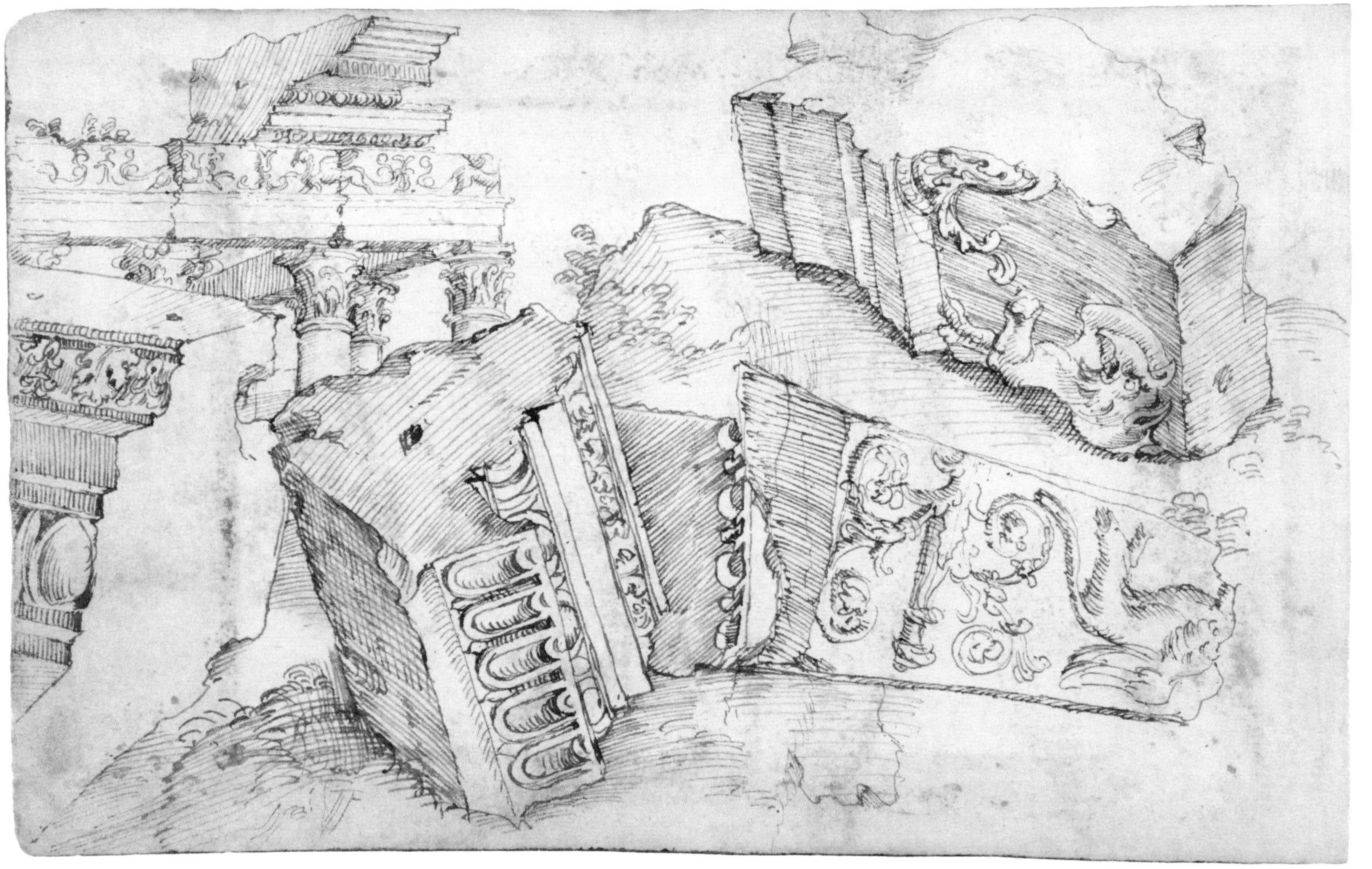

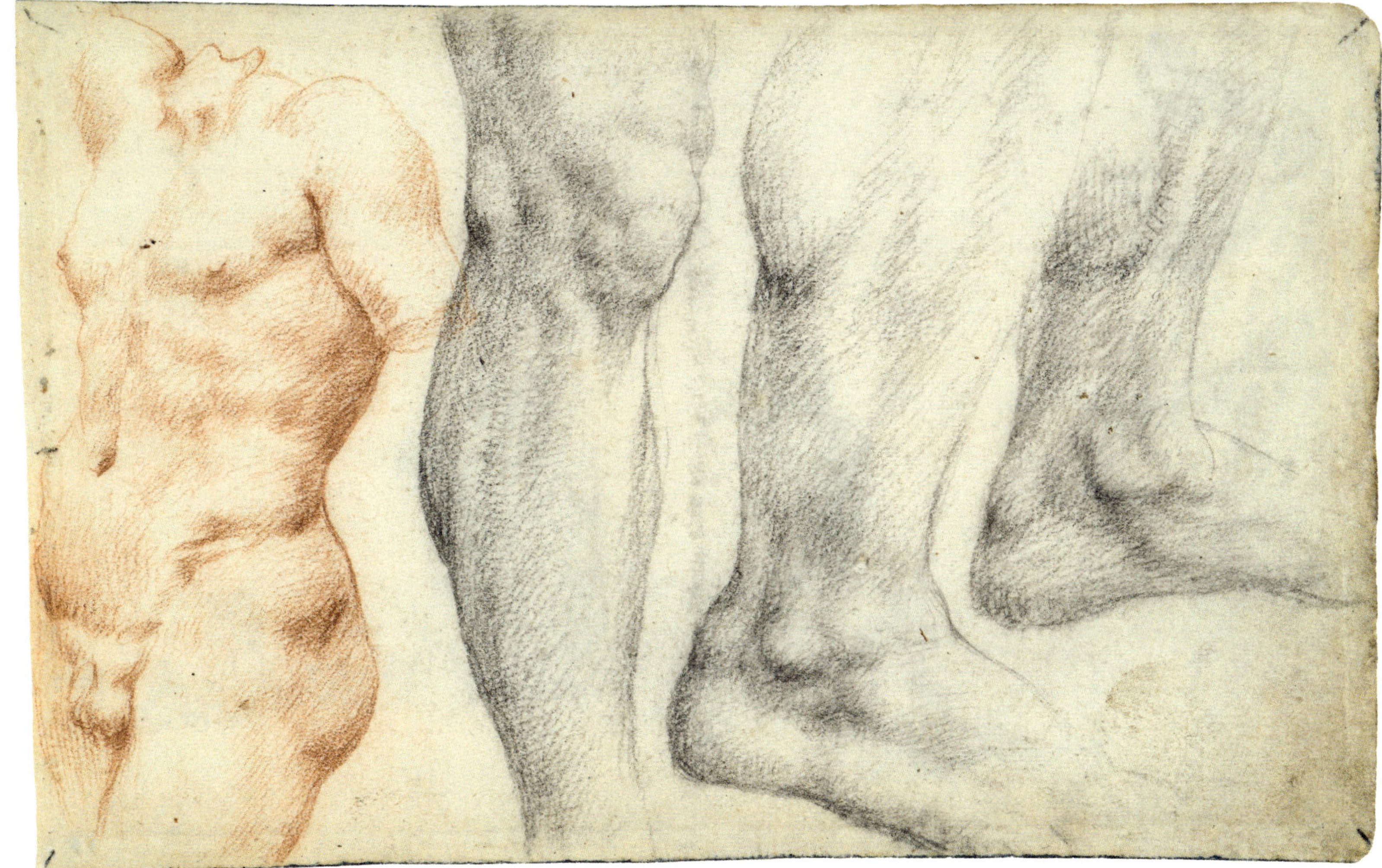

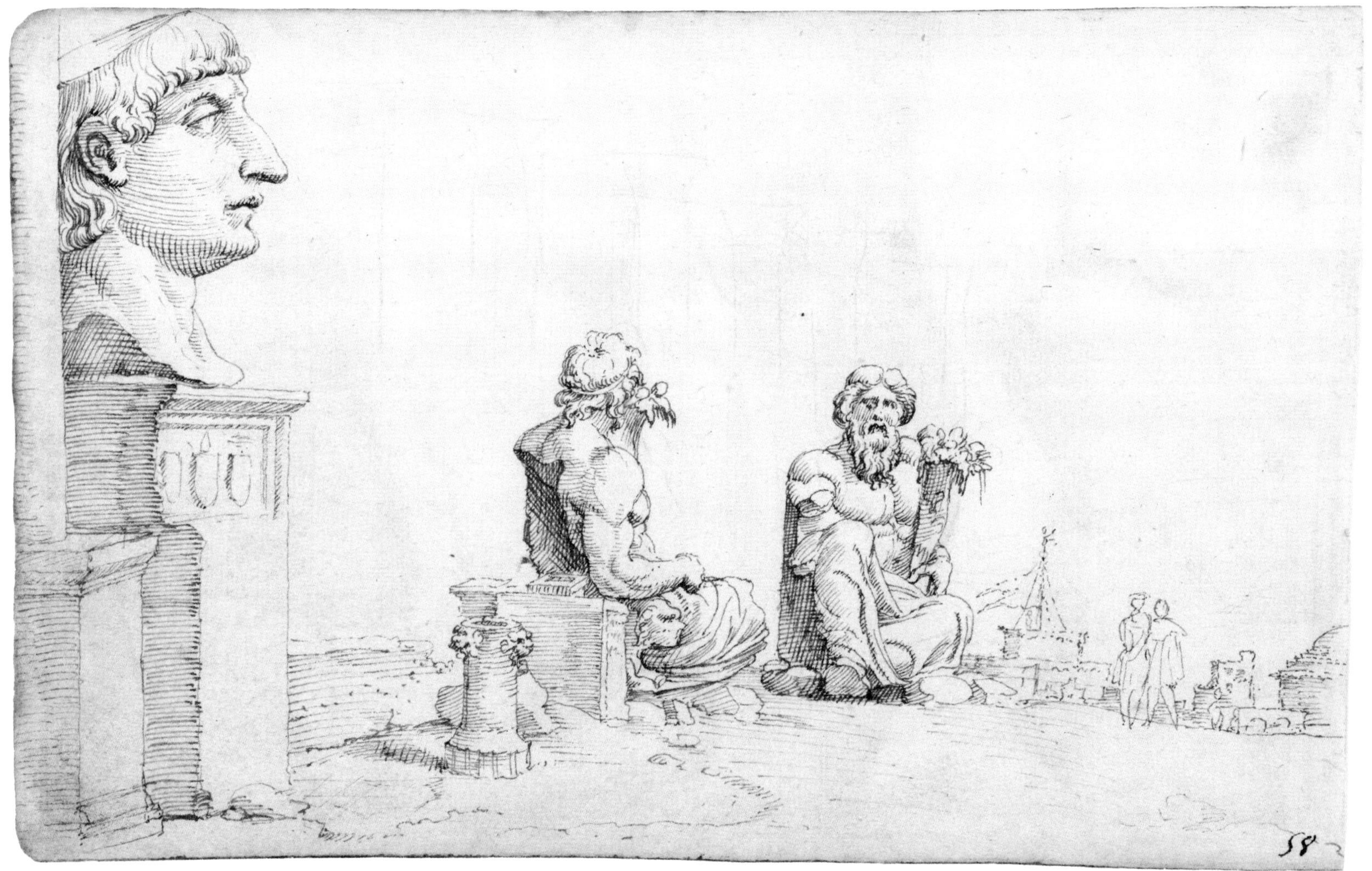

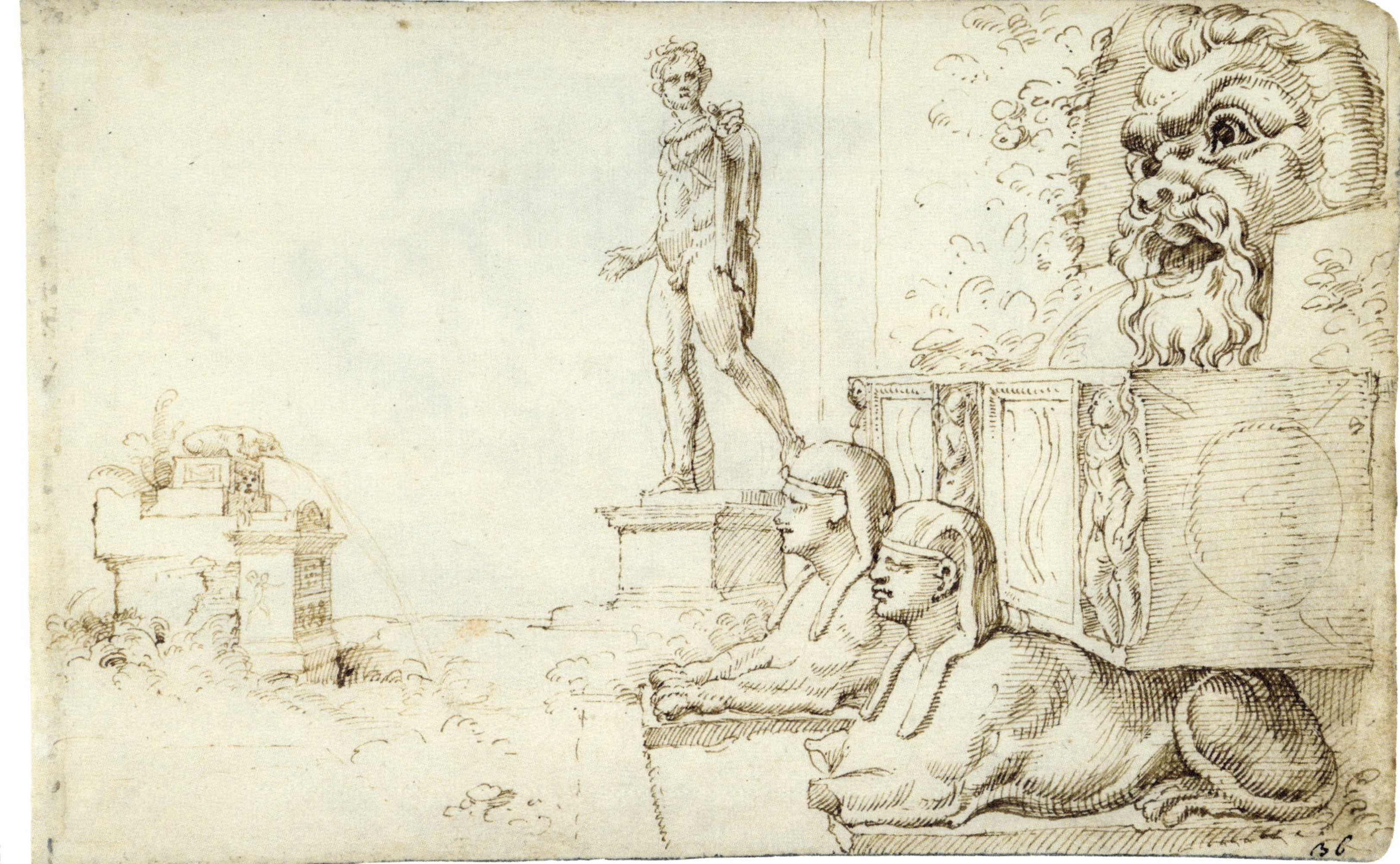

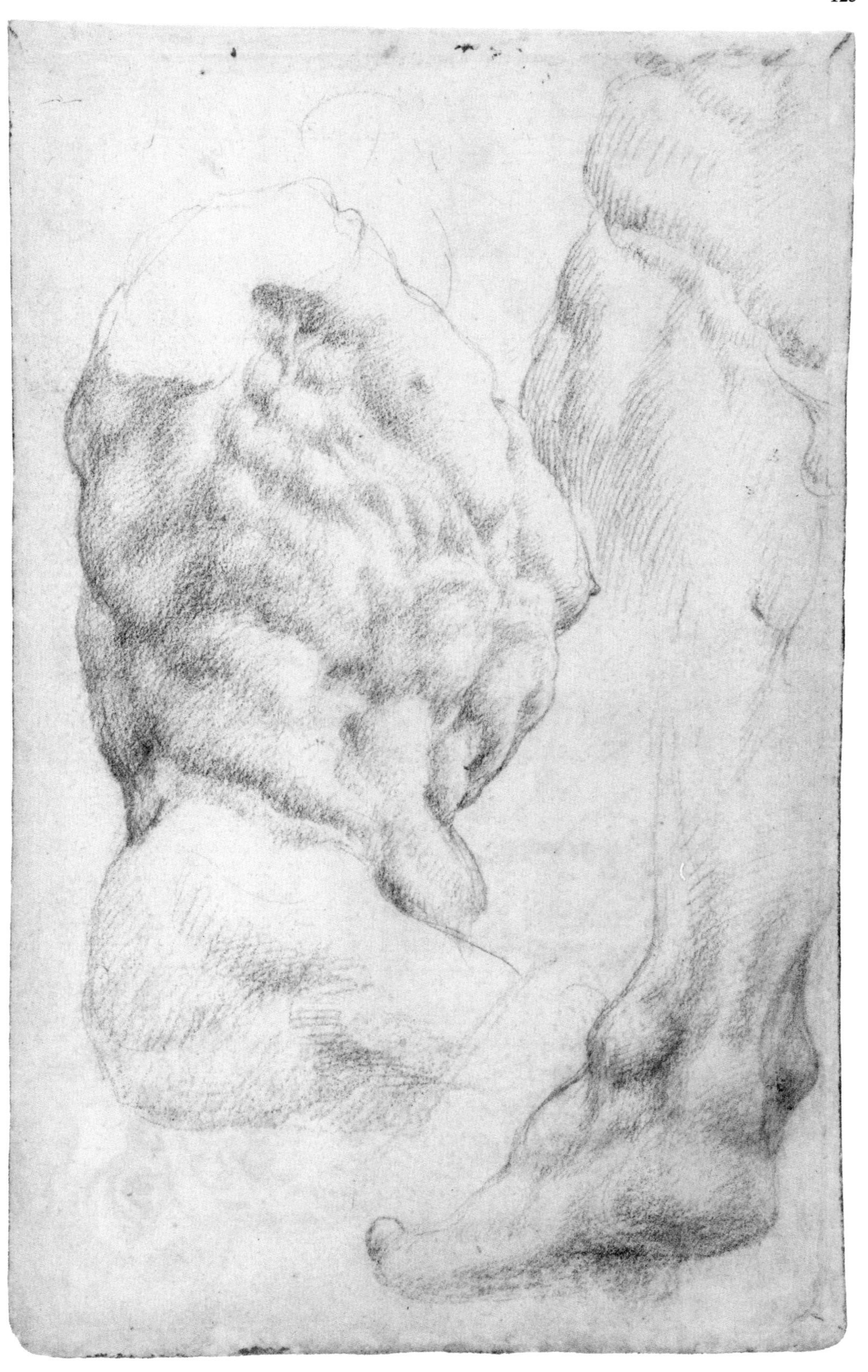

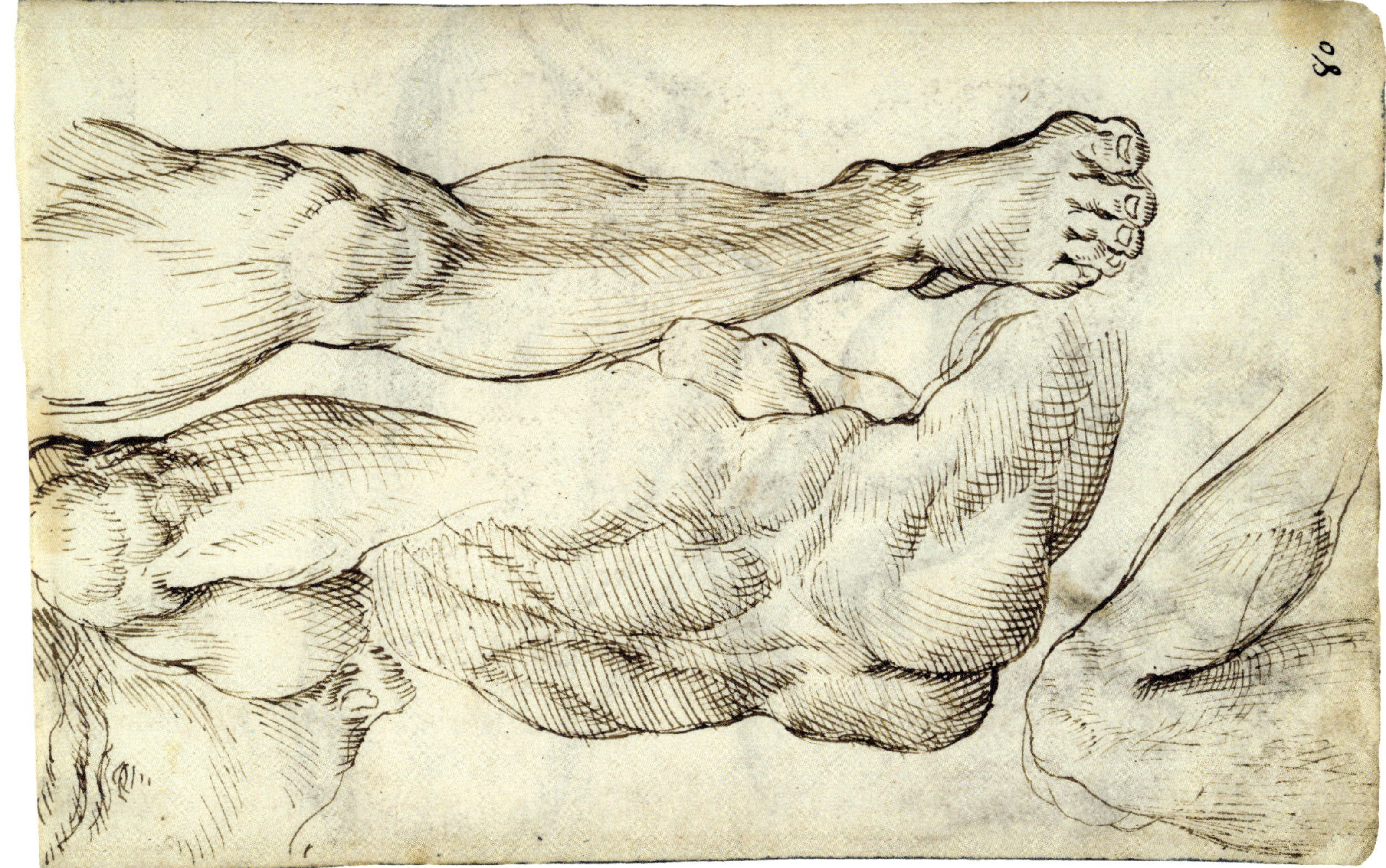

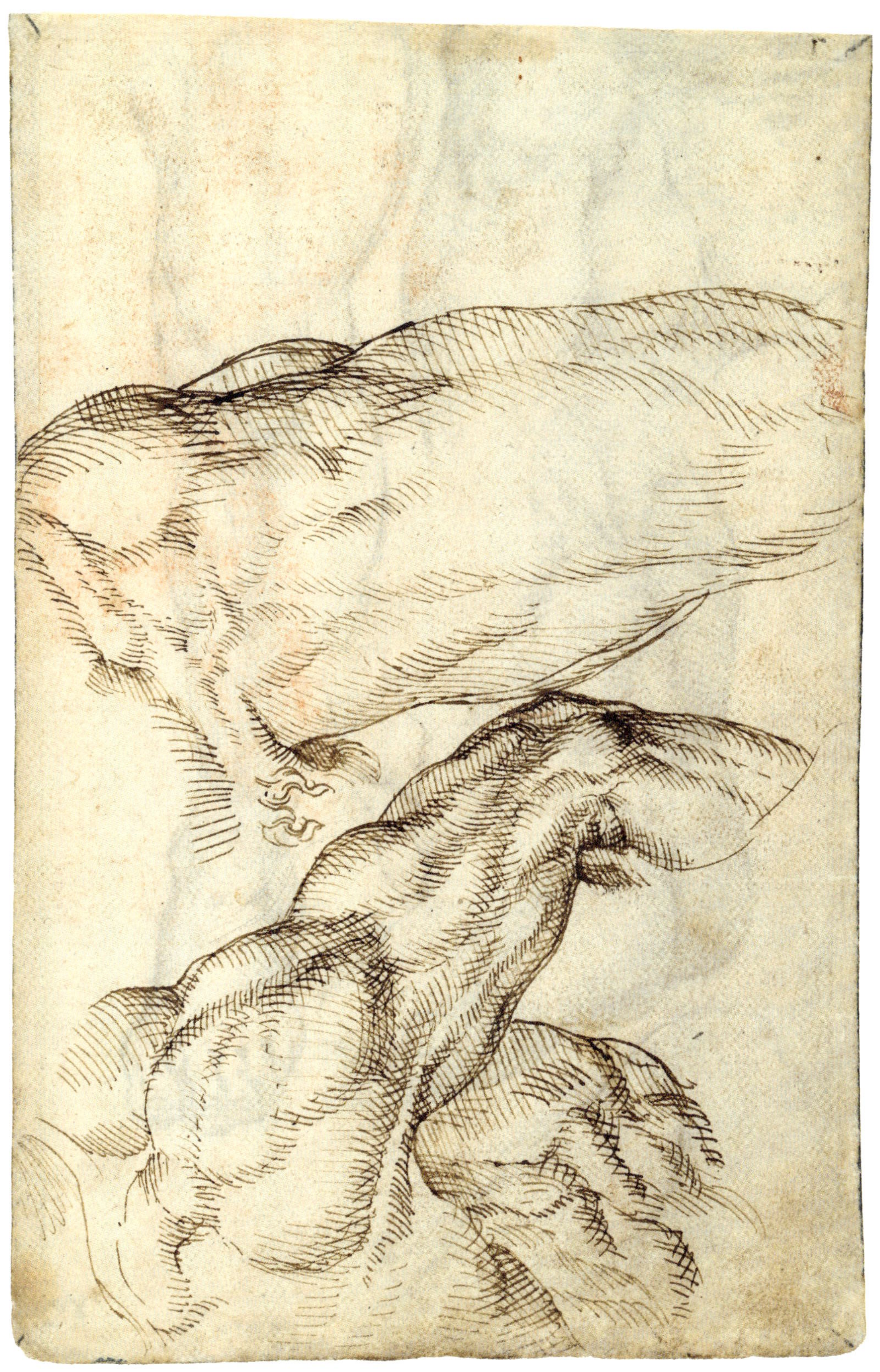

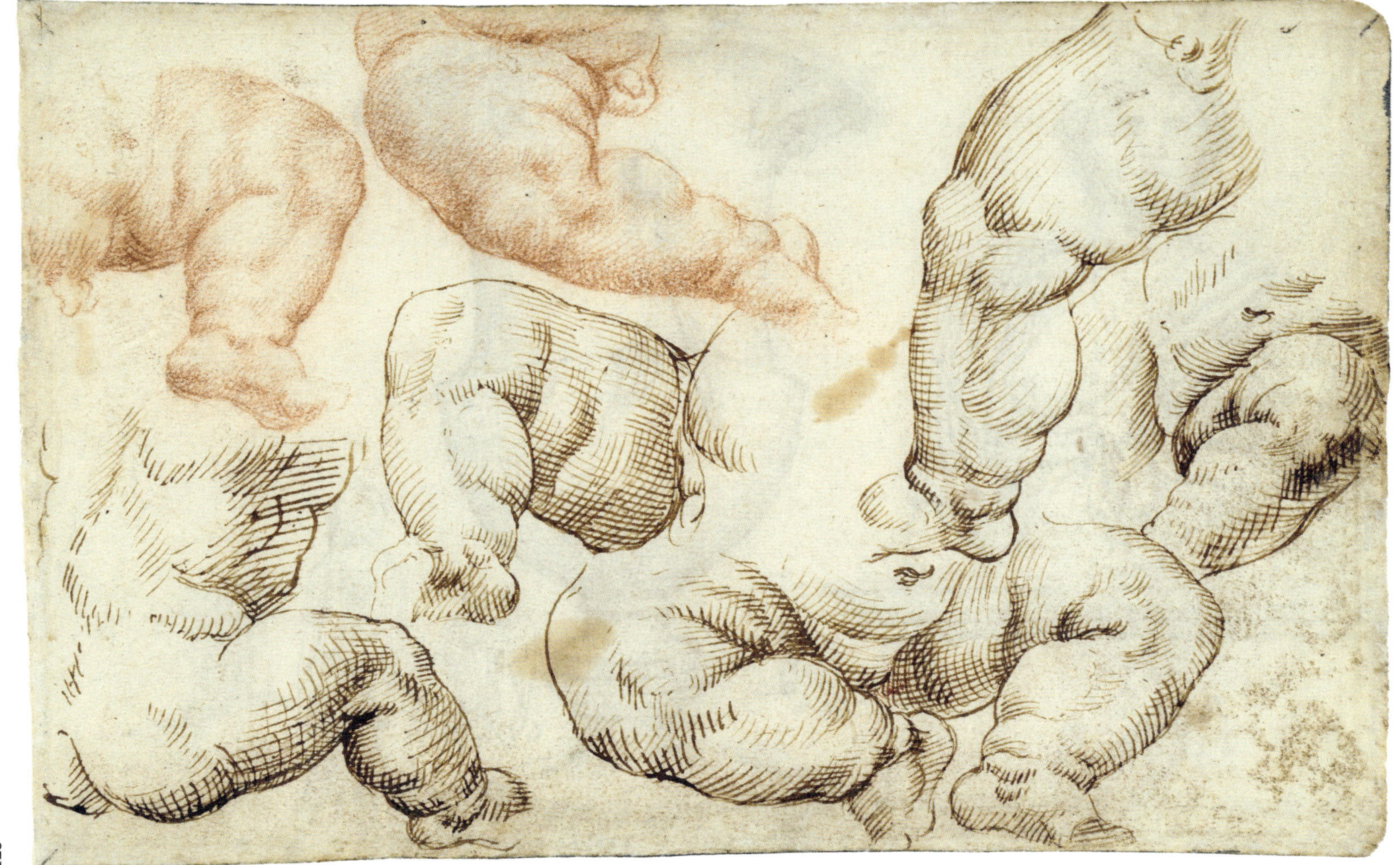

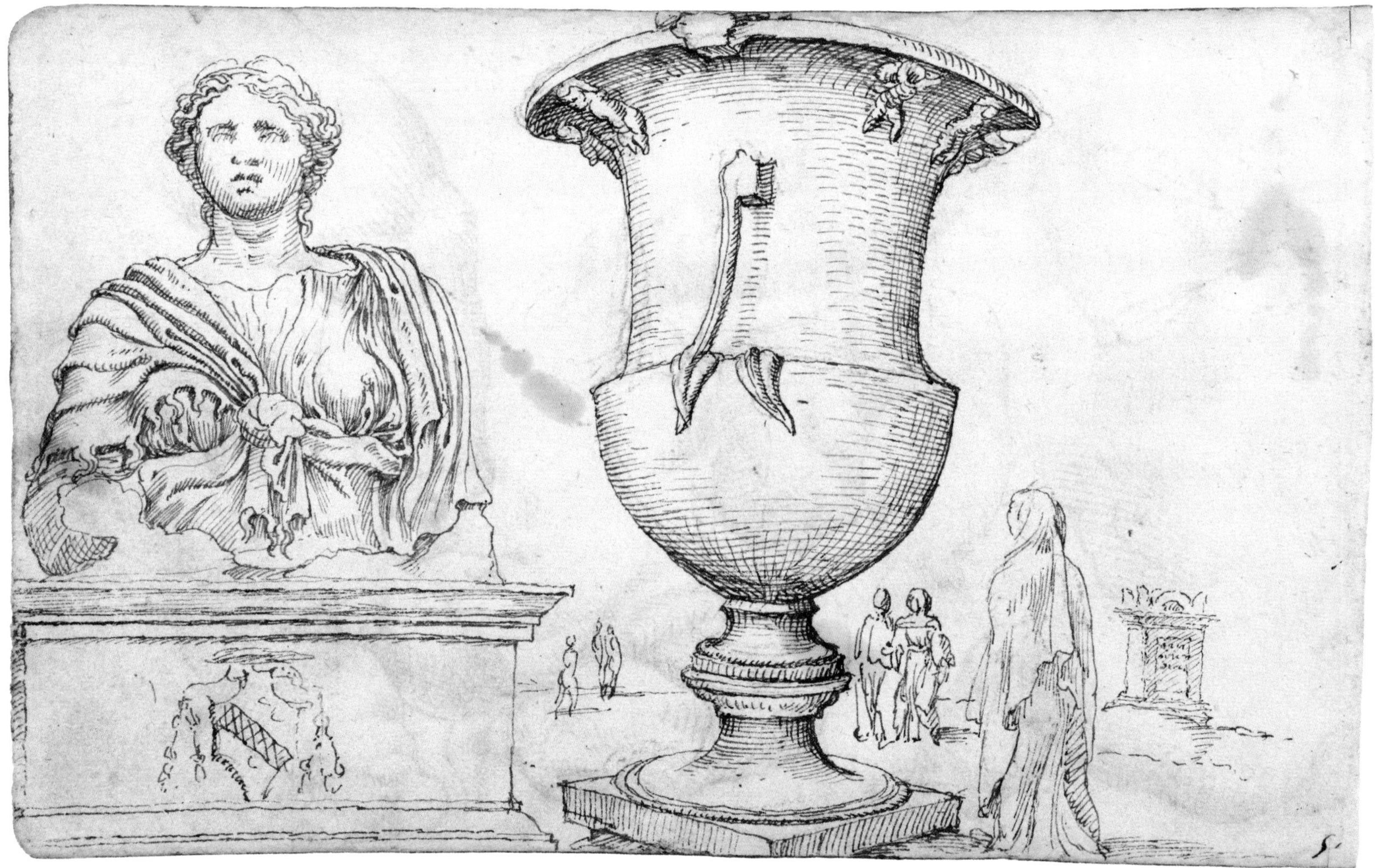

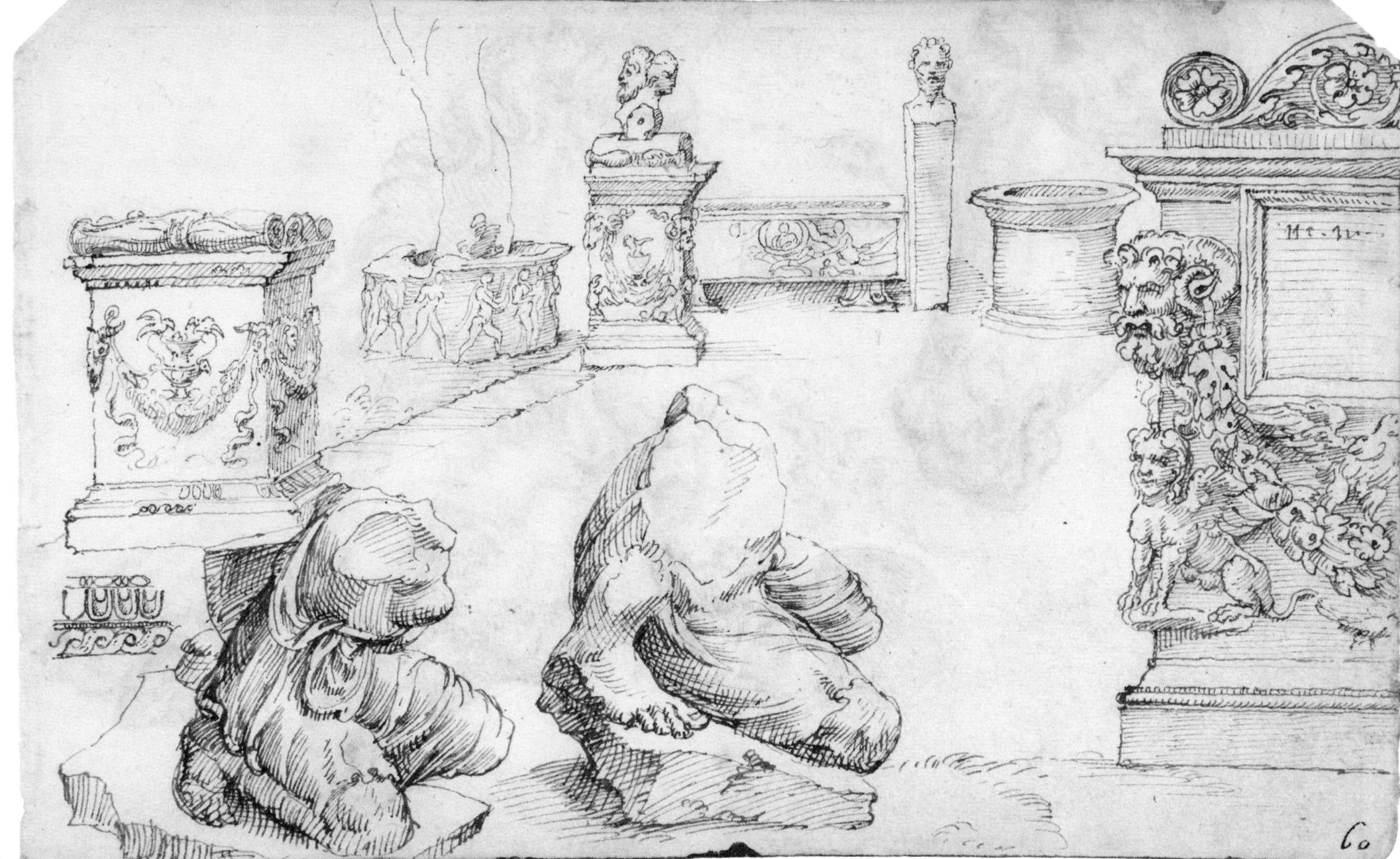

130
60

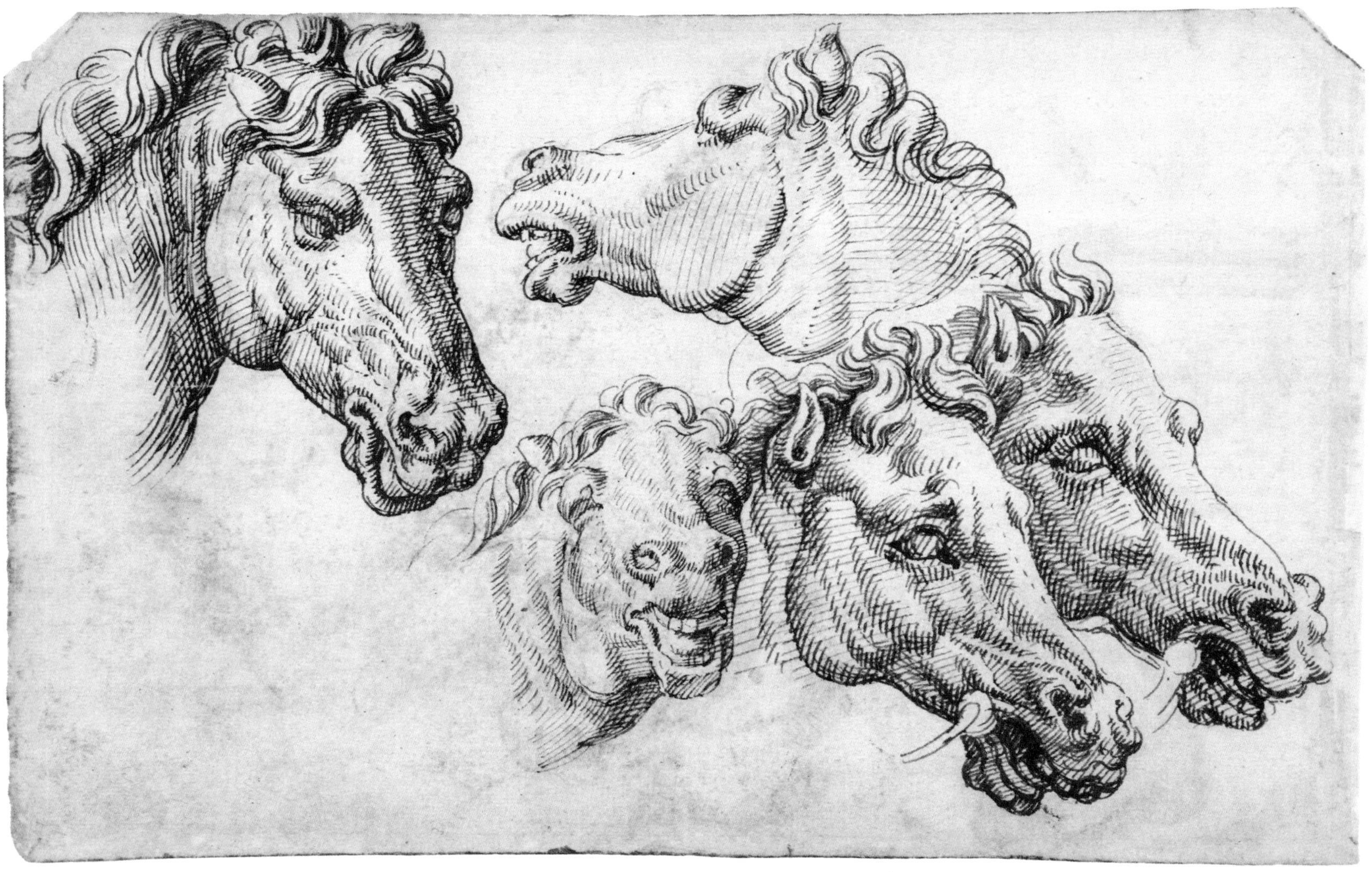

[ONE MISSING PAGE]

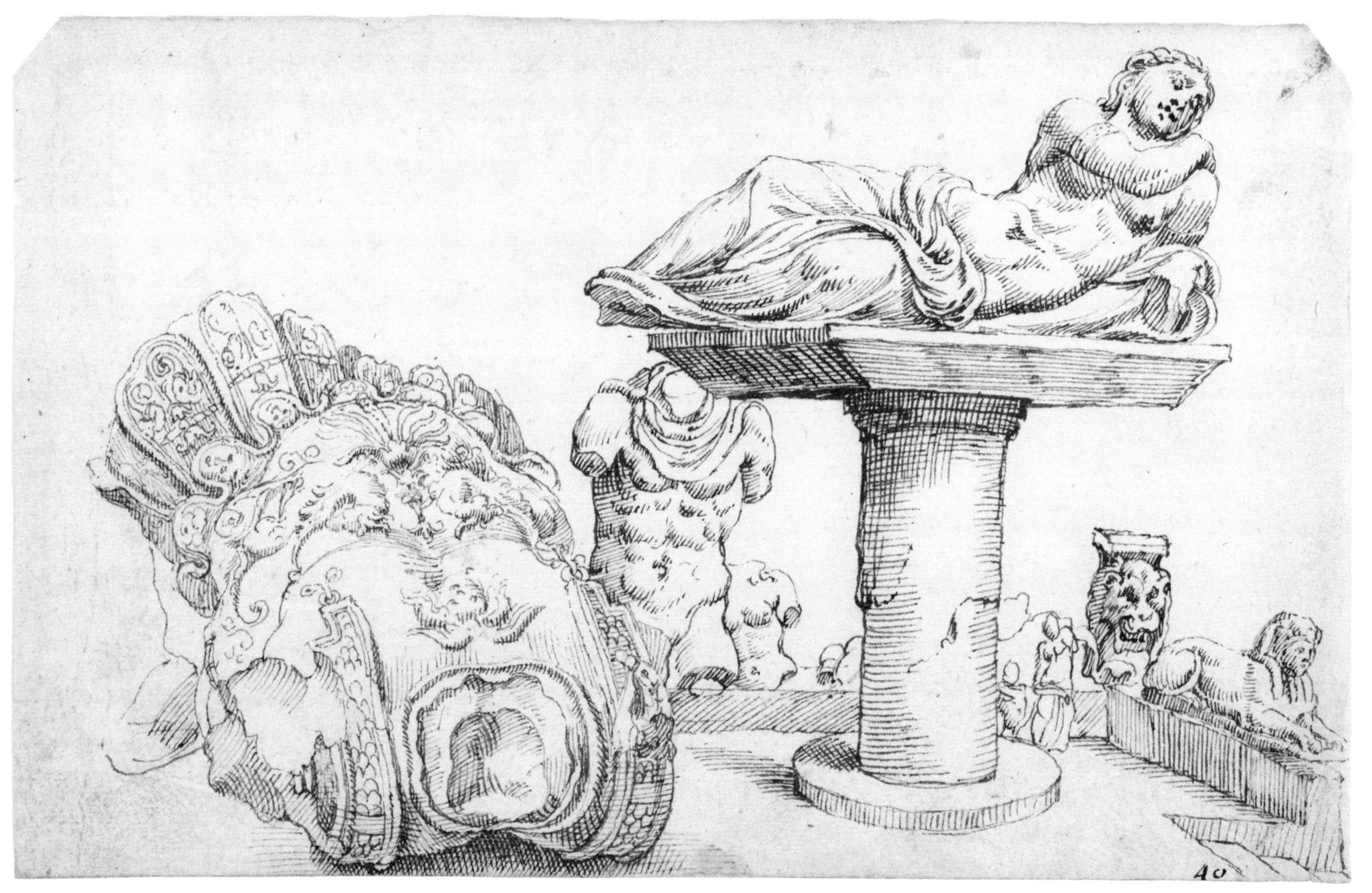

Tatjana Bartsch

THE ROMAN SKETCHBOOK OF
MAARTEN VAN HEEMSKERCK

"And then he went to Rome, which he had long very much wanted to do, so as to see the antiquities and the works of the great masters of Italy [...] And he neither slept away his time nor neglected it in the company of Netherlanders with boozing or whatever, but instead he copied many things, as much after antiquities as after the works of Michelangelo—also many ruins, ornaments, and all kinds of subtleties of the ancients which are to be seen in abundance in this city, the painters' academy. When the weather was good he usually went out sketching."[1]

These words by the art theorist Karel van Mander describe the journey undertaken by the painter Maarten van Heemskerck (1498–1574), who traveled from northern Holland to Rome to intensively pursue drawing.[2] Van Heemskerck arrived in Rome by a direct route without major stops, probably journeying on horseback and by ship. Shortly before his departure from Holland in May 1532, he gave a painting to the Guild of St. Luke, the painters' and goldsmiths' guild in Haarlem to which he belonged, as a farewell gift. By the summer of the same year he was already in Rome; there he met the Florentine artist Giorgio Vasari, who mentions the encounter in his *Lives*. The Eternal City seems to have been Van Heemskerck's only destination; from there he returned to Haarlem in 1536 or 1537, after a stay of about five years.

Over 110 pages with numerous drawings on both sides have survived from this journey, making the Roman oeuvre of Van Heemskerck one of the most extensive bodies of work by a traveling sixteenth-century artist still known today.[3] By far the largest number of drawings arrived in the collection of the Kupferstichkabinett in Berlin in 1886 and 1892, mounted in two albums. Windows had been cut into the album pages so that both the front and back of the sheets, which were glued only on the edges, could be viewed. These albums were probably assembled in the late eighteenth and nineteenth century. The original context of the drawings, however, was a different one: while the larger sheets, which vary in size, were probably used by the artist individually and stored loose in portfolios, the sixty-six smaller pages with almost identical measurements once belonged to a drawing book. The original binding had been lost over the course of the centuries and the sheets rearranged multiple times; accordingly, the pages were no longer in their original order and some were missing altogether. A single sheet that once formed part of the drawing book is now in the Rijksprentenkabinet in Amsterdam.

With their acquisition by the Kupferstichkabinett in Berlin, the two albums with the inventory numbers 79 D 2 and 79 D 2 a soon aroused the interest of archaeological scholarship.[4] For the Roman drawings of Maarten van Heemskerck show an unprecedented abundance of antique monuments—ruins, sculptures, reliefs, and inscriptions—as they existed in his time and in the context in which they had survived. For many of these works of art and architecture, Van Heemskerck's sketches are the earliest visual evidence, making them especially valuable for the history of preservation and collecting. Initially, therefore, scholarly interest in the drawings revolved primarily around the identification and analysis of the motifs depicted. For a long time, their role as antiquarian evidence overshadowed the reception and appreciation of their material characteristics and artistic quality, which was sometimes even denied. Only toward the end of the twentieth century did scholarly interest in Maarten van Heemskerck as a versatile, innovative artist begin to extend beyond his substantial painted and printed oeuvre to the collection of Roman drawings, which until then had often been considered in isolation from the rest of his work. The investigation of Van Heemskerck's concepts of artistic appropriation and the original contexts, functions, and interrelationships of the drawings pays tribute to their aesthetic dimension, which is characterized by remarkable precision as well as tremendous imaginative power.[5]

From this perspective, the altogether sixty-seven pages of the former drawing book deserve particular attention. The book is one of the earliest (if only partially) surviving examples of a Netherlandish artist's sketchbook and contains most of the extant studies, which represent a wide variety of motifs, techniques, and styles. Van Heemskerck drew with a quill pen and iron gall ink in various shades of brown,[6] using parallel- and cross-hatching as well as washes applied with the brush to evoke light, shadow, and volume. Many of the pen studies were executed over preliminary drawings in lead stylus; he also used red and black chalk. For the most part, different techniques appear on different pages of the book, although fourteen pages also show combinations of media.

Studies after antique sculptures are the most frequently represented subjects. Van Heemskerck probably admired these works not as an erudite antiquarian, but as a painter, with an eye for their role as models and guarantors of the highest aesthetic quality. They served him above all for the study of the nude human figure with its proportions and anatomical details. Some of the pages show random assortments of single motifs, while others group their subjects according to formal aspects, such as physiognomy or drapery. Buffalo, horses, goats, and exotic beasts such as an elephant, leopard, or ostrich—creatures he rarely if ever had opportunity to see in his homeland—bear witness to his interest in the depiction of animals. Many of these images are so specific and detailed that it seems as if the artist were already imagining a particular use for them. Past generations of scholars surmised that the occasional rendering of a knee, foot, or hip was drawn from nature; for the most part, however, such was not the case, since the studies were based on either antique sculptures or Renaissance frescoes.

Antique statues also appear as ensembles in their local contexts of display, whether private gardens, courtyards, or public squares. These are the very earliest known depictions of Roman antiquities collections; the same is true of the topographical views of ruins, which definitively shape our present-day image of Renaissance Rome. Van Heemskerck was interested above all in antique ruins, which he shows embedded in and overgrown by nature or integrated into the cityscape; here, too, he approaches his subject as a painter, not as an architect or antiquarian. The boundary to the *veduta*—the panoramic view from a distance—is fluid.

Van Heemskerck seldom drew from only a single vantage point. Many of his topographical views show wide-angle perspectives that enabled him to capture broad, sweeping vistas; for this purpose, however, he had to draw from different locations. A number of statues are rendered multiple times from different sides; this method of circling the object is also used for architectural studies, collection views, and topographical *vedute* of Rome. Often Van

Heemskerck depicts the subject from two or three different angles. These views combine to evoke a three-dimensional impression of the urban spaces, and sometimes the images are even grouped on a single page so that they can be experienced as a kind of tour. The drawings also betray a preference for unusual angles (from below or behind) and for views framed by other elements, such as a vista through an arcade, in order to emphasize a particular motif or create a picture within a picture.

From our few written sources as well as the surviving Roman oeuvre—which includes at least three commissioned paintings on canvas—we know that during his time in Rome, Van Heemskerck was in contact with other Netherlanders as well as with Italian artists. He copied drawings by Baccio Bandinelli and Antonio da Sangallo and studied the sculptures and paintings of Michelangelo with as much zeal as the frescoes of Raphael and Baldassare Peruzzi. He was also one of the first artists from Holland to draw in red chalk, a medium that at the time was still unusual in the Netherlands but was popular in Italy. He used it above all for figure studies, sometimes intentionally juxtaposing renderings in red chalk and pen on the same page in order to accentuate their expression. The warm reddish-brown tones of the chalk and its soft touch on the paper make the antique statues seem almost alive. The style of drawing, too, is indebted to Italian models, as evidenced by similarities to studies by Francesco Salviati, Polidoro da Caravaggio, Bandinelli, Peruzzi, or Michelangelo. Only a few of the sketches in Van Heemskerck's drawing book are annotated; these inscriptions served as memory aids for subjects previously unfamiliar to him and are limited to short notes.[7]

Van Heemskerck's drawing book was small enough to put in his bag and carry with him wherever he went. The use of sketchbooks as instruments for recording information, practicing, and remembering was also common in Italy and had been recommended already by Leonardo da Vinci, who himself filled dozens of such small and large books with sketches and thoughts. Since, as Leonardo said, "the forms and actions of things are so infinite that the memory is incapable of retaining them," the sketches "in a little book that you must always carry with you" (*tuo piccolo libretto, il quale tu devi sempre portare teco*) should not be erased, "but rather preserved with the greatest care."[8]

The decision made by the Kupferstichkabinett in 2021 to remove the former sketchbook pages from Album I and subject them to art technological analysis was of fundamental importance for the phenomenological investigation of the drawing book.[9] The back sides of the pages, which had previously been partially obscured, are now visible again in their entirety. The drawing media and materials could be precisely identified and the original structure of the book analyzed.[10] Proceeding from these new findings, conservators Antje Penz and Georg Josef Dietz proposed a reconstruction of the original sequence of pages in the drawing book, on which the order of this facsimile edition is based.[11]

The book pages are of uniform, oblong horizontal format and measure ca. 135 × 210 mm each; only in a few cases were they trimmed later. The outer corners are rounded and often show traces of wear from page-turning, making it possible to determine their original orientation in the book. A singular feature is the indigo-blue edging that both protected and adorned the book block on the three open sides and is still detectable on most of the sheets. The paper is of very good quality with a smooth surface and a high degree of whiteness. The two watermarks that occur (two crossed arrows with a six-pointed star above the intersection, and a crossbow in a circle) indicate that it was produced in the paper mills of Fabriano. In all probability, Van Heemskerck acquired the book directly in Rome. Drawings that extend across double pages as well as the presence of ink lines on top of the blue edging prove that the book was already bound when he drew in it. For studies in vertical format, he turned the book and opened it upwards; for drawings in red chalk, he generally used a fresh recto page.

The conservators of the Kupferstichkabinett used the following criteria for the reconstruction of the original sequence of pages: irregularities of the blue edging that repeat on opposite pages; the direction and shape of creases, folds, or bulges in the paper and their imprint on adjacent pages; the structure of the paper, including watermarks, felt side, and wire side as well as page thickness; ink color; imprints from other drawings (red or black chalk, ink), stains, and smudges; the general shape of the page as well as traces of wear; and relationships between the drawn motifs. A repeating pattern of four stacked double sheets (eight individual sheets) was identified, each group forming a gathering as part of the book block. The drawing book consisted of at least eleven gatherings; six of these can be joined together into a continuous fascicle, with an additional fascicle of two gatherings and three smaller fascicles of one gathering each. Finally, twenty lost pages and their former positions could be determined, although this makes it difficult to conclusively group the existing fascicles.

Both the quality of the paper and the finish of the edging bespeak a superior product whose original binding, though now lost, may have been made of parchment. The value of the small book is also reflected in the care with which many of its drawings were executed. The term "(travel) sketchbook" is thus applicable only to a limited extent: although it contains many rapid, spontaneous sketches made on location, it also includes elaborate, finished drawings based on preliminary studies and compilations of various motifs in new contexts, as well as painterly *vedute* of the city and panoramas that hold their own as autonomous works.[12] Van Heemskerck used his book as a repository of motifs and figures for later compositions, as an educational tool for assimilating new techniques and styles, and as a memory aid for recording new impressions and experiences. At the same time, however, it was also a safe place to explore creative ideas, which are articulated in mature, aesthetically ambitious compositions that evoke the fascination and passion of Maarten Van Heemskerck's own, very personal image of Rome.

1 Karel van Mander, *Het Schilder-Boeck, waerin Voor eerst de leerlustighe lueght den grondt der Edel Vry Schilderconst in Verscheyden deelen Wort voorghedraghen. Daer nae in dry deelen t'Leven der Vermaerde door luchtighe Schilders des ouden, en nieuwen tyds. Eyntlyck d'wtlegghinghe op den Metamorphoseon Pub. Ovidij Nasonis Oock daerbeneffens wtbeeldinghe der figuren. Alles dienstich en nut den schilders Const beminders en dichters, oock allen staten van menschen* (Haarlem 1604), fol. 245v; English translation in Karel van Mander, *Lives of the Illustrious Netherlandish and German Painters, from the First Edition of the Schilder-boeck (1603–1604)*, ed., annotated and transl. by Hessel Miedema, 6 vols., Doornspijk 1994–1999, vol. 1, 1994, 241.

2 Although the *Schilder-Boek* was not published until thirty years after Van Heemskerck's death, Van Mander's report is considered reliable, since he was well acquainted with the followers, colleagues, and friends of the older artist. On Van Heemskerck's life and work, see Ilja M. Veldman, *Maarten van Heemskerck (1498–1574)*, Zwolle 2024 (in preparation).

3 On authorship, content, reception and provenance of the drawings, see the extensive discussion in Tatjana Bartsch, *Maarten van Heemskerck. Römische Studien zwischen Sachlichkeit and Imagination* (Römische Studien der Bibliotheca Hertziana, 44), Munich 2019, as well as *The Allure of Rome: Maarten van Heemskerck Draws the City*, ed. by Christien Melzer and Tatjana Bartsch, exh. cat. Kupferstichkabinett, Staatliche Museen zu Berlin, Munich 2024.

4 The two albums were published in Christian Hülsen and Herman Egger, *Die römischen Skizzenbücher von Marten van Heemskerck im Königlichen Kupferstichkabinett zu Berlin*, 2 vols., Berlin 1913–1916.

5 See *Rom zeichnen. Maarten van Heemskerck 1532–1536/37*, ed. by Tatjana Bartsch and Peter Seiler, Berlin 2012 (Humboldt-Schriften zur Kunst- and Bildgeschichte, 8). See also Bartsch 2019 (as in n. 3); Arthur J. DiFuria, *Maarten van Heemskerck's Rome. Antiquity, Memory, and the Cult of Ruins* (Brill's Studies in Intellectual History, 287), Leiden 2019; exh. cat. Berlin 2024 (as in n. 3).

6 The ink contained no vitriol, which probably made it easier to mix while traveling. See Georg Josef Dietz et al., "Materials, Techniques, and Reconstruction of the Small Drawing Book," in exh. cat. Berlin 2024 (as in n. 3), 98–127.

7 On the relationship between text and image in the drawing book, cf. Emanuele Pellegrini, *La memoria in tasca. Taccuini, immagini, parole*, Rome 2021.

8 Leonardo da Vinci, *Trattato della pittura*, introduction by Marco Tabarrini, Rome 1890 (reprint La Spezia 1984), 71, § 169; English translation in Mary Pardo, "Leonardo da Vinci on the Painter's Task: Memory/Imagination/Figuration," in *Leonardo da Vinci and the Ethics of Style*, ed. by. Claire Farago, Manchester 2008, 58–95, here 69.

9 The analysis was undertaken for purposes of conservation and in preparation for the exhibition *The Allure of Rome: Maarten van Heemskerck Draws the City* at the Kulturforum in Berlin (April 26–August 4, 2024). It was conducted by conservators Georg Josef Dietz and Antje Penz in the Conservation Department at the Kupferstichkabinett, in collaboration with Susanne Grzimek. The analysis of the ink was performed by conservator Carsten Wintermann of the Klassik Stiftung Weimar. See also exh. cat. Berlin 2024 (as in n. 3), esp. Dietz et al. 2024 (as in n. 6).

10 Selective analysis of thirty-one drawings using X-ray fluorescence (XRF); chromatographical analysis of an ink sample; photographs of all drawings using multispectral imaging (MSI); detailed examination under a stereo microscope.

11 Cf. the detailed description with the reconstructed sequence of pages with composition of gatherings in the appendix of Dietz et al. 2024 (see note 6).

12 On drawing book terminology, see most recently Albert J. Elen, "(Artists') Drawing-Books and (Collectors') Albums. Similarities and differences," in *Libri e album di disegni 1550–1800. Nuove prospettive metodologiche e di esegesi storico-critica*, ed. by Vita Segreto, Rome 2018, 1–10.

*Compiled by Christien Melzer
and Tatjana Bartsch*

Maarten van Heemskerck
Small Drawing Book

66 + 1 sheets, mostly with drawings on both sides (65 + 1 sheets from the so-called *Album I*, dismantled since January 2023, Staatliche Museen zu Berlin, Kupferstichkabinett, Inv. 79 D 2; one sheet from the Rijksprentenkabinet Amsterdam, Inv. RP-T-1920-60)

after May 23, 1532–before November 30, 1537

ca. 135 × 210 mm, some pages later trimmed

Acquired in 1879 from Hippolyte Destailleur, Paris, for the Kunstgewerbemuseum, transferred to the Kupferstichkabinett in 1886 by the Ministerium der geistlichen [...] Angelegenheiten

Bartsch 2019 (as in n. 3), cats. 1–133 with additional bibliography; exh. cat. Berlin 2024 (as in n. 3), cat. 26

Preliminary note:
Missing pages are marked by placeholders. The folio numbers refer to the order and orientation of the pages in the former *Album I* and continue to serve as the inventory numbers. Dates are specified only when they can be established more precisely than the general time span of Van Heemskerck's stay in Rome. The pen drawings are executed in non-vitriolic iron gall ink, which can vary in color; thus in the following, only "pen" or "brush" is specified.

[indeterminate number of missing pages]

1 [fol. 38r]
Various Studies
Preliminary drawing in lead stylus, pen,
red chalk dust

2 [fol. 38v]
Three Studies after the Horse Tamers
Pen, red chalk impression

[two missing pages]

3 [fol. 28r]
Composite Capital and Colosseum
Preliminary drawing in lead stylus, pen

4 [fol. 28v]
Head of the Vatican Arno (Tigris), after 1533 (?)
Pen

5 [fol. 59v]
Head of the Vatican Nile
Pen

6 [fol. 59r]
Two Views of the Hercules and Antaeus Group
Preliminary drawing in lead stylus, pen

[two missing pages]

7 [fol. 44v]
Various Antique Studies
Preliminary drawing in lead stylus, pen

8 [fol. 44r]
Studies after an Antique Relief
Preliminary drawing in lead stylus, pen

[next gathering]

9 [fol. 49r]
Various Studies
Red chalk, pen

10 [fol. 49v]
Sketch of a Portico
Lead stylus

[two missing pages]

11 [fol. 20v]
Seated Griffin from an Antique Relief;
Ram Horns
Preliminary drawing in lead stylus
(partially erased), pen, red chalk impression

12 [fol. 20r]
Southwest Slope of the Palatine Hill
Preliminary drawing in lead stylus, pen

13 [fol. 75r]
Study of a Back
Red chalk

14 [fol. 75v]
*Studies after the Equestrian Statue of Marcus
Aurelius*
Preliminary drawing in lead stylus, pen

15 [fol. 63v]
*Two Studies after the Equestrian Statue of
Marcus Aurelius; View of a Female Torso from
the Rear (Medici Venus?)*
Preliminary drawing in lead stylus, pen,
red chalk

16 [fol. 63r]
Belvedere Torso and Fragment of an Obelisk
Preliminary drawing in lead stylus, pen,
red chalk impression

[one missing page]

— [fol. 73v]
Blank page

17 [fol. 73r]
Belvedere Torso
Pen

[next gathering]

18 [fol. 74r]
View of the Vatican Nile from the Rear and Leg Study
Black chalk, pen, red chalk impression

19 [fol. 74v]
Various Antique Studies, before June 1533
Preliminary drawing in black chalk, pen

20 [fol. 32v]
Various Antique Studies
Preliminary drawing in black chalk, pen

21 [fol. 32r]
Colossal Foot and Porticus Octaviae
Preliminary drawing in lead stylus, pen

22 [fol. 36r]
*Cantharus from Santa Cecilia in Trastevere and
Frontespizio di Nerone*
Partial preliminary drawing in black chalk,
pen

23 [fol. 36v]
Two Views of an Antique Head
Preliminary drawing in black chalk, pen

24 [fol. 13r]
North Transept and Crossing of New St. Peter's
Pen, brush, brown and gray wash

25 [fol. 13v]
Two Antique Heads
Partial preliminary drawing in lead stylus,
pen

26 [fol. 39r]
Head of Laocoön
Preliminary drawing in lead stylus, pen

27 [fol. 39v]
*Head of the Capitoline Brutus; Unknown
Antique Head*
Preliminary drawing in lead stylus, pen

28 [fol. 41r]
Head of Dionysos; Bust of a Double Herm
Preliminary drawing in black chalk, pen

29 [fol. 41v]
Two Studies after the Head of the Vatican Hercules,
after June 1533 (?)
Preliminary drawing in lead stylus, pen

30 [fol. 69v]
Ground Floor of Colosseum from the Northwest
Traces of preliminary drawing in lead stylus,
pen

31 [fol. 69r]
West Side of Arch of Constantine and Colosseum
Traces of preliminary drawing in lead stylus,
pen, red chalk impression

[one missing page]

[next gathering]

32 [fol. 54r]
View of the Vatican Nile from the Rear
Preliminary drawing in lead stylus, pen

33 [fol. 54v]
Head of the Cesi Mars
Pen

34 [fol. 57v]
Various Antique Studies
Preliminary drawing in lead stylus, pen

35 [fol. 57r]
*So-Called Knife Grinder; Two Sketches after
the Shoes of the Cesi Barbarians*
Pen and various colors of ink

36 [fol. 25r]
South Wall of the Cesi Garden
Pen and various colors of ink

37 [fol. 25v]
Three Views of a Venus Statuette
Preliminary drawing in lead stylus, pen

38 [fol. 6v]
Three Views of a Crouching Venus
Preliminary drawing in lead stylus, pen

39 | 40 [fols. 6r | 9r]
Double-page spread: *The Forum Romanum from
the South*, December 1535–March 1536
Pen and various colors of ink

41 [fol. 9v]
*Loggia of the Villa Madama with View of the
Tiber Valley*
Pen

42 [fol. 72r]
Lower Statue Court of the Casa Galli
Pen

43 | 44 [fols. 72v | 18r]
Double-page spread: *View of Rome from
the Janiculum*
Pen

45 | 46 [fols. 18v | 55r]
Double-page spread: *View of Rome from the
Aventine Hill; Winged Dragon*
Pen

47 [fol. 55v]
*Copy after an Elevation Drawing of the Palazzo
Branconio dell'Aquila*
Red chalk

[next gathering]

48 [fol. 16v]
*Tree Study, probably after a Sarcophagus Relief;
One of the Dioscuri from the Quirinal Hill, Viewed
from the Rear*
Pen

49 [fol. 16r]
View of Rome from Monte Mario; Two Studies
Pen and various colors of ink

[one missing page]

50 [fol. 65v]
Boot of the Genius Farnese
Red chalk

51 [fol. 65r]
Goats
Pen

52 [fol. 48r]
Goats
Pen

53 [fol. 48v]
Three Antique Foot Fragments with Shoes
Red chalk

[indeterminate number of missing pages; incomplete gathering]

54 [fol. 33v]
Three Studies
Red chalk

55 [fol. 33r]
Various Antique Studies
Preliminary drawing in lead stylus, pen

56 [fol. 26v]
Various Antique Studies
Preliminary drawing in lead stylus, pen

57 [fol. 26r]
Various Antique Studies
Preliminary drawing in lead stylus, pen

58 [fol. 34r]
Two Muses from the Villa Madama
Preliminary drawing in lead stylus, pen

59 [fol. 34v]
Antiquities from the Villa Madama
Preliminary drawing in lead stylus, pen

60 [fol. 24r]
View from the Loggia into the Garden of the Villa Madama
Preliminary drawing in lead stylus, pen

61 [fol. 24v]
Three Sailing Ships
Preliminary drawing in lead stylus, pen, grayish wash

62 [fol. 58r]
Two Antique Statues from the Villa Madama; View from the Frigidarium of the Baths of Caracalla toward the Southwest
Pen

63 [fol. 58v]
View of St. Peter's Square from the East; Two Studies, ca. 1535–before April 5, 1536
Pen, red chalk impression

[next gathering]

64 [fol. 8v]
Two Antique Studies
Red chalk in two shades

65 [fol. 8r]
Construction Site of New St. Peter's
Traces of preliminary drawing in lead stylus, pen

66 [fol. 30v]
Herm and Architectural Fragments
Preliminary drawing in lead stylus, pen and two colors of ink

67 [fol. 30r]
Two Nudes from the Sistine Ceiling and Other Studies
Pen and two colors of ink, red chalk impression

68 [fol. 51v]
Various Antique Studies
Red chalk in various shades

69 [fol. 51r]
Nude from the Sistine Ceiling; Pilaster Base; Two Views of a Draped Female Statue (Artemis)
Pen, red chalk impression

70 [fol. 61v]
Torso of a Young Man from the Santacroce Collection; Leg Study
Red chalk

71 [fol. 61r]
View from the Portico of the Palazzo dei Conservatori on the Capitoline Hill
Preliminary drawing in lead stylus, pen, red chalk impression

72 [fol. 60v]
Studies after the Santacroce Hercules and the
Capitoline Bronze Hercules
Red chalk in various shades

73 [fol. 60r]
Two Drapery Studies
Pen, red chalk impression

74 [fol. 52v]
Various Studies
Red chalk

75 [fol. 52r]
Various Antique Studies
Pen, red chalk impression

76 [fol. 19r]
Elephant Fountain of the Villa Madama;
Figure from the Sistine Ceiling
Red chalk in two shades

77 [fol. 19v]
Marforio with Fountain Basin and
Frieze Fragment
Partial preliminary drawing in lead stylus,
pen and various colors of ink

78 [fol. 3v]
Courtyard of the Casa Maffei
Preliminary construction drawing in lead
stylus, pen, gray-brown wash

79 [fol. 3r]
View into the Colosseum
Pen, compass pricks

[next gathering]

[one missing page]

80 [fol. 40r]
Elephant Fountain of the Villa Madama;
Baths of Maxentius
Preliminary drawing in lead stylus, pen

81 [fol. 40v]
Various Studies
Preliminary drawing in lead stylus, pen

82 [fol. 53v]
Motifs of an Augustan Frieze from San Lorenzo
fuori le Mura
Preliminary drawing in lead stylus, pen,
ocher-yellow wash

83 [fol. 53r]
Antique Statues from the Courtyard of the
Palazzo dei Conservatori
Pen, red chalk impression

[one missing page]

84 [Inv. RP-T-1920-60(R)]
Three Statues and Two Studies of a Ram's Head
Pen and brown ink

85 [Inv. RP-T-1920-60(V)]
Part of a Mantelpiece and Cartouche
Pen and brown ink, red chalk impression

86 [fol. 46v]
Cupid with Garland from an Antique Taurobolium
Relief; View of a Torso from the Rear
Red chalk

87 [fol. 46r]
Antiquities in the Garden of the Villa Madama
Preliminary drawing in lead stylus, pen

88 [fol. 35r]
Study after Raphael's Psyche from the Garden Loggia
of the Villa Farnesina; Five Antique Fragments
Preliminary drawing in lead stylus, pen

89 [fol. 35v]
Horse of the Dioscuri from the Quirinal Hill;
Toga Statue; Grotesques
Partial preliminary drawing in lead stylus, pen,
red chalk impression

90 [fol. 43v]
Two Studies after the Dioscuri from the Quirinal
Hill; Sketches after Stucco Decorations from the
Villa Madama
Red chalk, pen

91 [fol. 43r]
Draped Female Statue (Berenike); Candelabra and
Cupid Sacrificing a Bull from an Antique Relief
Traces of preliminary drawing in lead stylus,
pen

[next gathering]

92 [fol. 56r]
Various Studies
Red chalk in various shades, pen

93 [fol. 56v]
Various Studies
Red chalk, red chalk impression, pen

117 [fol. 64r]
Various Antique Studies, before June 1533
Pen, red chalk impression

118 [fol. 50v]
Various Antique Studies
Red chalk

119 [fol. 50r]
Various Studies
Red chalk, pen, red chalk impression

[one missing page]

[next gathering]

[one missing page]

120 [fol. 22v]
Detail Study after Laocoön
Black chalk, later framed in pen and
brown ink, light and dark-gray wash,
red chalk impression

121 [fol. 22r]
*Portico and Fragments of the Entablature from
the Temple of Antoninus and Faustina*
Preliminary drawing in lead stylus, pen,
red chalk impression

122 [fol. 45v]
Various Antique Studies
Red and black chalk

123 [fol. 45r]
Antiquities in Front of the Palazzo dei Conservatori
Preliminary drawing in lead stylus, pen

124 [fol. 23r]
Papal Statue Court and Fountain
Preliminary drawing in lead stylus, pen

125 [fol. 23v]
Antiquities from the Papal Statue Court,
before June 1533
Gray chalk

126 [fol. 67r]
Studies after the Older Son of Laocoön
Pen, lead stylus impression

127 [fol. 67v]
Two Studies after Laocoön
Preliminary drawing in lead stylus, pen,
red chalk impression

128 [fol. 37v]
*Leg Studies after the Nile Children in the
Papal Statue Court*
Red chalk, pen

129 [fol. 37r]
Various Studies
Preliminary drawing in lead stylus, pen

130 [fol. 47r]
View of an Unknown Antiquities Garden
Pen

131 [fol. 47v]
Horses' Heads
Pen and various colors of ink, impressions
of red and black chalk

[one missing page]

[next gathering]

132 [fol. 27v]
Landscape Sketch
Lead stylus

133 [fol. 27r]
Upper Statue Court of Casa Galli and Mars Torso
Pen and two colors of ink

This view forms a pendant to cat. 26.42, which
shows the lower part of the Galli courtyard
and the *Bacchus* by Michelangelo. There is some
doubt as to whether this sheet really belonged
to the drawing book, since it is the only one
with vertical chain lines; however, the quality
of the paper as well as the format and traces
of wear correspond to the other pages. It is
possible that it was inserted separately into
the book.

A publication by the Bibliotheca Hertziana –
Max Planck Institute for Art History and the
Kupferstichkabinett – Staatliche Museen zu
Berlin
Funded by the *Corpus der Italienischen
Zeichnungen 1300–1500*.

Editors:
Tatjana Bartsch and Christien Melzer

Translation:
Melissa M. Thorson

Project management:
Frauke Berchtig

Graphic design and typesetting:
Rutger Fuchs Amsterdam

Typeface:
Lexicon

Reproductions:
Schwabenrepro GmbH, Fellbach

Production:
Kati Klaeske

Paper:
Livonia Zero Offset by Lessebo Paper 140 g/m²

Printing and binding:
Livonia Print

Published by
Hatje Cantz Verlag GmbH
Mommsenstraße 27
10629 Berlin
www.hatjecantz.com
A Ganske Publishing Group Company

ISBN: 978-3-7757-5798-0

Printed in Latvia

Cover images:
123 [fol. 45r]: *Antiquities in Front of the Palazzo
dei Conservatori*
21 [fol. 32r]: *Colossal Foot and Porticus Octaviae*

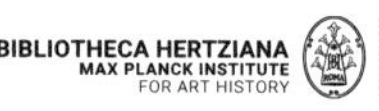
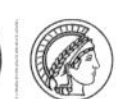

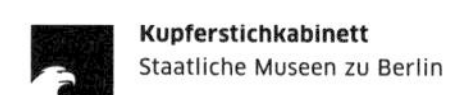